THE POLITICS OF GOOD INTENTIONS

DAVID RUNCIMAN

THE POLITICS OF
GOOD INTENTIONS

HISTORY, FEAR AND HYPOCRISY IN
THE NEW WORLD ORDER

PRINCETON UNIVERSITY PRESS   PRINCETON AND OXFORD

Library of Congress Cataloguing-in-Publication Data

Runciman, David.
   The politics of good intentions : history, fear and hypocrisy in
the new world order / David Runciman.
     p. cm.
   Includes bibliographical references and index.
   ISBN 978-0-691-12566-X (cloth : alk. paper)
   ISBN 0-691-12566-X (cloth : alk. paper)
   1. Political science—Philosophy. 2. World politics—21st century.
   3. Great Britain—Politics and government—1997–.
   4. United States—Politics and government—2001–.
   5. September 11 Terrorist Attacks, 2001—Influence. I. Title.

JA66.R75 2006
973.931—dc22   2005052164

British Library Cataloguing-in-Publication Data

A catalogue record for this book is available from the British Library

This book has been composed in Palatino and
typeset by T&T Productions Ltd, London
Printed on acid-free paper ∞
www.pup.princeton.edu

Printed in the United States of America

1 3 5 7 9 10 8 6 4 2

For Bee

CONTENTS

CONTENTS

PART TWO
Britain, Europe and the United States

PREFACE

What difference is there between the polemics of most of the representatives of the so-called "new morality" against the opponents whom they criticise, and those of any demagogue you care to mention? Someone will say: the nobility of their intentions. Fine! But what we are talking about here is the means which they use; and the opponents whom they attack claim likewise, with equal honesty from their point of view, that their ultimate intentions are noble. "They that take the sword shall perish with the sword", and war is war wherever it is fought.

Max Weber, "Politics as a Vocation", 1919

This book is about what is new in politics at the beginning of the twenty-first century, and what isn't. The language of "newness" has dominated political argument in recent years: new threats, new challenges, new opportunities, a whole new world order. The event that has given so many of these arguments their impetus is the attack on the United States that took place on September 11, 2001. That event provides the focus for a number of the chapters here, but the real purpose of this book is to get beyond the confines of the immediate past, and to place contemporary politics in a broader historical perspective, by comparing the character of political life and political thought now with their character at other times and in other places. It is impossible to know whether the nature of modern politics and the modern state have fundamentally changed in recent years unless we know something about how the modern state came into being, and how it has evolved over time. This book tries to use the long history of modern politics—from the time of Thomas Hobbes in the seventeenth century until today—to make sense of the brief present. History does not repeat itself, but it does not follow that the past has no lessons for the present or the future. Yet because history does not repeat itself, we need to be careful about what we think it is telling us.

As well as trying to use history, this book is also about the ways that history has been used and abused by contemporary politicians, as they seek to justify their actions under the dispensation of a new world order. Among the things that politicians have had to justify is the act of going to war itself. These justifications have had a profoundly polarizing effect, not just on narrow party-political argument, but also on the wider attitude taken to the question of what is familiar in early twenty-first-century politics, and what is new. There has been a tendency to see things in all-or-nothing terms: if we find anything familiar in the ways that politicians seek to justify themselves, then we often assume that nothing has changed; if we assume that something has fundamentally changed, then we tend to ignore the ways in which the self-justifying behaviour of politicians is all too familiar. The truth lies somewhere in between. Some things have changed, but many things have stayed the same. Some of the claims that have been made about how the present differs from the past deserve to be taken at face value, and some do not. This may sound obvious, but it has often been lost sight of in the welter of claim and counter-claim that has swamped political argument in recent years, from both the champions and the critics of a new world order.

But trying to decide what is new in contemporary politics does not just involve comparing the present with the past. It also means thinking about the future. The other central theme of this book is risk, and the fear that accompanies it. There is sometimes a temptation to treat these separately, and to assume that technical questions of risk are essentially unrelated to the problems of political justification. But risk is a political as well as a technical problem, and what is more, the worlds of politics and technology have become increasingly intertwined. The role of risk in politics is becoming something new, and I try to identify where that novelty lies.

This book is divided into two main parts, plus an introduction and an epilogue. The first part looks at Tony Blair and the war in Iraq. It explores the various ways that Blair has sought to justify that war and its aftermath, both in relation to the past and in relation to the future—that is, through history and risk. The second part looks at the wider divisions that have emerged between Europe and the United States, and explores some of the history that lies behind these divisions. It also asks what the history of European and American conceptions of the state can tell us about the prospects for a new kind of politics in the years to come.

The particular politicians whose actions and self-justifications this book analyses will not be in office forever, or even for very much longer. Things will happen that will demand new courses of action, new justifications, and in the end new political leaders, who will need to justify themselves in their own way. The politician on whom this book concentrates is Tony Blair, whose political career (in British domestic politics at any rate) is coming to an end. But it is not just about Blair. It is also about the way that politicians in general seek to use the idea of the new to escape the strictures of the old, and about whether they are justified in doing so.

Several of the chapters in this book started life as articles in the *London Review of Books,* but have been substantially expanded and updated for this publication: Chapter Two appeared as "The Politics of Good Intentions" on 8 May 2003; Chapter Three appeared as "The Precautionary Principle" on 1 April 2004; Chapter Four appeared as "Betting Big, Winning Small" on 20 May 2004; Chapter Five is a substantial expansion of "How Many Jellybeans", which appeared on 5 August 2004; Chapter Seven appeared as "A Bear Armed with a Gun" on 3 April 2003; Chapter Eight appeared as "The Garden, The Park, The Meadow" on 6 June 2002; Chapter Nine appeared as "Shockingly Worldly" on 23 October 2003.

I would like to express my thanks to Mary-Kay Wilmers and the editorial staff at the *London Review of Books* for providing much of the original impetus behind this book. I also thank my colleagues in the Department of Politics at Cambridge for their help and advice, above all Geoff Hawthorn, Glen Rangwala and Helen Thompson. I am very grateful to my successive editors at Princeton University Press, Ian Malcolm and Richard Baggaley, for all their hard work and encouragement, as I am to my agent Peter Straus. Finally, I would like to express particular thanks to Jeremy Mynott, who offered moral and practical support at a crucial stage, which enabled this book to be completed.

INTRODUCTION: SEPTEMBER 11 AND THE NEW WORLD ORDER

Did September 11, 2001, really change the world? This question was being asked across the globe within hours of the attacks taking place. But within days, it had become clear that there was to be no consensus on the answer. In Britain, at one remove from the raw emotion being felt in the United States, political commentators wasted no time in setting out their opposed positions. On 13 September, writing in *The Guardian*, Hugo Young, the most measured and reasonable of British political observers, declared:

> What happened on September 11th, 2001, changed the course of human history. We cannot yet grasp, by any stretch, all that this means. But already we start to imagine how it will poison trust, wreck relationships, challenge the world order, and vastly magnify the divide between the enemies and friends of democracy. It will harden the last vestiges of tolerance for compromise, and further reverse the presumptions of freedom—of travel, speech, politics, everything. It calls into question what power any longer is or means.[1]

Two days later, in *The Times*, Matthew Parris, an equally clear-sighted writer about politics, responded to Young. "And after September 11, 2001," he wrote, "and the horrible, horrible deaths of thousands of innocent people, one thing will be certain: the world will be the same again after all".[2]

Is it possible, after the passage of a few years rather than a few days, to say who was right? One thing now seems abundantly clear: Young was correct when he foresaw a poisoning of trust and a wrecking of relationships. There are few political relationships—between states, between political leaders, between politicians and their electorates—that have not suffered contamination from the fallout of that fateful day. Some important political institutions—NATO, the United Nations (UN)—may now be in permanent decline. Others, like the European Union (EU), are in flux, and it is impossible to be sure in what form they will eventually settle down, if they settle down at all. Yet does it follow from all this upheaval that we can no longer be confident what power is, or what it means? The turmoil in global politics over the last few years is a consequence of the exercise of political power in one of its most recognizable forms: the power of the determined leaders of well-armed nations to seek security through force. When politicians exercise this power, the results are invariably serious, and often deeply disorienting. But it does not follow that the power itself is unfamiliar, or that we should be doubtful about what it means. It means what it has always meant: war.

It was not what happened on September 11, 2001, that contaminated political relationships and destroyed trust; in fact, for a short while many traditional political ties, including those between Europe and the United States, seemed to have been strengthened by the challenge of confronting the terrorist threat. It was the Iraq war of 2003, its build-up and its aftermath, that did the damage. It is true that this war would never have happened as and when it did if the United States had not been attacked two years earlier. But to many observers, September 11 simply provided George W. Bush and his administration with a convenient prop on which to hang a set of military and ideological objectives that had been identified well in advance. The feeling has been widespread feeling among opponents of the Iraq war that the Bush administration exploited the opportunity provided by September 11 to pursue its own, preferred course in Middle Eastern politics, and it is this sense of exploitation which has generated so much of the mistrust. This mistrust only deepened when it emerged that in attempting to fit the case for war in Iraq onto a post-September 11 political framework—in attempting to justify it in terms of the terrorist threat—the Bush administration was forced to stretch the evidence about Saddam's weapons of mass destruction (WMD), and so misrepresented the nature of the threat he posed. Having been confronted with the evidence of this misrepresentation, Bush, and his ally Tony Blair, were repeatedly forced back onto their last line of defence. They had to argue that those who wished to pick holes in the arguments presented before the Iraq war for taking military action were missing the bigger picture. What was the bigger picture? It was, as Tony Blair put it in his speech to the Labour Party conference in September 2004, in which he defended his conduct in Iraq notwithstanding the mistakes that had been made over the intelligence, simply this: "September 11 changed the world".[3]

This, then, is the real difficulty with trying to determine whether the world changed on that day. The claim is not just a historical one, to be confirmed or rejected by historians at some point further down the line than we are at present. It is also a political claim, and it has frequently been made to serve some blatantly political objectives. It was a central plank, at times almost the only plank, of the campaign to re-elect George Bush. The message that Bush's opponent, John Kerry, did not appreciate the ways in which the world had changed after September 11 was hammered home by Bush and his running mate Dick Cheney throughout the campaign. "Even in this post-9/11 period", Cheney announced in his brutal, highly effective speech accepting the nomination of the Republican Party at their national convention, "Senator Kerry doesn't appear to understand how the world has changed".[4] In the first of their three presidential debates, Bush derided his opponent for what he notoriously dubbed his "pre-September 10th attitude". It was a charge that was to be reiterated endlessly until polling day. Bush lost the debate, but he did not lose the presidency.

The attraction for any incumbent politician of talking up the significance of epoch-making events is obvious. If the world has changed, then politics must change with it, and elected politicians can shirk some of their old responsibilities along the way. A new world order needs a new set of rules. The temptation always exists for politicians to use the appearance of a transformed world to avoid difficult questions about the particular consequences of their own immediate actions. But the countervailing temptation also exists: to dismiss all political claims to be operating under the dispensation of a new world order as inevitably self-serving and evasive. The idea that September 11 did not change the world— that things are, in Matthew Parris's words, "the same again after all"— can serve narrow political purposes of its own. Critics of the

Iraq war have repeatedly blamed its architects for not foreseeing the predictable, if unintended, consequences of a military occupation, because they were blinded by the transformative possibilities of September 11. Critics of the Iraq war, therefore, have every reason to want to argue that the world has not really changed at all.[5]

This is why it is so hard to determine what is new about politics at the beginning of the twenty-first century, and what is familiar. Much of what appears to be new has been exploited in ways that are all too familiar, and much of the familiar response to that exploitation neglects what appears to be new. This book is an attempt to disentangle some of these claims and counter-claims, in order to determine what has really changed. To do so, it explores not just the dynamics of the new world order, but the motives, arguments and deceptions of some of the politicians who inhabit it. Too often, these are treated separately, as though they occupied different universes. The torrent of writing about contemporary politics that has appeared in the wake of September 11 divides into two broad streams: those books and articles that use the attacks on New York and Washington to exemplify the new set of challenges politicians now face (many of the books were written or at least conceived in what George Bush would call a pre-September 10 setting, but when they appeared sought to demonstrate early inklings of a post-September 11 frame of mind); and those books and articles that wish to demolish the politicians who have used the attacks to pursue courses of action on which they were already determined. These books, like so many of the partisan political arguments on which they are based, often appear to be talking past each other. And it is not only books. For many critics of the Bush regime, the world did not change on September 11, because the day on which it really changed was 12 December 2000, when the United States Supreme Court finally determined, by a vote of 5–4, the outcome of that year's presidential election. Michael Moore's film *Fahrenheit 9/11*—which characterizes all the events consequent on Bush's election as a literal nightmare—perfectly captures the terms of this argument, which is no argument in any terms but its own. Moore's unwillingness to consider alternative scenarios to the one in which Bush steals the election and then contrives the war on terror serves only to enrage his critics. But

Moore's own rage is fuelled by his sense that the alternative scenarios have all been hijacked by the politicians, and put to work serving sinister purposes of their own.

This book does not seek to take sides in the sort of dispute that finds George W. Bush on one side and Michael Moore on the other. Instead, it tries to find a broader perspective in which to assess the claims of both politicians and their critics to have identified a new pattern in world-historical affairs. Of course, there are many books, and many academic books in particular, that also seek to locate recent events in a wider historical or theoretical context. But in this book, I try to do it without losing sight of the narrower political arguments, and without ignoring the motivations of the politicians who make them. I do not believe it is possible to assess whether we have entered a new phase of politics without considering the ways in which politicians have tried to exploit such claims. Nor, however, do I believe that the fact that such claims can be exploited means that they are necessarily untrue.

Tony Blair and the New World Order

The particular politician on whom I concentrate in a number of the chapters that follow is not George Bush but Tony Blair. This may appear a somewhat parochial choice for a book about world-historical politics. In global terms, the British Prime Minister is a much less consequential figure than the American president. Indeed, Blair has proved much less consequential than many of the members of the president's administration, as he has discovered to his cost.[6] Blair is a more conventionally articulate politician than Bush but, notwithstanding the silver-tongued reputation he acquired in the United States after September 11, I do not focus on him here because of his purported ability to articulate a more resonant defence of American policy than the architects of that policy have managed. Rather, I am interested in Blair because his articulation of the newness of politics since September 11 cuts across some of the arbitrary divisions imposed by that date, and by the American election that preceded it. The relative proximity of the contested election of late 2000 to the traumas of September 2001 has trapped much discussion of recent developments in global politics within a relatively narrow time-frame. It is all too easy to think of politics at the beginning of the twenty-first century

as defined by a choice between the relative significance of these
two events: either it was the arrival on the world scene of Osama
Bin Laden that made the all difference, or it was the arrival of
George W. Bush. But Tony Blair's political career, though likely to
be defined by his response to the same two events, is not limited to
the period begun by them. Blair, unlike Bush, is a political leader
of the late twentieth century as well as the early twenty-first. He
was deploying many of the arguments that were to justify his conduct after September 11 well before that date. Moreover, he is a
politician whose entire career has been built around his ability to
embrace what is "new". In the mid 1990s he rose to power on the
back of the rebranding of the Labour Party as "New Labour". By
the end of that decade, his attention had turned to international
politics.

In the speech Blair gave to the Economic Club in Chicago on
22 April 1999, under the title "Doctrine of the International Community", he used the example of the ongoing conflict in Kosovo
to make the case that the world had already changed. "Twenty
years ago", he announced, "we would not have been fighting in
Kosovo. We would have turned our backs on it. The fact that we
are engaged is the result of a wide range of changes—the end of
the Cold War; changing technology; the spread of democracy. But
it is bigger than that. I believe the world has changed in a more
fundamental way."[7] He went on:

> We are all internationalists now, whether we like it or not. We
> cannot refuse to participate in global markets if we want to
> prosper. We cannot ignore new political ideas in other coun-
> tries if we want to innovate. We cannot turn our back on
> conflicts and violations of human rights within other coun-
> tries if we want still to be secure. On the eve of a new mil-
> lennium we are now in a new world. We need new rules for
> international cooperation and new rules of organising our
> international institutions.[8]

If George Bush believed any of this in 1999, when he was Governor
of Texas, he gave little indication of it. But it was the doctrine by
which his presidency would ultimately be defined.

Blair's Chicago speech establishes an alternative time-frame in
which to view the politics of the new world order. On this account,
the defining moment came in 1989. The end of the Cold War

marked the beginning of a new set of opportunities in international relations, but also created new kinds of imperatives. Both the opportunities and the imperatives derived from the increasing economic, political and technological interdependence of nation states. After 1989, it was possible to contemplate humanitarian and, if necessary, military intervention in the world's trouble spots without having also to face the prospect of initiating a wider conflict between nuclear superpowers. At the same time, it became harder to ignore what was happening in the world's trouble spots, because of the ways in which information could be spread. With the spread of information came the potential to spread the political consequences of the trouble itself—consequences that might include terrorism, racial hatreds and the displacement of peoples. All these developments Tony Blair brought under the bland general heading of "globalization", and in 1999 it was globalization that he took to have changed the world, and to have fundamentally altered the terms in which national politicians should seek to engage with it. It was also this globalization that he used to justify the actions that he, Bill Clinton and the other NATO leaders had taken in Kosovo, without a UN mandate. In the post-1989 world, it was possible to confront a tyrant like Slobodan Milosevic without risking a catastrophic war with the former Soviet Union. It was also necessary to confront Milosevic, because the consequences of his tyranny could no longer be reliably contained. The doctrine of the international community, as Blair understood it, made intervention in such cases both possible and necessary.

What is striking about the arguments Blair deployed to justify the intervention he, George Bush and a few other national leaders were to undertake in Iraq four years later is how similar they are to what he said in Chicago, and how different. The core ideas of the Blairite philosophy did not alter. As he put it in a speech he delivered in his Sedgefield constituency on 5 March 2004: "Here is where I feel so passionately that we are in mortal danger of mistaking the nature of the new world in which we live. Everything about our world is changing: its economy, its technology, its culture, its way of living. If the 20th century scripted our conventional way of thinking, the 21st century is unconventional in almost every respect."[9] But three aspects of this doctrine shifted fundamentally after September 11, 2001. First, the tone changed, from one of moral uplift to something much darker and more foreboding. Speaking in 1999, Blair did not cast the challenges of the new world order in terms of "mortal danger"; instead, he spoke optimistically about the almost limitless possibilities available to progressive, well-intentioned politicians in a newly integrated international community. In this respect, Blair was still riding the wave of hope that had broken over much of Europe ten years earlier, with the collapse of the Berlin Wall. It was only with the collapse of the Twin Towers that the dark side of these limitless possibilities was revealed.

This change of tone also reflected the changing dynamics of American presidential politics. For Tony Blair, the idea of an international community is meaningless without the full support of the United States. To this end, he has always been willing to speak the same kind of language as the American political leaders on whom the whole project depends. In 1999, the leader whose support he needed was Bill Clinton, and the language he deployed was essentially Clintonian, with its emphasis on interdependence, technological change and open-ended opportunities for social and political betterment. Doubtless anticipating that Al Gore would succeed Clinton in 2000, Blair must have supposed that the need for this kind of rhetoric would only increase. But when Clinton was succeeded by Bush, and when Bush succeeded in defining his own presidency as an old-fashioned struggle between good and evil, Blair's own language had to change. Whatever his private instincts, he did not have the option of embracing the Manichean political theology of the Bush White House because the British public would not have been able to stomach it.[10] But he did have to show that he knew that the United States had embarked on a different sort of battle from the ones he had fought alongside President Clinton.

What he could not do, however, was buy into the most partisan accounts of what had happened in the transition from the age of Clinton to the age of Bush. For Clinton haters (of whom there were many), September 11 did not simply embody the downside of the new international order that emerged during the 1990s. Instead, September 11 marked a clean break with the Clinton years, and all their attendant fantasies, illusions and displacement activities— the years of Monica, OJ and the dotcom boom. Clinton had lulled

8

the United States into a false sense of security, from which all Americans awoke with a bang on September 11, 2001, when they discovered that while they had been playing the stock market and watching "reality" television, America's enemies had been plotting her destruction. On this view, it was the Clinton years, not the Bush years, that were the dream. After a brief interlude, the twenty-first century reverted to the type laid down by the twentieth—and to a quintessentially twentieth-century conception of the international order that rests, as Michael Ignatieff has put it, "less on hope than on fear, less on optimism about the human capacity for good than on dread of human capacity for evil, less on a vision of man as a maker of his history than of man the wolf towards his own kind."[11] This kind of brutal realism does not cover the views of everyone in the Bush administration, but it does cover some. "My friends, there never was a time when terrorism was just a nuisance; there never can be a time when terrorism is just a nuisance" was how the vice president chose (unfairly but efficiently) to dismiss John Kerry's approach to terrorism in the 2004 campaign.[12] For Cheney, September 11 changed the world by reminding the American public in general, and the Democratic Party in particular, that the world had never really changed at all.

Tony Blair needed something more than Cheney's brand of cynicism to explain the note of dread that entered his rhetoric after September 11 (not least because some of the cynicism was directed at him—"that preacher on a tank", as Cheney memorably dubbed him).[13] He could not abandon either the moral uplift or the technocratic impulses of the Clinton years, having invested so much in them, but nor could he carry on as though nothing had changed. He found the bridge he required between Clinton and Bush, and between the twentieth century and the twenty-first, in the language of risk. This represents the second big shift in the Blair doctrine of international community between Kosovo and Iraq. In place of an emphasis on interdependence and opportunity came an insistence on something called "the balance of risk", and on the fact that it had altered fundamentally on September 11 (see Chapter Three). The focus of this new anxiety was the possibility that terrorists would acquire WMD, and the apparent certainty that if they got them, they would use them. For Blair, this is the "mortal danger" threatened by the new international order. The

same interconnectedness that made it possible for the international community to act together against Milosevic is what makes
it possible for terrorists and rogue states to act together against the
international community, and threaten it with ruin. The dynamic
of globalization is the same as it was before September 11—it provides both the opportunity and the necessity for a new kind of
politics. But the stakes had suddenly become much higher.

The language of risk is nothing new in politics. The stakes for
which politicians play are invariably high, and every politician
has to make a judgment about what they can afford to lose, and
what they cannot (see Chapter Four). Moreover, the technological
changes of the twentieth century mean that the stakes have been
getting higher for quite some time. The idea that modern technology has created a new world of risk had become fashionable
among political scientists and sociologists long before Blair started
to deploy it in the wake of the attacks on New York and Washington. Ulrich Beck, who coined the phrase "the risk society" to
describe this new world order, has characterized late modernity
(or as he calls it "second stage modernity") as an age of "manufac-
tured uncertainty", in which the management of risk has become
the primary instrument of political power. The language of risk
serves politicians in two ways. On the one hand, as Beck puts it:

> The concept of risk reverses the relationship of past, present
> and future. The past loses its power to determine the present.
> Its place as the cause of present-day experience and action
> is taken by the future, that is to say, something non-existent,
> constructed and fictitious. We are discussing and arguing
> about something that is *not* the case, but *could* happen if we
> continue to steer the same course we have been.[14]

This open-endedness empowers politicians, placing a premium
on decisive action—*any* decisive action—in the face of uncertainty.
On the other hand, the mechanics of risk assessment are precisely
that—mechanical, and cautious, and impersonal—which allows
politicians to advise against a rush to judgment whenever it suits
them. The technocratic language of risk encourages the public to
place their trust in experts, who have the capacity to weigh up all
the evidence. In this way, risk allows politicians the twin luxuries
of certainty and uncertainty, to be deployed interchangeably, as
the occasion demands.

Blair's use of the language of risk in the aftermath of September 11 captures precisely these double standards. In his assessment of the threat posed by terrorists acting in conjunction with rogue states, Blair relied both on expert risk assessment and on his own intuitions. He highlighted the importance of knowing the risks posed by global terrorism, all the while insisting that when it comes to global terrorism the risks are never fully knowable. In his justification of the war in Iraq, Blair championed caution and incaution at the same time: this was not a moment to ignore the balance of risk, but nor was it a moment to weigh the risks indefinitely in the balance. Yet what is most striking about Blair's deployment of these double standards is not that he should seek to have it both ways, but that he should be so explicit about it. This is where Blair's risk society differs from Beck's. In Beck's account, political risk management appears as an attempt to conceal the true nature of the threats posed to the planet by the industrial order, particularly the threat of ecological disaster. Therefore, politicians use risk to downplay the possibility of catastrophe in order to make all threats appear manageable. But Blair uses the language of risk to raise the spectre of the total unmanageability of the new world order, so long as the threat of terrorism cannot be contained. Beck's conventional view is that politicians and industrialists are happy to hear talk of catastrophe so long as it is someone else doing the talking, allowing the politicians and industrialists to appear in control, relatively speaking. Blair is a practical politician who is nevertheless happy to talk the language of catastrophe himself.

Blair has also been surprisingly open about another side of political risk management, one that politicians have usually preferred to keep to themselves. The catastrophes he has been forced to contemplate since September 11 have not only been global ones. The possibility of terrorist attack has focused the minds of all democratic politicians on the risks they personally face when confronted with disasters they might have foreseen but failed to prevent. As Blair has put it, the risk is that individual politicians will not be forgiven if they are perceived to have taken a chance on any intelligence that turns out to have offered early indications of avoidable future disasters. In such circumstances, it makes sense for politicians to be highly risk averse. But equally, it makes sense for the publics they represent to remain relatively indifferent to these kinds of risks. Why should it matter to anyone but Tony Blair (and his immediate circle) whether the war on terrorism threatens Blair with catastrophic damage to his personal reputation? It is true that the general public has a very strong incentive to wish their political leaders to exercise sound political judgment when evaluating the terrorist threat. It is also true that the public will punish politicians who make serious misjudgments. But it does not follow that the private calculations of politicians concerning the huge political risks they face when assessing intelligence should encourage the electorate to give them the benefit of the doubt. Blair clearly thinks the opposite. He wants the public to recognize his predicament: to understand that the risks of the new world order are such that all politicians have to contemplate disaster on a daily basis, and act accordingly. Blair wants sympathy for being Prime Minister at such a time.[15] But democratic politics, in its traditional forms, is a notoriously unsympathetic business. Even though all politicians face personal risks in the decisions they take, that is their concern. If they get it wrong, a well-functioning democracy will have other politicians waiting in the wings, ready to take their chances.

It is Blair's highly personal use of the language of risk that is new, even if the risks themselves are not. September 11 did not change the balance of risk, in the sense that the world did not suddenly become a more dangerous place—it is in the nature of risk that a single event does not alter the balance of probability. What changed was the readiness of politicians like Blair to deploy the idea of an increasingly risky world to provide a bridge between two distinct aspects of the new world order: on the one hand, the growing impulse towards a technocratic, managerial style of politics, founded on the interdependence of the international community; and on the other hand, the increasing premium being placed on decisive political action, and on strong political leadership, in the face of that interdependence. The language of risk serves Blair's purposes because it is both personal and impersonal at the same time—the risks are his, and the risks are everyone's.

The same double standards are visible in the other big shift undergone by Blair's doctrine of the international community between the wars in Kosovo and Iraq. In his 1999 Chicago speech,

Blair recognized the dangers posed to the new internationalism by a potential falling out between the EU and the United States. But before the advent of the Bush presidency he understood this danger as coming from a failure on the part of both sides to recognize what was at stake in their relationship:

> The EU and United States should prepare to make a real step-change in working more closely together. Recent trade disputes have been a bad omen in this regard. We are really failing to see the bigger picture with disputes over the banana regime, or whatever else... The EU and the United States need each other and need to put that relationship above arguments that are not ultimately fundamental.[16]

After September 11, it was no longer possible to argue that any differences between the United States and Europe turned on issues that were not ultimately fundamental. Instead, Blair was forced to justify his unflinching support for President Bush in the face of widespread European opposition as a kind of risk assessment. For Blair, the risks of alienating the United States in a dangerous and uncertain world were greater than the risks of alienating swathes of European and global public opinion. As he put it in his speech in Washington to the Joint Houses of Congress in July 2003: "Believe me, if Europe and America are together, the others will work with us. But if we split, all the rest will play around, play us off and nothing but mischief will be the result of it."[17] Blair has also come to believe that Britain is uniquely placed to bridge the divide between the United States and Europe, because only Britain truly understands what is at stake for both sides. Where previously Blair saw his job as reminding both sides that there were more important things to worry about than bananas, now that nobody doubts it, his job is the more taxing one of trying to reconcile two distinct styles of politics that threaten to divide the world. On the one side is the consensual, managerial, legalistic style of the Europeans; on the other is the more robust, dynamic, self-willed style of the Americans. In the middle stands Tony Blair, who believes it is possible to combine them.

Europe versus the United States

Is it possible to combine them? The British Prime Minister is not alone in thinking that this is the most important problem facing the international order, now and for the foreseeable future. But he is wrong to assume that Britain is uniquely well placed to provide a solution, by offering a political bridge between the United States and Europe. The truth is that the Western world is divided by two distinct ways of doing politics, but the division does not run between any particular geographical areas or power blocs—it cuts across all of them. American politics has succumbed to many of the same regulatory and bureaucratic pressures as European politics, as legislative and executive activity become subject to ever wider forms of scrutiny and oversight.[18] Meanwhile, European political leaders are prone to many of the same self-assertive, bullying impulses as their American counterparts. The clash between the United States and France over the war in Iraq was a collision of world-views; but it was also a collision between two political leaders, each of whom was able to exercise extraordinary personal influence over national policy, an influence that their respective publics were willing to accept. Europe is a continent divided: not just between "old" and "new" (or anti-American and pro-American), but also between its impersonal governance arrangements—a technocratic, managerial, legalistic mode of politics perfectly captured in both the style and content of the now moribund EU constitution—and the personal authority of its political leaders, wherein caprice, charisma and strong tendencies towards egomania remain on powerful display. The United States is no different. As well as being split between the red and the blue states, the United States is being pulled in different directions by the conflicting trends towards the personalization and the depersonalization of its political affairs. George W. Bush's administration is centred to a remarkable degree on the personality of the president and a select group of his advisers, whose political authority is wholly conditional on the personal trust the president places in them. Yet neither Bush nor his advisers can inoculate the United States against the steady encroachments of an impersonal, interdependent, intrusive world.

There is nothing new in this tension between the impersonal demands of governance and the personal dynamics of governmental power. Indeed, it constitutes the central dilemma of all forms of modern politics—how to reconcile governance with government, so that states can be efficiently and justly administered but also flexibly and confidently led. The history of the modern state has been marked by frequent conceptual and constitutional readjustments in the attempt to bring the rule of men and the administration of things closer into line. None has been entirely successful—government and governance can never ultimately be reconciled, because they are not the same. Nevertheless, in the most successful modern states, the personal and the impersonal have been prevented from drifting too far apart, so that the foundations of modern politics have remained intact. These foundations now appear under threat. The increasing interdependence of nation states has led to a proliferation of rules and networks that no longer appear to be under the control of national governments. At the same time, many national governments have become increasingly centralized, and the domestic politics of nation states is focused more and more on the personal qualities of a narrow band of individuals. The question is whether this double tendency will simply result in another of the periodic readjustments in the conceptual underpinnings of the modern state, or whether it marks the beginning of the end for the state itself.

In this book, I argue in favour of the state as the only plausible site in which these tensions can be resolved. But I do not believe that the tensions themselves are negligible, and nor do I believe that they can be resolved simply by plumping for one style of politics over the other. One of the difficulties in deciding between them is that the forces producing personalized politics and impersonal governance are often the same. An integrated, globalized world of mass communication, mass transit and open markets requires a vast framework of impersonal rules to regulate, coordinate and oversee the transactions that take place within it. At the same time, a globalized world tends to personalize the experience of the individuals who inhabit it, since each person's encounters with this complex, overlapping set of rules and regulations may be different. There may be many more experiences shared by diverse individuals as a result of globalization, but a common set of shared experiences for all the people in a given geographical area has become much rarer. The internet, which is the cause of some of these changes, also serves as their most potent symbol. There is nothing more personal than trawling the internet for knowledge or advice or thrills that can be tailored to your particular individual preferences; at the same time, there is nothing more impersonal than receiving your knowledge or advice or thrills from a vast, rule-governed network of information-bearing machines.

The same forces are at work in politics. Electoral politics is increasingly tailored towards the personal preferences of diverse and often narrowly defined groups of voters. But electoral politics has also come to alienate many of these voters, because it appears to them as a technocratic, mechanical, passionless exercise. The information-gathering devices that make contemporary politics such a personalized business are also the ones that turn so many people off it, because it no longer speaks directly to them in a language everyone can understand. These trends are most obvious in the domain of 24-hour news, where the sheer variety of information available has led to a conformity in coverage, as newscasters seek to connect with their audiences by narrowing the scope of the stories they cover. What this means in practice is that politics is reduced to a series of discrete, self-contained events, through which individual politicians attempt to manage their relationship with a public whose experience of these politicians is invariably conveyed in personalized terms. The war in Iraq was one such event, and it was itself broken down into a series of such events (hostage crises, acts of torture, transfers of power, symbolic elections) (see Chapter Six). Terrorism has helped to create this climate of fractured political attention, but it also feeds off it. In the war on terror, we are taught all we could possibly need to know about a select band of politicians, terrorists and their victims, whose personal experiences and beliefs between them constitute the focus of global affairs. As a result, we learn almost nothing about what these experiences and beliefs might mean beyond themselves. A gap has opened up between politics as a rule-governed activity and politics as a set of personal experiences, and it appears to be growing (see Chapter Five).

This gap is not in itself evidence that we live in a changed world. The tension between personality politics and the impersonal responsibilities that individual politicians undertake has provided the central dynamic of representative democracy for over 200 years. What has changed is that some of the familiar political means for bridging this gap have started to fracture. Mass-membership political parties, large-circulation newspapers, robust representative institutions, and a stable and extensive system of welfare provision have served at various points to hold states together, by preventing power politics from becoming too detached from the impersonal requirements of democratic governance. But many traditional political parties are losing their members, newspapers are losing readers, some legislatures have seen their powers transferred elsewhere, or else simply dissipate, and welfarism is on the retreat as an electoral force. These changes are not uniform, and they are not irreversible. But they do present states with a new set of challenges. These challenges are most obvious in Europe, where some of the familiar structures of modern politics have started to fragment.[19] The guiding principles of a recognizable form of welfare state were intended to be enshrined in the new EU constitution: "The Union shall work for the sustainable development of Europe based on balanced economic growth, a social market economy, highly competitive and aiming at full employment and social progress, and with a high level of protection and improvement of the quality of the environment".[20] But because the constitution did not address the allocation of political power, questions of personal welfare were removed to the level of impersonal governance, leaving national governments with their powers undiminished, but their capacity to engage their electorates severely curtailed. This new constitution would not have abolished national politics. But it would have made it much harder to know what national politics are for.

Attempts by national politicians to sell this constitutional vision of Europe's future back to their electorates through the crude device of the plebiscitary referendum have served only to emphasize the divide between national power politics and the governance structures that now frame it. There were many things to be said for the vision of Europe contained in the constitution—it was a modest, sensible, pragmatic, if tedious, document. But it has proved to be a very hard sell, because it is very hard to recognize these qualities in the politicians whose job it is to sell it. This is not the politicians' fault—they are, after all, still engaged in the business of government, not just governance, and that means they have to compete for power with whatever tools are available. The constitution left them with the power, but also with fewer tools, though it has given them one extra tool, in the form of the constitution itself, over which national politicians have been playing out their power games for the last five years. This is a recipe for confusion and mistrust on all sides. The politicians cannot trust the electorate to judge the constitution on its merits. So the voters cannot trust the politicians to discuss it on its merits either.

The architects of the new constitution continue to hope that over time national politicians and their electorates will adapt to the new circumstances of European governance, and that new forms of national politics will evolve. If the European public eventually comes to see the merits of these constitutional arrangements, it is possible that they will also come to prefer national politicians who embody the aspirations contained in such a constitution, and the gap between government and governance will start to close again.[21] If it does, then Europe may well provide the world with the example of a new kind of politics to emulate, as so many of its supporters fervently wish.[22] However, there is currently no way of knowing whether this wish will be fulfilled. It is just as likely that government and governance will continue to drift further apart, as national electorates turn in on themselves, and national politics becomes ever more volatile, crass, fragmentary and personalized. If this happens—and there are hints of it, in the volatility and caprice of the voters recently displayed in various national elections, in the rise of minority parties, and in the decline across Europe in voter turnout—then it is hard to see how Europe's constitutional arrangements can be sustained.

The situation in the United States is different. The most recent presidential election showed that the traditional political parties are both still able to rouse the electorate, if skilfully managed, to feats of political engagement. The divide that clearly exists between the political rhetoric of many European politicians—consensual, managerial, evolutionary—and their political behaviour—confrontational, egocentric, power-hungry—does not hold for George Bush, whose manners match his message to a degree

rare in the history of modern politics. Bush is a master of partisan politics, and he has managed to breathe new life into some of
the traditional forms of electoral competition, leaving the United
States more divided than it has been in recent memory, but also
leaving no one in any doubt about the continuing importance of
central government for the governance of the nation. The United
States is still, in this sense, a familiar kind of modern state—albeit
a more powerful state than any other in the history of the world—
in ways that the core states of the EU can no longer claim to be.

Nevertheless, it would be a mistake to set the United States, as
a model of "modernity", against the open-ended and ill-defined
"postmodern" political institutions of the EU (see Chapter Eight).
Many of the differences between them are not fundamental, but
contingent. The most important is the fact that the United States
is currently at war, as Europe is not (see Chapter Ten). War has
traditionally provided the most reliable means for reconciling the
personal and impersonal sides of modern politics: a state at war is
able to connect the personal fate of its individual citizens with the
wider demands of the national community in ways that a state at
peace never can. Whatever one thinks about the conceptual and
practical viability of fighting a war against terror, there can be no
doubt that the Bush administration has successfully deployed the
idea to re-engage many individuals with their national political
institutions. This option is not available to the political leaders of
the EU. Although September 11 was a universal event, it was not
a universally personal one, and after the initial shock of the first
few days, many people outside the United States did not feel it
personally. It did not take long for this gulf to reveal itself, in the
mutual incomprehension displayed by individuals with similar
political viewpoints but widely different emotional ones, shaped
by their different nationalities.[23] In this sense, much of the divide
between Europe and the United States since September 11 has
simply been determined by where the attacks took place. The
contrast between the US's character as an aggressively modern
state and the postmodern, pacifist tendencies of Europe would
not be so clear if Europe had been attacked first. The contrast
remains real. But because the United States was attacked first, it
has been exaggerated.

The US's character as an emblematically modern state is also limited by the fact that this model of democracy is much harder to export than it once was. There are many reasons why the sort of state building that took place in the aftermath of World War II no longer appears a plausible option for transplanting democracy around the world. One is that the welfarist, corporatist mechanisms through which political stability was guaranteed in nations like Germany and Japan are now outmoded, and nowhere more so than in the United States itself. Equally, the spread of global governance institutions has coincided with a growth in national particularism; again, the United States has led the way in this respect, opting out of international agreements that do not suit her national political interests. Nationalism and anti-Americanism have gone hand in hand in many parts of the world, with the United States providing both an example and a target for resistance to the idea of creeping globalization. But the biggest problem with the idea of exporting democracy is that the sheer complexity and multiplicity of contemporary global governance arrangements means that no one is sure how it is done any more. States, particularly failed states, are no longer self-sufficient; yet it is far from clear what minimal degree of self-sufficiency is still necessary for them to participate in a democratic international order. Francis Fukuyama, who celebrated the end of history with the end of the Cold War, now acknowledges that "state building"— on which a stable liberal democratic order ultimately depends—is a very uncertain and complex business. Much of this uncertainty derives from what he calls the "bewildering variety of standards-setting and technical organizations" currently regulating international affairs.[24] But it also derives from the fact that no one can be sure where the balance between global governance and national government should ultimately lie. Fukuyama, who was one of the original signatories of the 1997 Project for the New American Century, recognizes that this is as much a problem for American as it is for European conceptions of the international order. A stable society of states appears to require both international oversight and national independence. No one on either continent has worked out how to square this circle (see Chapter Six).

In the face of so much uncertainty, it is not hard to construct a dystopian vision of an American twenty-first century, just as it is not hard to construct a dystopian vision of a European one. Philip Bobbitt, in his book *The Shield of Achilles*, imagines a world governed according to the Washington model, in which an ever more complex, interrelated, market-driven global society is overseen by ever cruder, more personalized, more brutal forms of power politics (see Chapter Eight). In such a world, rapid technological change quickly outstrips the capacity of political institutions to manage that change, with potentially catastrophic consequences. But equally, Bobbitt is able to imagine a utopian version of the Washington model as well. In this scenario, a stable world of market-driven politics provides the framework within which separate communities are able to experiment with their own voluntary social and political arrangements. Here, personal politics finds its own level under the umbrella-like protection of a dominant market state, allowing individuals and groups to choose the politics that suits them best, without those choices being implicated in any wider struggles for political power. The fantasy of a world in which there is global agreement about power politics, so that all lesser disagreements cease to be political, is an attractive, as well as an enduring, one. It is a fantasy nonetheless.

Much harder is to construct a realistic model of politics for the twenty-first century, in which global governance and national governments are able to coexist. Most attempts to construct such a realistic model contain a utopian streak of their own. For example, it is not enough to argue, as Robert Cooper does in *The Breaking of Nations*, that the challenge of contemporary politics is simply "to get used to the idea of double standards" (see Chapter Eight). Cooper believes that we need to be able to move freely, as the occasion demands, between modern and postmodern forms of politics, alternating a hard-headed military response to some threats with a readiness to pool national sovereignty when the opportunities present themselves.[25] Cooper explains why it might be desirable to adapt to these double standards, but he does not explain how. Yet the problem of double standards in political life is hardly a new one. Cooper, like so many other theorists of the new world order, fails to recognize that the most reliable mechanism we have for making ourselves accustomed to double standards in politics is the modern state itself. It is modern politics, not postmodern politics, which offers the best guide to understanding a world of flux and conflicting values.

The Liberty of the Moderns versus the Liberty of the Postmoderns

That is why, in trying to decide whether the world has changed, a long perspective is needed alongside a much shorter one. We need to view our current predicament against the backdrop of the historical development of the modern state. Many of the best-known recent accounts of the new world order have deployed the broad history of modern political ideas to frame their arguments about the novelty of our current predicament. But too often these historical ideas emerge as caricatures, and are used simply to categorize and parcel out various fixed and frequently obsolete alternatives.[26] For Robert Kagan, for example, the West divides up between Americans, who come from Mars, and Europeans, who come from Venus; at the same time, Kagan draws an equally rigid distinction between contemporary Hobbesians, who recognize the anarchic conditions of real power, and Kantians, who have given up on power in order to build their own fantasy world of peace (see Chapter Seven). Simplistic contrasts such as this one have served to reinforce the wider contrast that is often drawn between earlier doctrines of politics, with their stark certainties and rigid demarcations, and the uncertainty and complexity of the present age. When the political world we now inhabit is described as Hobbesian, it is meant to remind us that underneath all the intricacy of our endlessly varied lives, certain basic truths persist. Yet this is entirely to miss the point of what writers like Hobbes have to teach us. None of the truths of modern politics set out by Hobbes are basic, and most are a good deal more varied and complicated than the simple-minded platitudes that tend to characterize the discourse of the new world order. It is worth going back to classic theorists of the modern state like Hobbes, not so as to have convenient labels with which to impose an artificial order on the chaos of our own thoughts, but to see how other writers, as attuned to complexity as we are, tried to impose order on the chaos of their own time.

In the second part of this book, I move beyond looking at the attempts of politicians like Blair to justify themselves in the light of history, and explore the attempts of writers like Kagan, Cooper and Bobbitt to use history to make sense of the political world Blair has helped to create. In doing so, I go back to the original ideas of some of the great thinkers of the past, whose names are routinely bandied about in the political arguments of the present, to see what they really have to say. I also go back to the ideas of one writer whose name has been almost entirely forgotten: it is in the work of the great French revolutionary theorist Emmanuel Sieyès that some of the most significant lessons of modern political thought are to be found (see Chapter Nine). Sieyès understood as well as anyone that the task of modern politics was to find a way of accommodating the double standards of modern life: the personal and the impersonal, the private and the public. The modern state emerged as a practical response to the challenge of trying to combine the personal political authority of powerful leaders with the impersonal administrative capacity on which such political leadership had come to depend. The foremost interpreters of this new order recognized that a means had therefore to be found for reconciling two different modes of social and political existence, and two different styles of politics. They eventually found it in the idea of representation, which enabled modern politics to be personal and impersonal at the same time. But this idea also placed modern politicians, and modern political institutions, under severe strain, as the double standards inherent in representative politics threatened to pull them apart. The great political theorists of the emergent modern state—Hobbes in seventeenth-century England, James Madison in late eighteenth-century America, Sieyès in late eighteenth-century France, Max Weber in early twentieth-century Germany—understood both the risks and the opportunities of representative government. The risk was that the political and intellectual resources needed to hold the state together would be lacking. The opportunity was that if these resources could be found, it might prove possible to have the best of both worlds: strong government and good governance together.

The birth of the modern state also saw the attempt to combine an older way of doing politics along with the new. Many political theorists recognized the need to temper the values of modern politics with some of the virtues of ancient systems of government. One of the most resonant statements of this position was provided by the émigré Swiss philosopher and man of letters, Benjamin Constant, in his lecture "The liberty of the ancients compared to the liberty of the moderns", delivered in Paris in 1819. Constant was speaking in the aftermath of thirty years of epic turbulence in French politics, which he viewed as the consequence of a horribly misguided attempt by some revolutionary politicians to impose an outmoded conception of political liberty on what had already become a distinctively modern political society. The liberty of the ancients—the collective, martial, austere form of politics that had suited the highly regimented city states of the ancient world—simply did not fit a state like modern France, where too many separate, self-serving individuals were engaged in private pursuits of their own. Revolutionary politics celebrated valour, and discipline, and collective responsibility; but modern citizens were more interested in commerce, and money, and leisure, and they did not welcome political interference in their personal affairs. Any attempt, Constant believed, to force these citizens to give up their personal freedoms for the sake of the wider political community could only be sustained by the violent oppression of the citizens themselves.

Yet Constant was, if anything, even more clear-sighted about the dangers of celebrating the liberty of the moderns for its own sake. Simply to champion privacy, and the right of individuals to manage their own affairs within a framework of law, did not negate the danger of oppressive forms of politics. Instead, it increased the dangers, by removing personal freedom from the domain of politics altogether. Constant recognized the temptations of wishing politics away, but he also understood that politics never goes away.[27] Citizens who turn in on themselves will find that government turns in on itself as well, and starts to govern them in ways that they cannot control. Modern liberty, therefore, furnishes the pretext for its own kind of tyranny. What was needed was a defence of ancient liberty—a defence of participation, equality, virtue—in terms that suited the modern world. Constant found what he was looking for in the idea of representative government, which presupposed the independence of individual citizens, but also required their participation in the political life of the state. "Sirs," Constant concluded his lecture, "far from renouncing either of the two sorts of freedom which I have described to you, it is necessary, as I have shown, to learn to combine the two together." He went on:

> Even when people are satisfied, there is much left to do. Institutions must achieve the moral education of the citizens. By respecting their individual rights, securing their independence, refraining from troubling their work, they must nevertheless consecrate their influence over public affairs, call them to contribute by their votes to the exercise of power, grant them a right of control and supervision by expressing their opinions; and, by forming them through practice for these elevated functions, give them both the desire and the right to discharge these.[28]

We now live in a world where the liberty of the moderns contends with the liberty of the postmoderns. Modern political liberty has evolved in the ways Constant foresaw that it would—personal freedoms have been protected but also modified by the institutional demands of the representative politics of the nation state. But some of these demands now appear outmoded in the face of rapid technological and social change: individuals enjoy new kinds of freedoms in an increasingly borderless, hedonistic, information-rich, transient world. The idea that personal freedom still depends on a willingness to participate in the political life of a given nation state is no longer compelling for large numbers of people. Moreover, any attempt to impose modern forms of politics on progressively postmodern political societies is liable to generate its own kind of tyranny. The nation-state model of government cannot simply be relocated into the international arena and used to create modern political communities on a transnational or global scale. There are good reasons to think that the EU would oppress its citizens if it were to become a superstate of a conventional modern kind—it would be too cumbersome, too remote, too uniform for their diverse needs. Certainly, that is the view that most of its citizens currently take, and they are profoundly resistant to the kind of "moral education" that would be required to persuade them otherwise. A world state—on any conventional understanding of what that would mean—seems even more certain to be a recipe for violence, repression and civil disorder.[29]

But equally there are serious dangers in celebrating the liberty of the postmoderns for its own sake. Conventional modern politics is not going to go away, and national governments will turn in on themselves if postmodern governance arrangements are allowed to drift away from the domain of politics altogether. What is needed is a defence of modern politics for a postmodern world. This book attempts to offer such a defence, using history as a guide. The value of modern politics—the unifying, clarifying power of strong representative institutions—remains clear, even though the world itself has changed. Yet modern politics cannot provide any simple solutions to our current problems, given the inherent complexity of the thought that lies behind it, in the ideas of even its most clear-sighted champions. Constant himself is sometimes remembered as a great simplifier, as a result of the beguiling simplicity of the title given to his 1819 lecture.[30] But though Constant saw the sharp contrast between ancient and modern conceptions of freedom, he knew that political freedom itself could never be allowed to rest on the crude certainties of such an all-or-nothing divide. In this respect, Constant's diagnosis of the possibilities of modern politics has more in common with the formidably complex and intricate proposals put forward by his near-contemporary Sieyès than it does with the simplistic, all-or-nothing choices that so often characterize political discourse today.

The complexity of political existence generates a persistent temptation to seek out simplistic solutions to the problems of politics, as a means of cutting through the knotted difficulties that human beings have in living together in peace and prosperity. It also makes it tempting to recruit the great names of the past on one side or the other of some deep divide in contemporary politics, and to ignore the ones who do not fit. I end this book by looking at the thought of Sieyès, not because there are any easy answers to be found there, but precisely because he illustrates how few easy answers there are in the work of some of those who understood modern politics best, and who do not fit our contemporary divisions as a result. Constant himself drew on some of Sieyès's arguments, though he rejected others that he saw as unnecessarily complicated. Nonetheless, Constant too understood the deep perils of the siren call of simplicity. He saw the challenge of early nineteenth-century politics as that of finding a way of defending the liberty of the moderns, while recognizing that the best defence lay through the ancient value of participation. The challenge of early twenty-first-century politics is likewise the formidable one of finding a way to cope with the double standards of postmodern political life, while recognizing that the best guide for coping with any double standards in politics lies in the traditional theory and practice of the modern state.

The Politics of Good Intentions

What then of Tony Blair? The relative longevity and success of Blair's political career has been built out of his ability to straddle the divides of late twentieth- and early twenty-first-century politics: between old Labour and new Labour; Clinton and Bush; the United States and Europe; military power and international law; national sovereignty and global community. These divisions existed before September 11, 2001, but the terrorist attacks that took place on that day exacerbated them, and served to bring them to the surface of world affairs. The challenge for Blair has been to develop a style of politics that allows him to accommodate all of these divisions, without sacrificing either his own political identity, or his capacity to act decisively when the occasion demands. This he has managed to do, and though it has become increasingly difficult over time, it is a style that has continued to suit Blair well, as he demonstrated in the immediate aftermath of the London bombs of July 2005.

His method for achieving it has been to embrace the double standards inherent in contemporary politics, thereby bringing them to the surface of his own political rhetoric. His is a self-aware style of politics and he takes great pains to show that he understands the ways in which all national politicians must currently be prepared to be pulled in two different directions at once. It is also a very personal style, and he uses his self-awareness to personalize the difficulties and choices that he faces. Blair knows that trying to straddle the divides of contemporary politics leaves him open to accusations of hypocrisy from all sides. But it is a part of the genius of the style he has developed that its self-aware, personal, confessional character forestalls the charge of hypocrisy before it can be made. How, he seems to be saying, can I be a hypocrite if I know just how hypocritical I must appear? This self-knowledge provides the bona fides of his own good intentions.

Blair places a lot of weight on his good intentions, but he also recognizes that in politics good intentions are never enough. The role of good intentions in politics is the subject of the title piece in this collection (see Chapter Two). Blair's approach to this question is emblematic of many of the dilemmas currently facing the new world order, such as it is. But what his approach also shows is that awareness of these dilemmas is not sufficient to resolve them. Blair is a politician who has succumbed to the temptation to exploit complexity in an attempt to reinforce the appeal of simple-minded solutions. Paying lip-service to the double standards of contemporary politics does not serve to justify or to explain any particular course of action a politician might choose to take. In this sense, Blair's personal style of politics is part of the problem, not part of the solution. For all its appeal in times of heightened emotion (after the death of Diana, following September 11, and in the heady, traumatic days of July 2005), it has also caused him some acute personal political difficulties, as the British public have come to tire of its endlessly confessional character. But Blair's own fate also serves to expose some of the deeper difficulties faced by the forms of politics he has chosen to embrace. The new world order requires more substantial tests of a politician's judgment than their own sense of the difficulty of what they are undertaking, and their readiness to communicate this to a wider public. The best way to provide tests of political judgment is to have strong political parties, robust representative institutions, fiercely contested elections, and a fully engaged public, with all the difficulties that the coexistence of these things entails. Whatever Blair has done has been without these tests of judgment. There is no reason to suppose that it is possible to meet the challenges of the new world order without them. In this sense, nothing has really changed.

PART ONE

Tony Blair,
History and Risk

CHAPTER TWO

TONY BLAIR AND THE POLITICS OF GOOD INTENTIONS

On 1 April 2003, *The Guardian* newspaper admonished the British Prime Minister to remember the importance of living up to his good intentions in the Middle East, in the following terms:

> Putting Iraq to rights, in Mr Blair's view, should be the whole world's business. The more that all nations make common cause to do this, the better. The less this happens, the more vital it is to balance any absence of common cause with a sense of equitable and humanitarian initiatives—on the Middle East and on reconstruction in particular—which can help establish what Disraeli, seeking to justify the British invasion of Abyssinia in 1867, called "the purity of our purpose".[1]

Benjamin Disraeli is perhaps not the most obvious of Tony Blair's predecessors for *The Guardian* to have summoned in aid of its own, consistently high-minded opposition to the creeping imperialism of the new world order. It is true, nevertheless, that the British invasion of Abyssinia, which began in 1867 but only concluded in the spring of 1868, offers some striking parallels with the 2003 conflict in Iraq. Disraeli's Abyssinian adventure was, as its architect conceded in the House of Commons on 2 July 1868 after it had been successfully concluded, "a most costly and perilous expedition", the announcement of which was "received in more than one quarter with something like mocking incredulity".[2] Indeed, "when the invasion of Abyssinia was first mooted, it was denounced as a rash enterprise, pregnant with certain peril and probable disaster".[3] The risks were diminished, however, by the massive technological imbalance between the combatants, and in the end it was no surprise, as Disraeli put it, "if the manly qualities of the Abyssinians sank before the resources of our warlike science".[4] The decisive battle of the war—the battle of Arogi—lasted for an hour and a half, at the end of which the British forces had suffered 29 casualties; the Abyssinian force of 3000 lost at least 500 dead, and many more wounded. So the naysayers and doom-mongers at home were also routed, and Disraeli was able to tell the Commons "that we have asserted the purity of our purpose". He went on:

> In an age accused, and perhaps not unjustly, of selfishness, and too great a regard for material interests, it is something, in so striking and significant a manner, for a great nation to have vindicated the higher principles of humanity.[5]

The leader of the opposition, William Gladstone, seconding Disraeli's vote of thanks to the troops who had pulled off this masterly campaign, could only acquiesce.

Unfortunately, however, Disraeli meant by the purity of his purpose precisely the opposite of what was intended by *The Guardian* on Blair's behalf. The Abyssinian war was fought to free a group of nine hostages—the British Consul among them—who had been taken by the King of Abyssinia, Theodore II, to his fortress at Magdala in a fit of pique after Queen Victoria had refused his pleas for help, as a Christian, in his wars with his Muslim neighbours. The hostages were rescued, albeit at vast expense (the final bill for the expedition, at £9 million, was nearly double the original estimate), and Theodore committed suicide in his ruined fortress, shooting himself in the mouth with a pistol he had been given as a present by Victoria. The fortress was cleared, its armaments destroyed, and the town of Magdala burned. Then the British troops went home. The proof of Disraeli's pure intentions came precisely from the fact that they didn't hang around, didn't try to rebuild, or oversee, or maintain anything in the place they had sacked, but simply got out. Because Disraeli was a bona fide imperialist—a believer, like many of those around George Bush, in the twin principles of *Imperium et Libertas*—he could only demonstrate that he had no other goal than that of freeing the hostages and punishing their captors by sacking the place where they had been held. The "higher principles of humanity" he sought to uphold were

not what we would now call the higher principles of humani-
tarianism. Rather, they were the principles of biblical justice, the
idea that wrongdoers would be pursued, no matter how far away,
and no matter how relatively trivial the offence. Saddam Hussein
could have been treated in the same way. His technical offence—
the breach of UN resolutions—was also relatively trivial in the
grand scheme of things (trivial in the sense that it happens all the
time). The Abyssinian solution would have been to find Saddam's
WMD, destroy them and those responsible for them, and then
leave, no damage undone, in order to prove it really was about
the weapons, and not about something else. But there were two
problems with this approach. First, as we now know, there were no
weapons to destroy. Second, the invasion of Iraq was not simply a
punitive expedition, however much its architects might have been
forced at moments to pretend otherwise. It was also a mission of
liberation. It is a sign of the very different moral and political universe that Blair inhabits that his only chance of proving the purity
of his purpose has been to encourage the more punitively minded
members of the Bush administration to stick it out in Iraq, spend
more money and political capital, and try to repair some of the
damage they have done. And it is a sign of the complexities of
Blair's moral and political universe that this risks the charge that
Disraeli, the bona fide imperialist, was able to avoid—the charge
of imperialism.

Still, it is easy to see why *The Guardian* was so desperately rum-
maging for some historical precedent in order to pin the British
government down. The new world order is awash with good
intentions, many of them Tony Blair's. Yet the suspicion remains
that good intentions in politics don't count for much, if anything
at all. One of the things that has united all critics of the war in
Iraq, whether from the left or the right, is that they are sick of the
sound of Tony Blair trumpeting the purity of his purpose, when
what matters is the consequences of his actions. There he stands,
however, somewhere between left and right, trumpeting away.
Blairism as a force in international politics has proved very hard
to pin down, in part because Blair doesn't just believe in good
intentions; he, too, believes that what matters is outcomes, and
is prepared, as he often puts it, "to let history be my judge".[6] He
remains a third-way politician, and he believes in having things

33

both ways. What, then, is the worth of his good intentions? Does history provide any sort of guide?

The most celebrated, as well as the most sceptical, historical account of the role of intention in justifying political action is the one given by the sociologist Max Weber in his lecture "Politik als Beruf" (usually translated as "Politics as a Vocation")[7]. It was delivered on 28 January 1919 to a group of students in Munich, and Weber used it to warn them against, among other things, politicians who come flaunting their good intentions, but leave behind them a trail of blood. Munich was not short of examples of this type in early 1919. The most prominent was the journalist-turned-politician Kurt Eisner, who had stumbled into power at the beginning of November the previous year when he declared Bavaria a republic, two days before a similar proclamation was made in Berlin, and four days before the official end of the 1914–18 war. Eisner remained at the head of the state he had brought into being, despite the fact that the elections he called to the new Bavarian parliament in January had seen his group of Independent Socialists receive just 2.5% of the vote, and 3 out of the 180 seats available. Ignoring this result, and the unsurprising clamour for his resignation, Eisner clung briefly to office, arguing that for now practical politics had to give way before the purity of his purpose. His mission as he saw it was to cleanse the whole political life of Germany, starting in Bavaria, by embracing the idea of German war-guilt. In Eisner's world, everything that preceded November 1918 was immoral, sinful and corrupt; everything after could be beautiful, healthy and pure, if only German politicians would own up to the wickedness of what had gone before.

Eisner was not in Munich to hear Weber's lecture. He had better things to do. In fact, at the end of January he had a choice of three different conferences to attend as the representative of the new moral order in Bavaria—one in France, one in Germany and one in Switzerland. He could have gone to Paris, to witness the start of the peace negotiations that were to culminate in August in the Treaty of Versailles. Alternatively, he could have gone to Weimar, where he was expected for the opening of the constituent assembly that also produced in August a document of world-historical significance: the constitution of the new German republic. But instead, Eisner chose to go to Berne to attend a convention of European socialists, whose delegates included Ramsay MacDonald and Arthur Henderson from Britain, and which produced nothing. The convention was designed as a continuation of the regular pre-war gatherings of the Socialist International, at which various factions had been used to squabble and bicker before declaring their unshakeable class solidarity and confidence in the future. The elephant in the room this time, politely ignored by some of those in attendance, was the fact that the solid working classes of Europe had spent the last four years trying to blow each other to bits. Eisner was not a man to ignore an elephant in the room; rather, he dressed it up in ribbons and bows and tried to pass it off as a peace offering. Germany was to blame for the horrors of the war, he readily acknowledged. But because Germany was to blame, Germany was the best source of hope for the future. This was designed to be the beginning of a virtuous circle: expressions of guilt would mean a fresh start; a fresh start was the surest sign that the past was truly regretted. "We want to expiate our guilt", Eisner told his fellow delegates, "by going ahead on the path of socialism".[8] What did elections, or peace treaties, or constitutions, matter in the face of moral renewal? Nevertheless, Eisner decided to return from Berne to Munich, where his absence had been much resented, in time to attend the inauguration of the new Bavarian parliament on 21 February, where he planned to offer his resignation. Going to the opening ceremony on foot, and heedless of the repeated threats to his life he had received since coming to power, he was confronted by an embittered, anti-Semitic Bavarian aristocrat called Count Anton von Arco-Valley, who shot him dead. The moral renewal of Bavarian politics was over.

The mismatch between Eisner's intentions and the unintended outcome of his brief period of prominence would be comic, if it weren't so tragic. When news of the assassination reached the chamber to which he had been heading, one of his few remaining supporters produced a pistol of his own and shot the leader of the majority socialist party, wounding but not killing him. After that, things went quickly downhill. Within weeks a workers' soviet republic was declared, though it continued to be governed by those Weber called *litterateurs*—"poets, semi-poets, mezzo-philosophers and schoolteachers".[9] They sent an armed

Red Guard onto the streets of Munich, but insisted they mark their uncompromising opposition to bourgeois ways by pointing the muzzles of their rifles to the ground. The majority socialists fled the city, and soon more systematic killing began. This was enough for the government in Berlin, and for its nominal head, Friedrich Ebert, soon to be the first president of the Weimar Republic. He acquiesced in the suppression of the Bavarian revolution by the *Freikorps*, troops of mixed loyalties but confirmed anti-Bolshevism, and with a taste for vengeance. (He had earlier acquiesced in the murder of the leaders of the short-lived Sparticist uprising in Berlin, Rosa Luxemburg and Karl Liebknecht, an event which elicited from Weber the memorably heartless response: "They called up the street, and the street has despatched them".) In Munich, Red Terror was followed by White Terror, which was worse. By May, it was all over. Many thousands of people were dead, and political life in Munich became what it was to remain for the remainder of the Weimar years, a running sore for the new republic. Eisner had hoped to create in Bavaria a beacon for a new kind of politics, founded on good will and high moral purpose. After his death, Bavaria did quite quickly become the seedbed of a new political movement; it was, however, entirely malevolent. Munich was the birthplace of National Socialism.

Weber does not mention Eisner by name in the published version of his lecture, which appeared in October 1919. He probably felt he didn't need to. Nor does he refer to Friedrich Ebert, though it is possible to read parts of the text as a personal address to the new president, encouraging him to hold his nerve. Instead, Weber chose to discuss the thoughts of Professor Friedrich Förster, a celebrated moralist and pacifist, who was Weber's colleague at Munich University, as well as being a colleague of Eisner's in the new Bavarian government. Förster also happened to be in Switzerland at the beginning of 1919, where he had been sent by Eisner as his ambassador, charged with spreading the news of Germany's rediscovered sense of its moral responsibilities, and the sincerity of its good intentions. It was Förster's belief that in politics, only good can flow from good, and only evil from evil. For Weber, this was the political philosophy of a child. "Not just the entire course of world history", he wrote, "but any unbiased examination of daily experience, proclaims the opposite".[10]

36

Förster's mistake was to believe that a Christian ethic, and the benign categories of religious moral thought, could possibly apply to the world of politics. Politics is the devil's business. "Anyone who gets involved with politics", Weber declared in one of the best-known passages in the lecture, "is making a pact with diabolical powers".[11] It doesn't follow from this that we are all damned; only that no one should get involved with politics if damnation is what primarily concerns them. Förster, said Weber, was a man he could respect "because of the undoubted integrity of his convictions"; but for just that reason, he went on, "I reject him unreservedly as a politician".[12] It was of only small comfort that if such a man was to get involved in politics, ambassador to Switzerland (a nation Weber sometimes held up as a model of what can happen if you decide to opt out of power politics altogether) was probably the best situation for him.

Eisner and Förster were united by their sense that war-guilt was an essential vehicle of political renewal, and was to be encouraged. Weber thought their fixation not only childish but also perverse. In his lecture, he drew an analogy with the way some men behave when a love affair turns sour. Most, he argues, will seek some kind of self-justification, telling themselves that " 'she did not deserve my love', or 'she disappointed me', or offering some other such 'reasons'."[13] This is a "profoundly unchivalrous attitude", since it burdens the abandoned woman "not only with misfortune but also with being in the wrong". It has a counterpart in the attitude of the unsuccessful lover too, the man who takes his rejection as a sign of inadequacy, that he is of "lesser worth". The same kinds of things, Weber suggests, happen after a war.

> The victor will of course assert, with ignoble self-righteousness, "I won because I was in the right"... When the horrors of war cause a man to suffer a psychological breakdown, instead of simply saying, 'It was all just too much for me", he now feels the need to justify his war-weariness by substituting the feeling, "I couldn't bear the experience because I was forced to fight for a morally bad cause". The same applies to those defeated in war. Instead of searching, like an old woman, for the "guilty party" after the war (when it was in fact the structure of society that produced the war), anyone with a manly, unsentimental bearing would say to the enemy, "We lost the war—you won it. The matter is now

settled. Now let us discuss what conclusions are to be drawn
in the light of the substantive interests involved and—this
is the main thing—in the light of the responsibility for the
future which the victor in particular must bear." Anything
else lacks dignity and will have dire consequences.[14]

An obsessive preoccupation with guilt is a mark of irresponsibility, both in sexual relations and in political relations. In his lecture,
Weber cautiously extends the sexual analogy, calling questions
of past guilt "politically sterile (because unresolvable)".[15] But he
was more explicit in his private correspondence. In a letter he
wrote on 13 November 1918, he complained that "this wallowing in guilt feelings ... is a sickness—just as flagellation is one
in the religious area and masochism is in the sexual sphere".[16]
Weber was not alone in this view. Moritz Bonn, another professor
at Munich University during 1919, recalled long afterwards his
feeling that Bavarian politics were dominated during this time
by "neurotic temperaments to whom self-inflicted tortures are a
source of joy". For some, peace without honour was too good an
opportunity to pass by. "These Germans", Bonn wrote, "went at
it, as *flagellantes*."[17]

"Sterile excitement" is how Weber characterizes the temptations
of conviction politics. He contrasts them with what he calls "an
ethic of responsibility". Responsibility does not exclude conviction, but it does presuppose a particular attitude towards it. The
responsible politician knows that good does not always follow
from good. Even actions undertaken with the best intentions will
generate unintended consequences, and the mark of a responsible
politician is how they deal with these. The way to deal with them
is to take responsibility for them, which means neither denying
them nor wallowing in them, but accepting them for what they
are, the unintended but foreseeable consequences of any involvement in the dangerous business of power politics. All politicians
with real power have dirty hands, because real politics can be a
bloody business. The trick for Weber is not to try to hide them,
nor to parade them through the streets, but just to get on with the
task in hand, in the knowledge that dirty hands, and a soiled conscience, are the price that all politicians have to pay. Responsible
politicians will suffer, but they should suffer in silence, because

the test of politics is whether you can cope with the knowledge that you are not as good as you would like to be.

How easy, though, is it to distinguish this ready acceptance of suffering from some of the vices that Weber detects in the irresponsible politician? The American philosopher Michael Walzer— writing in 1973, in the dying days of another misjudged imperial war almost as horrible and irresponsible, though not so catastrophic, as the one Germany finally lost in 1918—detected in Weber's "mature, superbly trained, relentless, objective, responsible and disciplined political leader" a recognizable type: the type of the "suffering servant".[18] "Here is a man who lies, intrigues, sends others to their death—and suffers. None of us can know, he tells us, how much it costs him to do his duty."[19] The type remains a familiar one. The almost teary, always steely look on Vladimir Putin's waxen face—most notably as he apologized on Russian television for the deaths of innocents after the Moscow theatre siege in October 2002, or as he toured the hospitals of Beslan, dressed head to toe in black, following the school massacres there in September 2004—is pretty much its perfect embodiment. The responsible politician can apologize, but he can't do more than apologize, because that would mean passing the burden onto someone else. As a result, responsible politics in the wrong hands can look a lot like its opposite. "We suspect the suffering servant of either masochism or hypocrisy or both," Walzer writes, "and while we are often wrong, we are not always wrong."[20]

How can we tell? Weber does not give many examples in "Politik als Beruf" of politicians who fit his mould of responsibility, but the one who appears most often also happens to be the most notorious self-flagellant in modern political history. Weber does not discuss, and presumably knew nothing about, William Gladstone's predilection for scourging himself with a whip after his periodic encounters with prostitutes whom he was endeavouring to "save".[21] Instead, Gladstone appears as an example of two interrelated phenomena which Weber takes to be characteristic of modern, professional politics. First, Gladstone was a quintessential product of the age of machine politics, and a symbol both of its increasing prevalence and of its paradoxes. Gladstone was not a machine politician himself, in that he stood outside the party machine and simply required it to do his bidding. It did his bidding because he gave the machine what it required: electoral success. And he did this precisely by being something more than just a machine politician in the eyes of the public. It was what Weber calls "the ethical character" of Gladstone's personality, the sense that he was something more than just a vote winner, that gave him his hold over the new breed of political professionals who were interested in nothing more than getting out the vote. His electoral success, particularly after the Midlothian campaign of 1879–80, also exemplified another aspect of modern politics in Weber's eyes, the heightened sense of legitimacy that mass democratic politics can bestow on successful politicians, particularly in Britain and the United States. Gladstone was, for Weber, a kind of dictator, "the dictator of the electoral battlefield", and Weber admired the British parliamentary system precisely for its capacity to produce leaders of this type.[22] Gladstone may have been an ethical politician, but nothing about his political ethics was straightforward. As a successful conviction politician in an age of mass politics, he was, almost by definition, not simply a conviction politician at all.

In all this, Tony Blair is the political leader of the last 100 years who most obviously fits the Gladstonian mould. He is, like one or two before him, the dictator of the electoral battlefield, but he is also more than anyone since Gladstone a politician of a particular ethical type: moralizing, ruthless, self-serving, pious, visionary, partisan and thoroughly self-aware. He may or may not be a hypocrite—it is one of the marks of this kind of politician and this kind of politics that the charge of hypocrisy is almost impossible to prove and impossible to refute—but he has revealed an increasing taste for masochism. In the run-up to the war on Iraq, Blair's public performances were marked by a kind of relish for confrontations in which he could not hope to come out on top. All he could do was show us that he was willing to suffer the barbs of his opponents, and do so uncomplainingly, because it was his lot to suffer for his beliefs. This reached its apogee in the thoroughly bizarre encounter he had on 10 March 2003 with a group of women in the studios of ITV, at the end of which he was slow-handclapped for the first time since a notorious encounter with the Women's Institute three years earlier, something he hadn't seemed to enjoy at all. This time, he appeared, if not exactly to enjoy the abuse, almost to welcome it. His facial expressions—long-suffering, concerned, sincere, distressed, resolute—gave the whole thing the feeling of what Gladstone would have called "rescue work", although in this case no one wanted to be rescued. The audience included three women who had been bereaved by terrorism, two by September 11 and one by the 2002 bombings in Bali. Unsurprisingly, Blair had nothing to say in the face of their rage and pain except to let it wash over him. No politician in their right mind would choose the recently bereaved as their interlocutors for an argument about the rights and wrongs of a proposed course of action that involved killing. But this was not an argument—it was an exchange of feelings, conducted in an atmosphere of mutual incomprehension and barely suppressed emotion. The point, so far as one could tell, was for Blair to be able to say, as he did say, repeatedly, that just as he understood the strength of feeling of his opponents, he needed them to understand that he felt just as strongly too.

The difference between Blair's rescue work and Gladstone's is that Gladstone's really was rescue work—it was private, and personal, and more-or-less secret. Like the self-scourging that followed it, it lay deep in the background to his politics, and though some hint of its tone may occasionally have leaked into his political rhetoric, it was not a political strategy (public exposure would have been catastrophic). Blair's masochism is a political strategy, and has, one presumes, no echoes in his private life.[23] In this respect, Blair has more in common with Eisner than with Gladstone: he makes a parade of his guilt. But of course, Tony Blair is really nothing like Kurt Eisner or Friedrich Förster or any of the other wishful moralizers who briefly and disastrously flitted across the scene of German politics in the Weimar period. He is not nearly wishful enough, and much too successful. He is also much too keen on war (five in six years, at the last count). Eisner and Förster were expressing guilt for a war they had done what they could to oppose, and wholeheartedly repudiated. Blair has displayed the public symptoms of guilt for a war he did everything he could to engineer. In this sense, Blair is a new kind of politician, one who doesn't really fit into Weber's typologies of political responsibility and irresponsibility. He seems to be both types at once.

Take Weber's injunction that responsible politicians should always weigh their intentions against the consequences, both intended and unintended, of what they do, and not simply contrast their own motives with the ill will of their opponents. "What distinguishes the polemics directed by most exponents of the supposedly new ethics at the opponents they criticize from the polemics of other demagogues?" Weber asked in his lecture. "Their noble intentions, some will say. Very well. But the claim under discussion here is the means, and their enemies lay just as much claim to noble intentions, and do so with complete sincerity."[24] It was a distinction of this kind that even the moralizing Gladstone sought to uphold. Though he made clear enough his personal revulsion at the antics of his Tory opponents, he was careful not to impugn their motives, for it was not motives that mattered. Gladstone made much of his principles—at Midlothian it was "the sound and sacred principle that Christendom is formed by a band of nations who are united to one another in the bonds of right; that they are without distinction of great and small."[25] But he went on:

> I hold that he who by act or word brings that principle into peril or disparagement, however honest his intentions may be, places himself in the position of one inflicting—I won't say intending to inflict—I ascribe nothing of the sort—but inflicting injury on his own country, and endangering the peace of all the most fundamental interests of Christian society.[26]

Tony Blair is not usually so cautious. He has not shirked from questioning the motives of his opponents, from the wicked Saddam, to the malicious French, to the self-serving Tories, to the cynical media. Moreover, it is central to the political philosophy of Blairism that actions that may have the potential to endanger the unity of the international community can be justified by the good intentions that lie behind them. Yet, as Weber says, what matters here are the means.

Disraeli was able to show that there was no mismatch between the means and the end of his adventure in Abyssinia, because he only set out to liberate nine hostages, not a whole captive people. Blair does not have this luxury. There is an unavoidable mismatch between what Blair intends and the methods he employs, because he intends peace, and he has chosen war. Nor does he have the

luxury of the nineteenth-century politician in the face of this paradox, which is to invoke God's unfathomable purposes. Abraham
Lincoln, who also fought a war for peace, and was in some ways
the embodiment of what Weber meant by a responsible politician,
did not have to take full responsibility for the war he fought.[27] In
a letter of 4 September 1864, he wrote to a friend:

> We hoped for a happy termination of this terrible war long
> before this; but God knows best, and has ruled otherwise ...
> Surely He intends some great good to follow this mighty con-
> vulsion, which no mortal could make, and no mortal could
> stay.[28]

Blair may think like this, but he couldn't say it, even among
friends, for fear of ridicule. Lincoln also spoke of the purity of
his own purpose ("Having chosen our course," he told Congress
on 4 July 1861, "without guile, and with pure purpose, let us renew
our trust in God, and go forward without fear, and with manly
hearts"), but he had the further advantage of being able to prove it,
in adversity.[29] The warlike science available to Lincoln's armies,
newly terrible as it was, was also available to a large extent to
the other side, so that neither could hope to win without being
prepared for a long, hard, bloody conflict, which is what they got.
Purity of purpose here means, among other things, a willingness
to fight to the end. Blair can't really talk in these terms, because
the fights he picks are too one-sided. It is true that he likes to point
out that in each of his major wars (Kosovo, Afghanistan, Iraq) he
stayed the course when the doubters were writing his political
obituary. But it was in each case just *his* obituary they were writing, and just a political one; the killing remained for the most part
the killing of unknowns on the other side. Moreover, staying the
course meant holding his nerve for a few weeks in the face of
attacks mounted in television studios and on the pages of unsympathetic newspapers, and in the face of large, but largely peaceful,
popular demonstrations, whose political momentum was quick
to fade away. Blair has shown courage, but he has not had to show
all that much courage; certainly he has not been given the opportunity to demonstrate his integrity solely by dint of what Lincoln
and Weber might have called his "manliness".

Instead, in each conflict Blair has fought, he has been forced to
offer a different kind of justification for the mismatch between

means and ends. He has explicitly conflated the two types of politics Weber sought to distinguish—responsible and irresponsible politics, or the politics of unintended consequences and the politics of good intentions. He has sought to show that he is well intentioned by showing that he takes the unintended consequences of his actions seriously. In some ways, this is such a familiar argument that it is barely noticed anymore. But it is only familiar because Blair has made it so. For example, speaking in the House of Commons on 28 April 1999, during one of the "difficult" phases of the Kosovo conflict, when innocent civilians were being killed by stray bombs but little progress seemed to be being made, Blair defended himself in these terms:

> The difference [between us and them] quite simply is this. Whenever there are civilian casualties as a result of allied bombs, they are by error. We regret them, and we take precautions to avoid them. The people whom the Serb paramilitaries are killing are killed deliberately. That is the difference between us and them.[30]

This statement contains the three classic elements of Blairite self-justification in wartime. "We" are to be distinguished from "them", first by our "regret", second by our "precaution", and third by the fact that in our case the killing is not "deliberate"—it is unintended. Of these three, the second carries least weight, both morally and politically. The best way to take precaution against the killing of innocents is not to drop bombs on them in the first place. It is perfectly possible to believe that one should do everything one can to avoid causing unintended harm or injury, but that means being willing to abjure politics, where such things are unavoidable. The Kosovo war was hardly an abjuration of politics, but rather something like an attempt to adhere to what Weber calls the politician's maxim: "You shall resist evil with force, for if you do not, you are responsible for the spread of evil."[31] Hence, inevitably, a limited role for precaution. There is also something problematic about the "we" here, since by "we" Blair can't just mean the forces that he controls, but also those of his allies, above all the Americans. American conduct in recent wars, whether in Kosovo, Afghanistan or Iraq, has occasionally been cautious—the high altitude from which the bombs were dropped on Kosovo, for fear of Serb artillery; the "operational pause" before Baghdad while the Republican Guard were pounded into dust—but this is not the same as taking precautions against the unnecessary loss of life among non-combatants. In fact, it's the opposite. Taking precautions in Kosovo would have meant flying bombing missions at a low enough height to make accurate identification of targets possible. In Iraq, it would have meant more special forces operations, and fewer large explosions. Bunker-busters, and cluster-bombs, and daisy-cutters are not precautionary weapons.

So, that leaves regret and good intentions. What does Blair mean by regret? Presumably, he means that "we" take the deaths of the civilians seriously, that we do not discount them or consider them nugatory in the light of the justness of the cause, that we do not simply accept that some people's lives are means while others' are ends. It is true, in war, that some people's lives will be means in the cause of saving others, but this is not a fact without moral significance; on the contrary, it is precisely because it is morally significant that these deaths are regretted notwithstanding the justness of the cause. This is the language of political responsibility, expressing a willingness to take seriously what Weber calls "morally suspect or morally dangerous means" without being incapacitated by them. However, regret is, on Weber's account, a "personal" matter, something that a politician will have to deal with and something from which no politician should suppose themselves immune. What it is not is a justification for political action, as it is used by Blair here. This incongruity is emphasized by the fact that in the same breath as expressing his sense of responsibility, Blair also employs the argument from good intention, by stating that these are deaths by error. In other words, if we discount the line about precaution, Blair is saying that the difference between him and Milosevic, or Bin Laden, or Saddam Hussein, is that, on the one hand, he (Blair) regrets what has happened, and, on the other, he has less to regret, because he did not mean to do the things he regrets. Which somewhat diminishes the quality of the regret.

Precaution, regret and the absence of malice have become something of a mantra for what Noam Chomsky calls "the new military humanism", of which Blair is perhaps the leading exponent.[32] In this philosophy the old methods of power politics are allied to a new ethic of good intentions to produce ostensibly beneficent results. This ethic is not really new, since it draws heavily on the just-war tradition, with its emphasis on fighting wars for the right reasons, and with restraint. What is new, in Blair's versions of these arguments at least, is the collapse of the separate principles into each other—the collapse of the distinction between *jus ad bellum* and *jus in bello*. Too often, Blair takes restraint as evidence of good intentions, and good intentions as evidence of restraint. This is circular—you can tell we mean well from the fact that we didn't mean to kill those people; you can tell we didn't mean to kill those people from the fact that we mean well. Moreover, just-war theory is not designed to help us distinguish "us" from "them"; it is intended to enable us to distinguish good wars from bad ones. The reason we fight a particular war cannot be to distinguish ourselves from the enemy in the way we fight it. If that were the motive, we would best distinguish ourselves from the enemy by choosing not to fight at all.

The other striking thing about these Blairite formulations of just-war theory is their pervasiveness in the philosophy of New Labour. They do not just apply in the case of war. Indeed, politics in New Labour circles often looks like the continuation of war by other means. For example, Blair's defence of his Kosovo strategy found an echo in the aftermath of that war's successful conclusion in the words of Ian McCartney (then a minister at the Department of Trade and Industry, subsequently Labour Party Chairman) when seeking to defend the government's domestic record. Speaking in an interview published on 12 July 1999, and wishing to answer the accusation that the Labour government had abandoned its principles in office, particularly with regard to welfare provision, McCartney said:

> The difference between a good minister and one who just performs is that you have to make difficult choices. Sometimes you have to make decisions which disappoint people, but I don't think this government has made a single decision which was malevolent. Every one has been taken for the right reasons and we are really making a difference to people's lives.[33]

There is at least no talk here about precaution, or trying to cause as little damage as possible. It is a straightforward conflation of the argument from responsibility (or in Blair's version "regret") and the argument from good intentions. First, McCartney sets out the credentials of the responsible politician, who knows that there will be difficult choices—what Gordon Brown prefers to call "tough decisions"—and that the attainment of political ends always involves treating some people as means and not as ends (or in the sanitized version here, "disappointing" them). In other words, New Labour understands about unintended consequences. But in the second half of what he says the tone changes from one of self-knowledge to one of justification: the difference, he suggests, between *us* and *them* (i.e. the Tories, who would also treat some people as means, but would do so with "malevolence", or, as Blair might put it, would disappoint people "deliberately") is precisely that we do not intend these things. As a result, what were difficult choices a sentence previously have now become easier, because each one is taken for the right reasons. Just as regret, justified in terms of intention, sound less like regret, so tough decisions, justified in terms of intention, sound more like foregone conclusions. Because we regret, we have less to regret. Because we know the choices are difficult, they are not difficult for us. Weber warned against politicians whose saintly intentions were taken to sanctify the unforeseen results of their naiveté. McCartney's is the cynic's version of saintliness—a kind of sanctification by other means. Because we know we are not saints, he seems to be saying, you are not to judge us as though we were, and as though we were not fully aware of what we are doing. Knowing we are not saints serves to sanctify the consequences of what we do.

This line of argument can be used to defend anything, even the indefensible. The journalist-turned-politician Siôn Simon (who currently sits as the ultra-Blairite MP for Birmingham Erdington) offered the absurdist version when seeking to justify another of Blair's pet projects, the grotesque and idiotic Millennium Dome. Writing in the pages of *The Daily Telegraph* on 13 November 2000, by which time it was quite clear that the Dome was a monstrous white elephant that no amount of bows or ribbons could disguise, Simon defended it by reminding his readers of the intentions that lay behind its creation.

> Blair's decision to go with the Dome was everything it should have been. It showed the confidence that befits a British Prime Minister. The complaint of arrogance is

irrelevant—all confident acts are called arrogant when they go wrong; the word usually employed when they go right is "brilliant". That the entire Cabinet was against it matters even less. Since assuming the Labour leadership in 1994, Blair has been opposed by the entire Shadow Cabinet and 95% of the party in virtually every important decision he has made. If Labour had been a democracy rather than an elective dictatorship, the party would now be on a philosophical par with the German Social Democrats. Probably in power and probably headed for another term, largely thanks to the Opposition, but with no sense of purpose or direction.

Most important, the Dome was a visionary project … It was bold, confident, proud, unembarrassed, modern, European, grand. We were none of these things under John Major, and only partly one or two of them under Mrs Thatcher when we went to war. Furthermore, it was a very open, self-imperilling and therefore very trusting thing for a leader to do. Blair didn't just take the national mood as fixed, he set about changing it. The paradox is that although the means failed, the ends were achieved.[34]

This is a longer and bolder version of the "non-apology" apology that Blair himself offered at the Labour Party conference that year, when in a carefully choreographed moment of contrition, he said that although he took full responsibility for the fact that the Dome had not achieved what it set out to achieve, he wouldn't apologize for "trying". It also has its direct parallel in the "non-apology" apology Blair offered at the Labour conference of 2004 for the intelligence failures that preceded the Iraq war: "The problem is I can apologise for the information that turned out to be wrong, but I can't, sincerely at least, apologise for removing Saddam."[35] In other words, as Simon puts it, although the means failed, the ends were achieved.

Simon's account of the thinking behind the Blairite world-view is strikingly Weberian. He invokes the confidence that is both a responsibility and a resource of the office of Prime Minister, which derives from the particular relation between party and leader that is generated within the British parliamentary system, and which is documented by Weber in the first part of "Politik als Beruf", culminating in his description of Gladstone's mastery of the party machine. Simon recognizes, and celebrates, the fact that

Blair too is dictator of the electoral battlefield. His dig at the German Social Democratic Party picks up on a further preoccupation of Weber's political writings, which was how to reconcile the Caesarist demands of modern mass democracy with the limitations placed on it by a system of proportional representation, and with the interests and principles that the so-called "ethical" parties of the left seek to represent within such a system. But alongside these Weberian and mock-Weberian themes Simon runs another set of claims, which are quintessentially Blairite. This is the argument that Blair's courage, the "self-imperilling" nature of the whole enterprise, can justify it after the event, when it has gone wrong. Certainly, the Dome was a very risky thing for a British Prime Minister to have got involved with, in that it was hideously expensive, horribly managed, and full of rubbish. But this can hardly serve to justify the decision to proceed. Simon suggests that the fact that this was such a risky project should excuse its unintended outcome; but if it does excuse it, then the project turns out not to have been so risky after all. The Dome cannot both have endangered the Prime Minister and be cited as the reason why we should give him the benefit of the doubt.

Simon takes the us/them distinction that Blair maintains in the international arena, and McCartney insists upon in the domestic arena, and runs it through the party machine. The "them" here are the rest of the cabinet and 95% of the party; above all, the "them" is Gordon Brown, Blair's most consistent, and only serious, rival for power throughout his premiership, who is known to have opposed the Dome in cabinet, and would not therefore, had he been Prime Minister, even have "tried". Simon also makes explicit the connection between this kind of self-serving visionary politics and war (and, as Blair's outriders have repeatedly chosen to remind the press, Brown doesn't really "do wars"). But the war in Iraq shows the limits of this kind of self-justification. Not even Blair would have been able to save himself, if the military campaign in Iraq had gone wrong, by claiming to take responsibility for the failure, but refusing to apologize for "trying". He would have had to resign (as, in a perfect world, he should have had to resign over the Dome, which was one of the biggest public accounting scandals of recent British political history).[36] What's more, Blair has been compelled to hitch his wagon to an American president who, unlike his predecessor, doesn't really do philosophical contortion. George Bush is more like the Texan version of Friedrich Förster, who believes that good will follow from good, and evil-doers will pay the price of evil. In a sense, this has freed Blair up to be more straightforwardly moralistic about the Iraq war than he was able to be about Kosovo, where he was hedged in by the caution of his allies. It is also true that for the Iraq war, the moral equation was simpler, in utilitarian terms at least: it is almost certainly true that it would have done more harm to leave Saddam's regime in place than to remove it by force (this was also true of the Serbian regime in 1999, but complicated by the fact that regime change was not the aim of that war, and much of the visible harm inflicted by Milosevic in Kosovo took place after the allies started dropping their bombs). But if Blair has been more straightforward about his claim that the war against Saddam was a good war, he has also been more straightforwardly hypocritical as well. His insistence, for example, following his failure to secure a second UN resolution, that he could bypass the UN Security Council if one of its members threatened a veto that was purely "capricious", makes a mockery of the international legal system he also wishes to uphold. If French vetoes are "capricious", and American and British vetoes are not, then we are back in a world where intentions count more than outcomes. If this is true, then no vote on the Security Council or anywhere else carries any weight, because what matters in not the show of hands but the presence or absence of malice among those who raise them. This is the same reasoning that led Eisner to seek to discount the outcome of elections to the Bavarian Parliament in 1919, and the reason it was hypocritical (and foolhardy) of him to attend its opening ceremony.

Some commentators have periodically taken the brazenness of Blair's hypocrisy as evidence that he is not simply foolhardy, but has gone mad. Matthew Parris, writing in *The Times* at the height of Blair's "masochism strategy", cited Blair's serene attitude to his rebuff in the Security Council, along with his increasing self-righteousness, his Iraq fixation, and the strange look in his eye, as symptoms of mental unbalance, and possibly the beginnings of mental collapse.[37] Max Weber, in "Politik als Beruf", warned that mental breakdown was indeed the risk that all conviction politicians run, because the dirty reality of politics always chafes against the clean, straight lines of conduct they try to follow. As these become frayed, the temptation is to go into denial, and to declare: "The world is stupid and base, not I. Responsibility for the consequences does not fall on me but on the others, in whose service I work and whose stupidity and baseness I shall eradicate."[38] Anyone who really believes this is indeed mad. But Blair is not mad, and the predicted mental collapse never arrived. He knows that because the world is stupid and base, it doesn't pay to think in these terms. He also knows that madness is not an attractive quality in a responsible politician. Indeed, just as it is part of the intellectual architecture of Blairism to equate political responsibility with an absence of the malice that marks one's opponents, so it is traditional to question their sanity as well. The Blairite response to the charge of mental unbalance is to say: "Look, we know politics is a devilish business, which is what distinguishes us from our enemies—the 'mad' and the 'crazy', like Milosevic and Saddam, the simply 'weird', like most of the Tory opposition, or just poor, troubled Gordon Brown with his 'psychological flaws'. Seeing what it does to other people is what keeps us sane."[39]

What is distinctive about Tony Blair's version of political responsibility is that he takes what is "internal" in Weber's account—that is, what belongs to the interior life of the politician, or the party machine—and plays it out on the surface of politics, so that the inner workings of his political conscience are laid bare for all to see. Gordon Brown's problem, and before him Gladstone's—another "Iron Chancellor" who was thought by many even in his own party to be mentally unbalanced, and therefore unfit to become Prime Minister—is that they keep it all buttoned up inside. Blair has been able to talk about his good intentions by making a parade of his awareness of their limitations. This is not a tactic that would work for everyone—George Bush, for example, prefers to make a spectacle of his own personal limitations, his very "ordinariness", in order to highlight the strength of his convictions—but it works for Blair. What it does not do is justify any particular course of action. Knowing that good intentions aren't enough isn't enough.

51

In the end, a course of action is justified by its outcome, including both its intended and its unintended consequences. This doesn't mean that Chomsky is right to refuse to talk about "motives" at all, since a motiveless politics would be completely pointless. Nor is Chomsky right to insist that the exponents of the new humanism must either be true to its principles, and pursue injustice everywhere they find it, or stop claiming to have principles altogether. No politicians can be entirely true to their principles, but it doesn't follow from this that they should cease to have any. It is possible that war with Iraq may ultimately prove to have been justified, and justified for many of the reasons that Blair set out before it began: that it was worth fighting a war, and taking the lives of innocent civilians, in order to take away the destructive capabilities of that particular regime, given its continued intransigence in the face of international censure. It is even possible that Iraq will become the beacon for a new kind of politics in the Middle East, founded on principles of democracy and the rule of law. But this depends on everything that happens as a result of the war, and how the destructive forces it served to unleash are contained (see Chapter Six). Nothing Blair has said about his agonized awareness of this can justify it, any more than his expressions of regret at the loss of innocent life can justify the taking of it. All politicians ought to be aware of the difficulties they face, just as they all ought to regret the loss of innocent life. But if a politician needs to talk about these things, simply in order to justify what he is doing, he should get himself a therapist.

Blair has not sought therapy (so far as we know) as a way of confronting his demons since the conclusion of the Iraq war. He has, however, been forced to confront the fact that the primary rationale for the invasion—to disarm Saddam of his WMD—can no longer be deployed as part of his armoury of self-justification. In the absence of these weapons, he has been compelled, since the war's end, to make use of a different set of justifications for the ousting of Saddam. These have continued to play on his protestations of good faith, and an insistence that critics of the war need to accept the sincerity of the motives of those who undertook it. At the same time, he has continued to recognize that protestations of good faith alone can never be enough to sustain either his own sense of purpose or his party in office.

Instead, he has had to resort to a new range of consequentialist and pseudo-consequentialist arguments to run alongside the politics of good intentions. These are the subject of the next chapter, which explores some of Blair's post hoc justifications for the conflict, once it was clear that Saddam's WMD would not be found, in the language of "risk".

CHAPTER THREE

TAKING A CHANCE ON WAR:
THE WORST-CASE SCENARIOS

On 5 March 2004, Tony Blair gave a speech in his Sedgefield constituency in which he sought to justify his actions in Iraq by emphasizing the unprecedented threat that global terrorism poses to the civilized world. He called this threat "real and existential", and he argued that politicians had no choice but to confront it "whatever the political cost".[1] This is because the alternative— the possibility that terrorists might get their hands on WMD—was too awful to contemplate. In the days that followed, this speech, like everything else Blair has said and done with reference to Iraq, was picked over by wave upon wave of journalists and commentators. Those who had supported the war concluded that it was a passionate and heartfelt defence of what had been a brave and justified decision. Those who had opposed the war found it strong on rhetoric but short on substance, and wondered whether all the passion might not, as so often with Tony Blair, be concealing baser political motives. But what almost no one bothered to ask was whether the central claim in the speech was true. Is it true that the threat of global terrorism has altered "the balance of risk", as Blair called it, so that actions like the one against Iraq can be justified by considering the worst-case scenario if action is not taken? Should worst-case scenarios, if they are sufficiently terrible, trump all other considerations when politicians have to decide what to do?

There can be no doubt that these are extremely weighty questions. Indeed, it is hard to think of any that carry more weight, given the exotic array of worst-case scenarios we are now faced with. The British cosmologist Martin Rees puts the chances of the human race surviving the next 100 years at around 50:50.[2] His list of things that could go horribly wrong ranges from the highly unlikely—a giant asteroid strike—to the frankly bizarre—rogue scientific experiments rolling the cosmos up into a tiny ball—to the all too familiar—global warming, viral mutation, and, of course, nuclear and biological terrorism. In light of all this, it is hard to dispute Blair's claim that considerations of how to deal with catastrophic risks are far more important than any of the questions that are still being asked about who said what to whom in the immediate run-up to the war itself. But that is just why it has proved so hard to take him at his word. For Blair's opponents, it is impossible to concede the importance of these large questions about risk without also seeming to have accepted Blair's plea that they should move on from seeking to hold him to account for his own conduct before the war. For Blair's supporters, it is not necessary to concede their importance, because they have already decided that largely speaking Blair did the right thing. The issue has been prejudged both ways—either the war was wrong, in which case these can't be the most important questions, or the war was right, in which case these are questions to which we already know the answers. The problem is that Blair has raised the issue of risk in order to defend his own course of conduct, which immediately trivializes it. But that does not mean that it is impossible to think seriously about the broader ramifications of what he was saying. It just means that to start with it is necessary to divorce what was said from the devious and somewhat desperate politician who was saying it.

Blair's basic argument is easily confused with what is often called the doctrine of pre-emption, which states that in the war on terrorism governments cannot and should not wait to be attacked before fighting back. But Blair's case does not have to be put in such incendiary terms, which serve only to collapse arguments about risk into a political ideology—neoconservatism—and reduce them to a form of warmongering. Blair's position can just as well be expressed in the more neutral language of precaution, rather than pre-emption. What lawyers, bureaucrats and even some philosophers like to call the precautionary principle states that when faced with risks with uncertain and potentially catastrophic downsides, it is always better to err on the side of caution. In such circumstances, the burden of proof is said to lie with those who downplay the risk of disaster, rather than with those who argue that the risks are real, even if they might be quite small. This appears to be Blair's preferred post hoc justification for the war in Iraq. As he conceded in his Sedgefield speech, he understands how "sensible people" might have come to opposite conclusions about the threat posed by Saddam:

> Their argument is one I understand totally. It is that Iraq posed no direct, immediate threat to Britain; and that Iraq's WMD [programme], even on our own case, was not serious enough to warrant war, certainly not without a specific UN resolution mandating military action. And they argue: Saddam could, in any event, be contained.[3]

But what this stance does not take into account, according to Blair, is precisely "the balance of risk", meaning it does not take seriously enough the downside of getting things wrong. Blair can accept that his opponents might have been right (containment might have worked at less cost and armed intervention without explicit UN sanction might have set a dangerous precedent), and he acknowledges that their case has been strengthened by the failure to find any evidence of Iraq's WMD since the war ended. But they might also have been wrong, and the consequences of their being wrong, of containment not working, were potentially much more serious than the consequences of his being wrong, and Saddam not having any weapons. This is why Blair is able to argue that the failure to find WMD in Iraq is not, ultimately, the issue. "The key point," he says, "is that it is the threat that is the issue."[4]

The precautionary principle is sometimes summed up by the familiar proverb: "Better safe than sorry." Like most proverbs, this one doesn't help much if you stop to think about it: of course it is better to be safe than sorry (safe is good, sorry is bad, so it is hardly a tough choice). What the precautionary principle states is that if there is a chance you might be sorry, it is better to be sorry but safe. This is the crux of Blair's argument, though for a while he couldn't quite bring himself to spell it out in these terms, because he was still hoping the WMD would be found, so that he wouldn't even have to say sorry. But when he did have to apologize for getting that part of the equation wrong, this line of defence has the

advantage that it was not the exclusive preserve of neoconservative warmongers. The precautionary principle is championed by
all sorts of people who were not at all keen on the war in Iraq. For
example, it is often used to urge much stronger interventionist
action to deal with the threat of global warming.[5] Even if some of
the science is uncertain, it is argued, the balance of risk requires
acting as though the gloomiest predictions about global warming
were the most accurate, because getting that wrong is less dangerous than acting on the basis of more sanguine predictions and
getting that wrong. Some risks, in other words, are just not worth
taking. Why, Blair might say, should we be willing to think this
way about one threat to our very way of life, but not to think this
way about another?

The easy answer is to point out that, in the case of Iraq, taking precautions meant dropping bombs on innocent civilians,
whereas in the case of global warming, it simply means insisting on more responsible use of energy resources. But this answer
only works if it can be assumed that restricting the practices that
produce global warming is without serious cost. In reality, limiting the practices that produce global warming would inevitably
inhibit economic growth, including in those parts of the world
where economic growth is desperately needed to increase standards of living and life expectancy. If it turns out that the gloomy
science is wrong, lives would have been sacrificed for little or
no gain. Therefore, the precautionary principle may require the
needless sacrifice of innocent life whether it is applied to war in
Iraq or to the emission of carbon dioxide. In both cases, the argument must be the same: it is worth taking a chance on the needless
sacrifice of innocent lives only because the risks of not taking that
chance are so much greater.

It is not possible to argue that the precautionary principle only
makes sense when applied to environmental issues and not to
military ones. But it is possible to argue that it doesn't make sense
in either case. Indeed, this is what its application to the war in
Iraq brings out—how can something be called precautionary if it
involves a readiness to throw away lives on a supposition? As the
legal philosopher Cass Sunstein has recently made clear, the precautionary principle is flawed however it is used—whether the
issue is the environment, food safety, terrorism or war—because

it is self-contradictory: it can always be used to argue both that we should be more careful and that we should not be too careful.[6] Tony Blair captured this double standard perfectly in his Sedgefield speech. "This is not a time to err on the side of caution," he said, "not a time to weigh the risks to an infinite balance; not a time for the cynicism of the worldly wise who favour playing it long."[7] And yet his speech also argues exactly the opposite—that what matters is taking precautions against future disaster, seeing the big picture, weighing the overall balance of risks. In the very next paragraph, he remarks: "It is monstrously premature to think that the threat has passed. The risk remains in the balance here and abroad."[8] This, then, is not a time to err on the side of caution and not a time to err on the side of incaution. Such an argument can also be used to justify anything.

The trouble with the precautionary principle is that it purports to be a way of evaluating risk, yet it insists that some risks are simply not worth weighing in the balance. This could only make sense if it were true that some risks are entirely off the scale of our everyday experience of danger. Presumably, this is what Blair was getting at when he said that global terrorism posed an "existential" threat. But existential is a slippery word, in politics as well as philosophy. If global terrorism posed a threat to the existence of all human life on Earth, in the way that, for example, a ten-mile-wide asteroid heading towards Earth would, then it might make sense to place it in a different category to all other risks, even if the chances of disaster were extremely slight. But it is simply not plausible that terrorism does pose a threat of this kind, or at least that it poses any more of a threat than all sorts of other things, including a war between states that are permitted to hold onto their large nuclear stockpiles. If terrorism poses an existential threat, it is not to our very existence, but to our very way of existence: it threatens our prosperity, our security, our ability to live as we choose, our peace of mind. But while all this is true, it is not clear that it makes for a qualitative difference between terrorism and the other sorts of risks that we face. Threats of disruption to our way of life, even of the massive disruption that would be caused by a large-scale terrorist attack, can still be compared with the threatened disruption that would be caused trying to prevent them. Yet the precautionary principle implies that in the end there is no comparison. In his Sedgefield speech, Tony Blair discussed at some length his decision a few months previously to place armed guards and barricades around Heathrow airport, in response to an intelligence warning of a terrorist attack that never came. He asks us, as ever, to put ourselves in his shoes:

> Sit in my seat. Here is the intelligence. Here is the advice. Do you ignore it? But, of course, intelligence is precisely that: intelligence. It is not hard fact. It has its limitations. On each occasion, the most careful judgement has to be made taking account of everything we know and advice available. But in making that judgement, would you prefer us to act, even if it turns out to be wrong? Or not to act and hope it's OK? And suppose we don't act and the intelligence turns out to be right, how forgiving will people be?[9]

This passage captures the essence of the precautionary principle: risk assessment will only take you so far, at which point you have to start thinking about the worst that could happen. It also captures something else about the existential threat posed by global terrorism. A large-scale terrorist attack could have cataclysmic consequences for the political existence of whichever politicians happen to be in charge when it takes place. "How forgiving will people be?" Blair asks. The truth is no one really knows until something happens. The evidence of September 11 and of the bombings in Madrid and London cuts both ways. Some people, undoubtedly, will always blame the government. But many others seem to accept that no government can act on all the intelligence it receives without destroying the way of life it is trying to protect; and even when it does act, it cannot always be sure that its actions will work. What people seem to mind most, if the Spanish elections of 2004 are anything to go by, is a rush to judgment after the event rather than a failure to exercise the correct judgment before it. The example of 9/11 also suggests that following a really traumatic incident the public are as likely to unite around whoever happens to be in charge as they are to seek out someone to blame. Still, because no one can be sure, the precautionary principle comes into play here too. The worst-case scenario is that a major terrorist attack, about which there were plausible intelligence warnings, might destroy not only the careers of individual politicians but perhaps the existence of some political parties, maybe even the viability of an entire system of government. Why take a chance? So much, then, for Blair's claim that politicians should act "whatever the political cost".

It cannot be argued that terrorism confronts us with risks that are somehow off the scale. An attack on London's main airport, like an attack on the London underground system, though bad, is by no means the worst thing that can happen. But it could be argued that terrorism confronts us with risks that cannot be measured on any reliable scale, because the evidence is always so uncertain. In this respect, terrorism does pose different sorts of problems from, say, global warming. Although we may not know which scientific accounts of climate change are the most accurate, the different theories are at least scientific ones, and therefore provide the basis for various kinds of risk assessment, because it is possible to compare the predictable outcomes of different trends. (If the world is warming up at 1 °C per decade, that will have consequences that can be predictably contrasted with what will happen if the world is warming up at 1 °C per hundred years.) But there is no comparable social or political science of terrorism. It is indeed, as Tony Blair says, a question of "intelligence" rather than "hard facts". Moreover, even if the intelligence is as reliable as it can be, the predictable outcomes are far from certain. Were Saddam Hussein to have acquired nuclear weapons, would that have increased the likelihood of their falling into the hands of people willing to use them by a factor of 1, or of 10, or of 100? In the face of such radical uncertainty, it seems to make sense to fear the worst. It also seems to make sense to suppose that any terrorist organization that is seeking to get hold of nuclear weapons would be willing to use them.

It would be a mistake, however, to assume that because certain risks are unquantifiable in their own terms, no comparative judgments can be made with respect to them. We cannot begin to know what the real likelihood is of Al Qaeda acquiring WMD, not even if we had an accurate record of who else has such weapons, which we don't. But we can compare the likely costs and benefits of trying to deal with this unquantifiable threat at different times and in different places. Indeed, the best case that might have been made for seeking to disarm Saddam Hussein by force is one that relied on this kind of comparative risk assessment, rather than depending on the precautionary principle. Faced with a wholly unknowable threat, the rational thing to do is to compare those outcomes we can predict, and ignore those we cannot. We might not know, in the end, whether Al Qaeda was likelier to acquire nuclear weapons from Iraq, from North Korea or from Pakistan (though perhaps we can now guess). But we could know with a reasonable degree of certainty that a military confrontation with Iraq carried far fewer risks than a military confrontation with either North Korea or Pakistan. Equally, if Iraq was to be attacked, another old proverb looks quite plausible: "The sooner the better." Going to war in 2003, when Saddam was relatively weak, carried fewer risks than waiting for five years, or for ten, by which point he might have become much stronger. So, the best available answers to the questions most often posed before the war—why Iraq and why now—were in both cases the same: because other places and other times carried too many risks. Blair seems to have recognized this, at least in private. In Peter Stothard's *30 Days*, which tells the story of the war from the point of view of those inside Downing Street, we hear the response the Prime Minister liked to give behind closed doors to those who asked the questions, why Saddam, and why now: "Because we can."[10]

If there was such a case to be made in terms of comparative rather than absolute risk, and if Blair was willing to allude to it in private, why has he not been more willing to pursue it in public? The answer is because he can't. It is not a defensible position, or at least it isn't for Blair's government. One problem is that any justification of the war in these terms depends on being able to demonstrate that all the risks of an invasion were taken seriously, including a range of worst-case scenarios for its aftermath. But if any of the champions of war seriously considered that things would turn out as they have—no real WMD and no real security for the people of Iraq either—then they have not been letting on. There has not been enough visible evidence of long-term planning for this war to be plausibly defended in cost–benefit terms. Equally, once it becomes a question of relative risk, it is no longer possible for politicians to rule out of bounds questions about whether going to war increases or decreases the risk of terrorist reprisals. If the British government were warned, as we now know they were, that an invasion of Iraq was likely to increase the threat posed by Al Qaeda to British targets, at least in the short term, then the case has to be made that these losses are a price worth paying for the possibility of long-term benefits.[11] It is not enough to argue, as British Foreign Secretary Jack Straw did following the Madrid bombings, that "Al Qaeda will go on and would have gone on irrespective of the war in Iraq, until they are firmly stopped". Nor is it enough to say, as he also said, that "We did it for the best of motives".[12] This is the very weakest version of the precautionary argument: we had to do something; Iraq was something; Iraq was justified. It assumes that faced with a threat like the one posed by Al Qaeda, nothing can be weighed in the balance until the threat is finally vanquished. Yet if the Iraq war is to be justified in cost–benefit terms, it can only be because the real costs, recognized as such, are outweighed by the benefits.

This, though, points to the deeper difficulty. A rational risk assessment of war, or of anything else, is an incredibly hard sell for any politician. It carries too many political risks of its own. Thus no British politician could conceivably have risked arguing that the deaths that occurred in London on 7 July 2005 were a price worth paying for freeing the world from Saddam Hussein, even if (perhaps particularly if) that was what they believed. Politicians invariably have little to gain, and much to lose, by seeking to present their arguments in strict cost–benefit terms. What they have to gain is that they can claim to be behaving rationally. What they have to lose is that behaving rationally about risk leaves even the most sympathetic politicians sounding cynical, and heartless, and lacking in conviction. It means admitting in advance that you might be wrong, because being wrong is one of the risks that have to be weighed in the balance. It also means putting a price on human life, and measuring its loss against the alternatives. Of course, politicians, like insurance agents, do this all the time, but unlike insurance agents they don't like to be seen doing it. Nor can politicians leave the business of cold calculation up to the technocrats, and then simply argue that they are acting on the advice of the experts. To do so would be to suggest that the politicians are no longer in control. In an email released at the Hutton Inquiry into the death of Dr David Kelly, Blair's chief of staff Jonathan Powell wrote to his communications director Alistair Campbell and his foreign policy adviser David Manning about an early draft of the so-called "September dossier" on Iraq's WMD programme: "I think it is worth explicitly stating what TB [Tony Blair] keeps saying: this is the advice from the JIC [Joint Intelligence Committee]. On the basis of this advice, what other action could he as PM take?"[13] But although Blair might have been saying this in private to Jonathan Powell, what he eventually told the British public in the final version of the dossier was: "I believe that faced with the information available to me, the UK government has been right to support the demands that this issue be confronted and dealt with."[14] In other words, what matters is what the Prime Minister believes to be right, given the information available. He had no choice but to confront the issue. But it was important for the British public to know that the decision to confront the issue was still his choice.

The precautionary principle fits neatly into this way of thinking. Because it can be used to justify both precaution and incaution, it can also be used to plead either necessity (we have no choice) or discretion (we have to make a choice), or both, depending on the circumstances. The ability to dress up choice as necessity and necessity as choice was an indispensable part of the Prime Minister's armoury in the run-up to the Iraq war, and he deployed it to devastating effect. Looking back over the four set-piece debates on Iraq in the House of Commons (24 September and 25 November 2002 and 26 February and 18 March 2003) it is striking how in the first three the government made it clear that there was no need yet to take a final decision about war, because all the options had to be kept open and the course was not finally set. But in the fourth and decisive debate, Blair made his position clear at the outset: "This is a tough choice indeed, but it is also a stark one: to stand British troops down now and turn back, or to hold firm to the course that we have set."[15] Whatever else might be said about this, it is brilliant politics, and it worked: the government survived the first three debates by offering the prospect of a decisive vote down the line, and it survived the decisive vote because the earlier debates had allowed it to pursue its policy to the point of no return. A rational risk assessment would have meant laying bare the real necessities and the real contingencies at each stage of the decision-making process. The September dossier, which provided the subject for the 24 September debate, did not do this.

The job of the JIC is to weigh the risks associated with different pieces of intelligence, including the risk that some of them might be wrong, so that politicians can exercise their judgment. But the dossier, which was said to reflect the view of the JIC and not the politicians, made no mention of risk. It merely judged the intelligence to be true. Which allowed Tony Blair to judge that it had to be acted on. Which allowed him to persuade parliament of the same.

Once the war was over, and it turned out that the intelligence was not so reliable as had been thought, Blair ordered an inquiry into how it was gathered and assessed, but not into the political decisions that followed, because the ultimate "democratic" judgment belonged to parliament. This inquiry, which was conducted by the former head of the civil service Lord Butler, reported its findings in July 2004. It concluded that, notwithstanding a number of serious flaws in the way that the government and intelligence services had handled the available intelligence, the failures had been collective ones, and no one individual was personally to blame. In his response to the report in the Commons, the Prime Minister emphasized this last point: "Everyone genuinely tried to do their best in good faith for the country in circumstances of acute difficulty."[16] On the wider question of whether the war had been justified, about which Lord Butler had been compelled by his terms of reference and by constitutional propriety to remain silent, Blair stated: "I can honestly say that I have never had to make a harder judgment. But in the end, my judgment was that after September 11th, we could no longer run the risk; that instead of waiting for the potential threat of terrorism and WMD to come together, we had to get out and get after it."[17] It was this judgment that parliament had endorsed in March 2003. But what parliament cannot be said to have done is to reach its own judgment on the nature of the risks, because it was not provided by the government with the raw material on which to make such an assessment. The road from the precautionary principle leads by a long and winding route to the terms of reference of the Butler inquiry, and to the subsequent exoneration of the Prime Minister. All are founded on the same, unjustified supposition: that, in the face of an existential threat, some risks are just not worth considering.

Blair's ultimate ability to escape from the clutches of the Iraq war, and the failure of the occupying powers to unearth any WMD, was partly confirmed, partly confounded by the result of the 2005 general election, which saw him returned to office with a sizeable but nevertheless greatly reduced majority, on what was by historic standards a very small share of the popular vote. During the election campaign, Blair was forced to downplay the rhetoric of risk aversion when explaining away his own errors of judgment and miscalculations in the run-up to war, and to talk up the sincerity of his intentions (in order to counter the repeated opposition charge that he had "lied" about the threat posed by Saddam). Nevertheless, it was Blair's skilful and ruthless manipulation of the language of risk that helped to engineer his political survival to this point. Blair has revealed himself to be an expert at deploying the double standards of the precautionary principle to wrong-foot those who have sought to pin him down on the consequences of his actions in Iraq. It would be a mistake, however, to suppose that Blair has always been in control of the politics of risk manipulation. In questions of risk, as in everything else in politics, a lot depends on individual temperament. As well as providing a device that enables politicians to try to absolve themselves of some of their personal responsibilities, risk also helps to lay the personalities of individual politicians bare. The next chapter looks beyond Blair's exploitation of the language of risk to see what the Iraq war says about his personal risk temperament, and how it compares with that of other politicians. Blair's attitude to risk has often been his salvation, but it has also served to threaten him, on more than one occasion, with ruin.

TAKING A CHANCE ON WAR: SUEZ AND IRAQ

> **Bush:** Blair wants to keep on the right side of us.
>
> **Rice:** That's right.
>
> **Bush:** If he's not pro-American, he's nothing. Look at it his way round. He's staked the house. He's not going to quit. On the other hand, his government can fall. That's a real thing. It may really fall. So. [Bush looks round.] I'm sorry, gentlemen. We have to do what we can.
>
> David Hare, *Stuff Happens* (2004)

There was a time, during the spring and summer of 2004, when it briefly looked as though Iraq might turn out to be Tony Blair's Suez, and destroy him. The parallels were certainly striking, and Blair's critics were not slow to point them out. First, there was the strong suspicion that, like Suez, the whole Iraq escapade was the result of a private deal cooked up between the belligerents. The decision to send British and French troops to Egypt in 1956 was sealed during a secret meeting at Sèvres in France, where British, French and Israeli representatives agreed on a plan that would allow the Israelis to attack the Egyptians, and the British and French to intervene in order to separate them, reclaiming the canal in the process. The decision to send British and American troops to Iraq appears to have been sealed at a meeting between Blair and Bush at Crawford in Texas in April 2002.[1] We cannot know for sure what was said, but it seems likely that an understanding was reached, whereby Bush made it clear that he was going to disarm Saddam by force come what may, and Blair made it clear that come what may he would help him. If so, then the strong suspicion also exists that Blair, like Anthony Eden in late 1956, misled parliament and the public over the nature of the undertaking on which he was engaged. Eden insisted that he had had no direct foreknowl-edge of Israeli intentions; he was able to respond decisively, he said, only because he had prepared for such a contingency, not because he had initiated it. This was a lie. The Israeli action was a pretext for British and French intervention, and Eden himself had helped to concoct it. Tony Blair has repeatedly insisted that the diplomatic manoeuvres of the autumn and winter of 2002–03 were not intended to serve as a pretext for armed intervention in the spring, but were genuine attempts to avoid the use of force by persuading Saddam to disarm peacefully. It is not possible to demonstrate that this is a lie, but it remains very hard to believe, if only because nothing Saddam could have done would have persuaded the Americans and British that he could be trusted to disarm without the use of force. Like Blair, Eden went through the motions at the UN, though without even the appearance of conviction, which Blair possessed in spades. Yet it is the appear-ance of conviction that came to look so suspicious, because so much of the evidence of Saddam's weapons programmes pro-duced by the British and Americans at the UN turns out to have been unfounded. Like Eden, Blair committed himself to a story that became harder to sustain with each retelling. If he really con-tinues to believe it, then he must be self-deceived; if he ceased at some point to believe it, or never believed it to start with, then he has been deceiving everyone else.

Above all, though, what seems to unite Eden and Blair is the sheer recklessness of their military adventures, their willingness to stake everything on wars they could have avoided if they had wanted to. Both Suez and Iraq were huge, and seemingly fool-hardy, political gambles with the futures of their respective gov-ernments. Neither of them were in entirely clear political waters before they went to war, but they were each in a pretty secure posi-tion: both had recently won decisive election victories, and though they both had critics within their own parties, there was nothing there or on the opposition benches that called for drastic action. Certainly, nothing in domestic politics demanded from either of them an all-or-nothing roll of the dice. Yet while it is true that both Eden and Blair were ready to risk everything on the outcome of military conflicts they could not ultimately control, these were in fact very different kinds of gamble, from very different kinds of gambler. What distinguishes Blair's Iraq from Eden's Suez is the different attitudes towards risk that these episodes reveal. These differences are as telling as any similarities between them.

No one is entirely rational about risk, certainly no politician. Everyone's perception of danger and uncertainty is shaped in part by what they are familiar with, and what they choose to recognize. This is one of the reasons why most politicians take the threat of terrorism so seriously. Violent threat is what they are familiar with, and so they see it as more threatening than other kinds of risks; this is what you would expect of anyone who was forced to spend much of their time in the company of soldiers and police officers. But as well as being shaped by professional circumstances, individual attitudes to risk are also shaped by personal temperament. Different individuals have different risk temperaments. Some people like to take chances and some don't. Some like to take chances on certain things—say, their health—but are extremely conservative when it comes to other areas of their life—say, their money. It is not possible to know what chances Tony Blair has been willing to take in his private life, though he appears to be a fairly conventional man in that respect. However, it is possible to surmise what his political risk temperament is, on the evidence of his long tenure as party leader and, for almost as long, Prime Minister. Tony Blair is a highly risk-averse politician who nevertheless likes to play for very high stakes. This is not quite as eccentric, nor as uncommon, as it sounds. Some poker players like to wait until they have what they feel certain is a winning hand, and then put everything on the table, even if it risks driving everyone else out and shrinking the size of the pot. The thought that they can drive everyone else out is what keeps them going. Some roulette players believe that the way to play is to be willing to bet big, in order to be certain of winning something, however small. If you put £100 on red, and then if you lose put £200 on red, and then if that loses put £400 on red, and so on, you will eventually be guaranteed to win £100 when red comes up. Or at least, you would be guaranteed to win if there wasn't the danger that a bad run of luck will bankrupt you before you get the chance to reclaim your losses. This superficially risk-averse strategy is said to have been responsible for more suicides at Monte Carlo than any other. Its appeal lies in its veneer of security; its danger lies in the certainty of ruin, if you play it regularly against the bank, or against anyone else who can sustain a longer run of misfortune than you can.

Iraq did not in the end lead to Tony Blair's political suicide. It has been one of his great strengths that he has always had a pretty sure sense of when he has more political capital in the bank than his opponents. When he does, this is the risk strategy he likes to adopt: to be ready to stake everything to guarantee some success, even if the rewards are relatively small. They are not always small, of course. One early example of this strategy was his approach to the reform of the Labour Party constitution, which established his reputation for being willing to lay everything on the line. He demanded, and won, the party's backing for the repudiation of Labour's traditional commitment to nationalization. In that case, his opponents stayed in the pot long enough for the eventual victory to be well worth the winning. The apogee of this kind of brinkmanship came during the Kosovo conflict, when Blair's absolute confidence that he had more political reserves to draw on than Milosevic led him to offer a personal guarantee to the thousands of Albanians fleeing their homes at the start of the campaign that he would return them to their homes before it was over, which he did.[2] But still, this is an approach to risk that always carries the same hazards, no matter how it is played, or by whom. An extended run of bad luck, or a single moment of spectacular misjudgment, can be fatal. And even when it does not result in ruin, there are bound to be times when having to empty your pockets and borrow everything in your friends' pockets as well, just to win that elusive £100, will look undignified, and faintly ridiculous. For example, Blair's performance during January 2004, in the run-up to the decisive parliamentary vote on his policy of introducing variable university tuition fees, was both uncertain and undignified. Having turned the occasion into a vote of confidence in his government, he was trapped into risking too much for too little, and very nearly lost everything (he won by five votes, having made enough concessions to leave the policy hardly worth the winning). It left him with a huge amount riding on the result of the Hutton Report into the death of David Kelly, which appeared the next day. Here, however, Blair could be pretty confident that his luck would hold. He knew, as everyone else subsequently discovered, that Lord Hutton's wheel was tilted heavily the government's way. Instead, it was BBC Chairman Gavyn Davies and Director General Greg Dyke, foolishly trying to play Blair at his own game, who bet the farm, and lost (both resigned within 48 hours of Hutton making his findings public).

This risk-averse, high-stakes strategy is one of the things that sets Blair apart from the two other most significant British politicians of the past decade. His friend and rival Gordon Brown is another risk-averse politician, but one who prefers to play for low stakes, endlessly and tirelessly working the percentages to build up his political reserves, never willing to put all his eggs in one basket. Blair's erstwhile opponent Ken Livingstone, by contrast, is a politician who has been genuinely happy to take big risks, and to gamble everything on uncertain ventures that offer the prospect of spectacular rewards. Blair has frequently been frustrated by what he sees as Brown's excessive caution, particularly over British entry into the euro, about which his Chancellor has never been willing to take any chances. Likewise, Blair has invariably been appalled by Livingstone's cavalier disregard for the safe option, and for the finer details of political calculation. Nevertheless, he has found enough in common with each of them to be able to work with both. With Brown he shares a loathing of wishful political speculation; their risk aversion was jointly forged by having to listen to fantasies of Labour election victories during the 1980s. With Livingstone, Blair shares a readiness to play for high stakes once it is clear how the cards are stacked (this is what allowed the two men to unite behind London's successful bid for the 2012 Olympics).[3] The popular success of Livingstone's brand of political brinkmanship as mayor of London persuaded Blair to throw in his lot with the man he once warned would be a disaster for the city, and to readmit him as the official Labour candidate in the 2004 mayoral election. For Blair it was worth courting ridicule in order to end up on the winning side. Equally, when it comes to risk, Brown and Livingstone have never had anything in common, and they can't stand each other as a result.

Blair's personal attitude to risk helps to explain why he was ready to commit himself so early to George Bush's military plans for dealing with Iraq. In one sense, this represented a huge gamble. By allying himself with a staunchly right-wing American president, against the wishes of many in his own party and a large section of British public opinion, Blair was risking his own political reputation and that of his government on what appeared to be a whim. But in Blair's eyes, this was absolutely not a whim; rather, it was the only risk worth taking. Blair is drawn to the Americans because of their overwhelming strength. He recognized that nothing would stop George Bush getting his way in Iraq in the end. In these circumstances, he seems genuinely to have believed that it was too risky to allow the United States to go it alone. Everyone involved in the Iraq crisis thinks that everyone else has behaved recklessly in one way or another ("reckless, reckless, reckless", as his International Development Secretary Clare Short memorably described Blair on the eve of war, notwithstanding the fact that she herself recklessly remained in Blair's government for two more months, thereby destroying her own reputation). Blair's view is that those who opposed the war, including the French and German governments, were risking the unity of the West for the sake of an argument they could not win. It is simply not in Blair's nature to believe that it is worth taking a chance on weakness rather than strength. But nor is it in his nature to believe that, once you take a chance, it is worth holding anything back.

This is what makes Iraq so different from Suez. Both were huge gambles, but Eden's government staked its reputation on what was essentially an enormous bluff. To succeed, it needed its opponents to believe that it was stronger than it was. When Eisenhower's administration withheld military and financial support for the operation, that illusion could not be sustained, and the bluff was exposed. It is inconceivable that a politician like Tony Blair would ever allow himself to get into such a position. This is in part a matter of risk temperament. But it is also because Blair's personal attitude to risk coincides with the central lesson that the British political establishment drew from the Suez debacle: it is never worth bluffing the Americans. In this respect, Blair's Iraq policy was a deliberate inversion of Eden's recklessness at Suez, because the one thing Blair was not willing to contemplate was being frozen out by the United States. Indeed, he seems to have

been prepared to risk almost anything to avoid that fate. He ratio-
nalized this position by claiming that the Bush administration
would only be open to influence by those who offered it unques-
tioning support, despite all the evidence that the Bush administration, like most other administrations, is only open to influence
by those who offer it either money or votes. But the truth is that
Blair does not believe in placing bets against the biggest player at
the table. He had no choice but to stand "shoulder to shoulder"
with Bush, because that is the only way he could see what was in
the president's hand.

The fact that Blair's attitude to risk matches that of the British
political establishment is no mere coincidence. Blair is the first
Prime Minister for more than a generation to have been brought
up squarely within that establishment. He is not old enough to
remember Suez at first-hand (he was only three in 1956), but he
is old enough to have seen something of what it meant to the
world to which he belonged. Fettes, the ultra-establishment public
school that Blair attended, was one of the places where the humiliations of Suez would have been most keenly felt. Selwyn Lloyd,
Eden's hapless Foreign Secretary and go-between at Sèvres, was
a former pupil, and the school was very proud of the link, even
though Suez did his reputation great damage. Moreover, it had
been at Fettes on 5 November 1956, at the very height of the crisis, that an effigy of Hugh Gaitskell (a Wykehamist, and leader of
the Labour Party in its opposition to war) was burned in place of
the guy.[4] Those who were there at the time now insist that this
was a joke, but joke or not, it would have been part of the folk
memory of the school when the young Anthony Blair, then still a
Tory, arrived in 1966. Suez offered a young man with an interest
in politics a series of case studies in the price to be paid for political recklessness, whether it was the recklessness of those who
embarked on a war they could not finish, or the recklessness of
those who opposed a war they lacked the means to prevent. Blair's
political career has been marked by a determination to avoid all
such risks.

One of the ironies of Suez, and one of the contrasts it offers
with Iraq, is that the risks taken were out of character for many of
the leading players. The highly respectable Selwyn Lloyd was certainly not a man used to doing secret deals at clandestine locations

73

in the French countryside, and the French and Israelis found his evident discomfort at Sèvres almost comical. Gaitskell talked himself round from a position of cautious support for the government over the summer of 1956 to passionate opposition by the autumn, which left him with little room for manoeuvre. Eden had previously shown himself to be an expert player of the game of international power politics; the recklessness of his Suez policy was shocking to many who knew him, in part because it was so unexpected. The one person who seems to have behaved in character is also the only senior British politician who benefited directly from the Suez crisis. Hugh Thomas, in his book *The Suez Affair*, describes the behaviour of Eden's Chancellor, Harold Macmillan, as that of someone who derived "an almost aesthetic satisfaction from danger and risks".[5] It was Macmillan who did most to persuade Eden that an Anglo-French invasion of Egypt without either United States or UN backing, though clearly risky, was a gamble worth taking (he is said to have put the chances of success at 51 to 49, odds to make even the most nerveless politician blanch).[6] Yet it was also Macmillan who pulled the plug on the invasion after less than a week, when he told the cabinet that he could not stem a run on the pound that was threatening to bankrupt the currency. Macmillan revealed himself to be a born risk taker who was happy to play for high stakes, so long as the stakes were not his own. When he was gambling with Eden's reputation, he was willing to risk everything, but when his own reputation as Chancellor was at stake he was no longer willing to play. Macmillan was as responsible as anyone for the disaster of Suez. But it was Macmillan, rather than any of his more circumspect colleagues, who succeeded Eden when he resigned in January 1957. Thus Suez also offers a case study in how a Chancellor can use an unpopular war to supplant an otherwise secure Prime Minister, but only if he is a risk taker of a particularly unscrupulous kind.

Because the risks involved in Suez were different from those involved in Iraq, the lies were different too. Eden had to persuade parliament that the Israeli invasion of Egypt, an event over which he exercised almost complete discretion, was actually a fait accompli, and so beyond his control. Blair, by contrast, had to persuade parliament that the American invasion of Iraq, an event that he knew to be inevitable, was not a fait accompli, but something over which British politicians might be able to exercise some control. Eden dissembled in parliament because the gamble he had made depended on secrecy for any chance of success. As he told the Backbench 1922 Committee of the Conservative Party on 18 December 1956, when it was all over: "Some half-truths were necessary, and always are, in this sort of operation, which demands extreme secrecy."[7] For Blair, the opposite was true. The half-truths he told, in the two dossiers he published about Iraq's WMD, were demanded by the need he perceived for complete openness.[8] He had to persuade parliament and the public that there was a case for going to war beyond the fact that the Americans were going to war anyway. Blair had to put everything he had on the table, so that he could pretend to be a player in his own right. Eden's problem was that he was a player in his own right, and increasingly out of his depth. He had to keep everything as close to his chest as possible, in the hope that no one would find out.

In many ways, the Iraq crisis offers a kind of mirror image of the Suez crisis, with everything the same, and everything different. The Iraq war was fought over the issue of WMD, but when it was won, and the weapons weren't found, it became a war about something else—the wider threat of global terrorism and the need to spread democracy. The Suez conflict was fought over the ownership of a canal, but when it was lost, and British ships carried on using the canal anyway, it became a war about something else— the wider threat of Soviet domination and the need to counter tyranny. In 1956, the British government downplayed the nuclear threat before the war, because it was so real—there really were Russian WMD pointed at London. In 2003, the British government played up the nuclear threat before the war, because it was so unreal—there weren't even Iraqi WMD pointed at Cyprus, as had been suggested in the September dossier. Suez and Iraq both did considerable damage to the reputation of the UN in the run-up to war, because of the brazen way in which the major powers used the Security Council as a place in which to play the game of high politics. But both conflicts offered some comfort to the champions of the UN once formal hostilities were over, as it became clear that the major powers would be hard pressed to sort out the mess they had made without UN help. The same arguments were heard on both occasions, only with the leading roles reversed. In his memoirs, Eisenhower recollected the nagging question of autumn 1956: "What was the purpose of the French and British in going to the United Nations? Was it ... a sincere desire to negotiate a satisfactory peaceful settlement (as the British insisted) or was this merely a setting of the stage for the eventual use of force?"[9] The French president would be asking almost exactly the same of the Americans nearly half a century later.

The Suez crisis broke the health and the career of the British Prime Minister. Eden had fallen seriously ill at the beginning of October 1956, with a fever that reached 106 °F, and it seems likely that he was heavily medicated from then until the final collapse of his Suez policy in November, when his health deteriorated further and he was advised by his doctors to take a holiday. He reluctantly agreed, spending three weeks at Ian Fleming's somewhat spartan Jamaican hideaway, even though British troops remained on the ground in Egypt. When he returned, it soon became clear that he could not continue in office (at the 18 December meeting of the 1922 Committee Eden was forced to admit that he no longer "held in his head" the details of Britain's treaty obligations in the Middle East, at which point even his most loyal supporters lost confidence in his ability to carry on). In January he resigned on the grounds of ill health, allowing his Chancellor to succeed him. For a while, there was speculation that Tony Blair, whose health also appeared to suffer during the Iraq conflict, would do the same. But this was wishful thinking. Blair seems to be a reasonably healthy man who sometimes looks ghastly; Eden was a seriously ill man who did his best to appear well. Blair also took a Caribbean holiday when the war was over (staying at Sir Cliff Richard's luxury holiday home on Barbados), but unlike Eden, he showed no sign of having lost either his appetite or his nerve on his return. Indeed, Blair and his colleagues—with their jogging machines and their smoke-free workplaces and their infant children—seem almost ridiculously healthy compared with the Suez generation of politicians, most of whom appear to have been ill (not only Eden but also Eisenhower, Dulles and Ben-Gurion were incapacitated at one point or another during late 1956). Only Dick Cheney remains as a throwback to the days when politicians were prepared to risk their health in the selfless pursuit of wealth and power.

Though Eden forfeited his premiership, his physical well-being and his peace of mind as a result of Suez, the one thing he did not sacrifice was his popularity with the British public. Where Blair's approval ratings steadily declined following the end of a war he won, Eden's approval ratings steadily rose following a war he lost. In late November 1956, when the ruin of what Eden had tried to achieve was laid bare for all to see, over 60% of the British electorate said they approved of his performance as Prime Minister (and among Tory voters the figure stood at an astonishing 95%).[10] Even a year later, long after he had resigned, both Eden himself and the war that ruined him were recording positive approval ratings in the opinion polls. The fact that Eden had gambled, and bungled, and lost counted for less than the fact that he had stood up for what he believed in, against overwhelming odds. In the words of the time, Eden became in the public mind the man who "lost everything save honour". Blair, by contrast, was the winner who seemed unable to do anything to reclaim his honour. The risk Blair took in going to war in Iraq was not that he would lose, but that he would win too little for what he had been willing to stake, and end up looking like a fool.

Blair has done what he can to try to escape from this fate. The mere act of remaining in power can do much to diminish the appearance of foolhardiness, just as Eden's hasty departure from office eventually came to overshadow his lingering reputation for honour and decency. But it is also true that Blair's willingness to expose himself to ridicule has helped to inoculate him against its most corrosive effects. The consistent message of Blair's political career has been that ridicule doesn't matter; what matters is staying in the game. This brazenness has been reflected in Blair's preferred political strategy, which is to make sure that the opposition have no cards left to play: the repeated complaint of the Tory Party, ever since Blair came to power, is that whenever they get a good idea, he steals it. It is also reflected in the other great gamble of his political career: his decision to allow a future referendum on the EU constitution. This decision, which was taken in April 2004, at one of the low points of his premiership, was widely seen as a sign of weakness, or even desperation, and routinely described at the time as "the gamble of his life". But it was also the sort of gamble he has been taking all his life. It has all the hallmarks of Blair's risk-taking style: capricious yet calculated (the calculation being that a referendum was one of his opponents' few popular policies, so he would appropriate it), Blair showed himself willing, if necessary, to stake everything on a final spin of the wheel, even if the ultimate rewards might be quite small (the big prize, replacing the pound with the euro, has always been beyond Blair's grasp). But Blair also calculated that there would be quite a few spins of the wheel before the point of no return was reached—including the referendums that were to come in the other EU member states, any one of which might get him out of trouble by voting no, as both France and the Netherlands eventually did. Conversely, if all had voted yes, he knew that he would be better placed to present the vote to the British people as an all-or-nothing choice between staying in the EU or quitting altogether. The decision to offer a referendum on the EU constitution was an exercise in the kind of risk-averse brinkmanship in which Blair has always specialized.

Blair's attitude to risk has helped to make him one of the longest-serving Prime Ministers of modern times. He has proved consistently lucky throughout his career, in the weakness and division among the political opponents he has faced, and in the caution of Gordon Brown, the only person who could have supplanted him, yet someone who consistently shied away from the opportunity. But Blair's good fortune has been coupled with the remorselessness of his gambling instincts. In order to remain in office, Blair had to renege on a series of deals he made with Brown to quit before the end of his second term.[11] No one can be sure of the details of these deals, or what motivated Blair to break them. But part of it appears to stem from a sense of missed opportunity, the idea that, for all the risks taken during his time as Prime Minister, the rewards have been relatively small. Like the Monte Carlo gambler who goes through hell to win £100, Blair has found it very hard to walk away from the table; he appears haunted by the sense he should have got a greater return for his money. He has also been consistently worried that his successor might squander what little has been gained. It is this, more than anything, which seems to have driven him on, to the point where a dignified exit from the game becomes increasingly difficult, if not impossible, to achieve.

Like all Prime Ministers, Blair is concerned about how history will judge him. Whatever happens, he will be judged to have done better than Anthony Eden, who routinely occupies last place in historians' lists of the most successful premiers of modern times.[12] But to have done better than Eden is scarcely enough to justify what he has been through. His ultimate reputation will depend on what follows him, and the prospects look uncertain at best. If his successor does well—if, say, Gordon Brown turns out to be another Gladstone—Blair may be eclipsed. But if his successor does badly, it may be concluded that Blair left too few solid gains for any successor to build on. This is the ultimate risk that Blair has been running. When all the drama and the excitement of his various gambles has faded, history may only see the paltry rewards, and decide that it wasn't really worth it.

CHAPTER FIVE

WHO KNOWS BEST?

The degree to which British politics has been dominated in recent years by the risk personality of a single politician has done nothing to diminish the widespread distrust that is currently felt towards elected politicians in general. The highly personal nature of Blair's approach to the risks of war with Iraq, coupled with the ruthless way he exploited those risks to secure his own political survival, has inevitably led many people to wonder whether any Prime Minister should be allowed to place such faith in their own judgment. Equally, the relative ease with which Blair was able to co-opt the upper reaches of the British political establishment—its elite bureaucrats, special advisers and spymasters—to back his judgment, has raised questions about whether politicians in general should have so much discretion on matters of security risk in the first place. The Iraq war, and the wider war on terror, have exposed the danger of politicians getting certain kinds of threat out of proportion, while neglecting others. But is there any way of doing it better? Would we have been better off trusting in someone else's judgment—that of other politicians perhaps, or of individuals other than politicians? Or is the problem that we have become too reliant on individual judgment altogether, and should learn to put more faith in the formal impartiality of general rules, and in the impersonal insights of unruly crowds? This chapter looks at the question of who knows best when it comes to making judgments about terrorism and other threats to national security—politicians, judges, or the general public?

Politicians versus Judges

Most of us, most of the time, are deeply prejudiced in favour of individual over collective judgments. This is hardly surprising, since we are all biased. First of all, we are biased in favour of our own opinions, which we tend to prefer to those of anyone else. Second, we are biased in favour of individuals generally, because we are all individuals ourselves, and so are broadly sympathetic to the individual point of view. We like to think of people exercising their personal judgment, and not just blindly following the rules. For example, who wouldn't prefer, when appearing before a judge, to learn that the judge was willing to hear each case on its merits, and exercise some discretion if necessary? General rules, we think, are likely to be discriminatory, because they cannot take account of special circumstances. Individuals, by contrast, can use their own judgment, and make exceptions.

However, though we are right to suspect that all general rules are discriminatory, we are wrong to suppose that it is therefore better to trust to individuals. This is because no individual is truly capable of judging each case on its merits; rather, they simply bring their own personal generalizations to bear on the case in question. These are likely to be just as crude and inflexible as the mandatory guidelines of some far-distant committee. It is easy to forget this. Because general rules are cold and impersonal, the injustices they inevitably create seem crueller and more pernicious. In his recent study of the general squeamishness that currently prevails about stereotyping anyone, Frederick Schauer gives various examples of the seeming cold-heartedness of general rules, including the cases of perfectly friendly dogs put down because they fell foul of the terms of dangerous-dog regulations, or airline pilots forced by United States law to retire at the age of sixty, regardless of their proficiency, expertise or health.[1] It is not only airline pilots who think this latter rule absurd. The first commercial flight into space was piloted in 2004 by a sixty-three year old who had been forced to quit his day job as a domestic airline pilot. When he appeared on television talk-shows to publicize this feat, he pointed out that he was only available to fly in space because the government had deemed him unfit to fly underneath it. How audiences laughed at this spectacle of a bureaucracy gone mad, that a man should have been reduced by ageism to becoming an astronaut!

Because of glaring examples such as this, it is tempting to think that there must be some way of deciding such questions as who is and who is not fit to fly that would not be so inflexible and discriminatory. There isn't. For example, why not test pilots when they reach sixty to see if they are fit to carry on? But specialized tests rely on generalizations no less than general rules do. A blood pressure test, for instance, designed to ascertain the likelihood of sudden incapacitation, will seem discriminatory to anyone who falls below its arbitrary threshold and then goes on to enjoy thirty more years of healthy existence. So why not dispense with formal tests altogether, and simply get individual doctors, perhaps in conjunction with other experienced pilots, to exercise their own judgment in assessing a person's fitness to carry on after the age of sixty? The answer is that these individuals will simply be applying their own generalizations, and these are likely to be as arbitrary as any. Some doctors will be particularly alert to incipient heart trouble; others will be on the lookout for mental instability; some pilots will simply prefer those of their colleagues who remind them of themselves ("I like a drink now and then, and I can still fly, so why not this person?"). It is almost impossible to overstate the tendency of individuals to prefer the judgment of those other individuals they happen to know personally, or work with, or who simply give them a good feeling. These are the very reasons we have general rules in the first place, to protect us from the arbitrary judgments of individuals.

This does not mean, of course, that it is impossible to argue against general rules on the grounds that they could be fairer—a law that forced pilots to retire when they went bald or converted to Islam would clearly be grotesque. What it does mean, though, is that it does not make sense to argue against general rules on principle, simply because they are general. What matters is to distinguish between what are essentially spurious and what are essentially non-spurious generalizations. Spurious generalizations include those where there is no statistical correlation (as in the case of baldness and flying ability), as well as those where the correlation is irrelevant (it is true that in recent years a high percentage of the airplanes to crash in the United States have been piloted by Muslims, but the non-spurious fact is that they were also piloted by terrorists, who certainly should be prevented by law from flying airplanes). What then matters is to decide which non-spurious generalizations are useful in making the general rules. By no means all of them are useful. For example, it is almost certainly true that there are non-spurious generalizations to be made about the likelihood of certain types of passengers posing a threat to airline security, on the basis of age, gender and ethnic background—the likeliest terrorists are young males of Middle Eastern origin. But this does not necessarily mean that young males of Middle Eastern origin should be singled out as a general rule for special attention from security officers. This is because individual security officers are likely to have devised such a rule for themselves, which they would apply, and probably over-apply, regardless. More useful would be guidelines that identified other dangerous groups who might be missed (other kinds of terrorists, other kinds of criminals, other kinds of security threats). Once it is clear that all judgments, including all individual judgments, rest on various kinds of generalization, then rules can be devised that take account of the inadequate generalizations of individuals.

It does not follow from this, however, that because sweeping generalizations are unavoidable in law and public life, no individual using their own judgment could outperform the rulebook. For instance, it is probably true that a really skilled and sensitive judge, well versed in all the vagaries of individual human experiences, and willing to trust in their own instincts, would do better if they exercised some discretion when sentencing than if they followed a fixed grid that insisted on particular sentences for particular crimes. Mandatory life sentences for murder under English law seem a particularly egregious example of excessive rigidity, since in some cases of murder there are, of course, extenuating circumstances. The problem, though, is knowing who are the really skilled judges. Most judges tend to think that it is them, which is why judges as a whole tend to oppose mandatory sentencing regulations. It is possible, as Schauer writes, that

> the judges are right, and that the judgement of judges as a whole (itself a generalisation) will produce fewer mistakes than would be produced by a systematic application of the guidelines. But in determining whether this is true, it may not be the best strategy to listen only to the judges, for it should come as no surprise that judges, just like carpenters,

police officers, customs officials and university professors,
are hardly the best judges of the frequency and magnitude
of their own errors.[2]

Even if the guidelines make more mistakes than the best judges,
the fact that not all judges are the best is a good reason for having
sentencing guidelines.

The same principles, of course, should also apply to politicians,
who are as prone as anyone to misjudge the frequency and magnitude of their mistakes. But politicians have an argument to deploy
in favour of their own personal discretion that cannot so easily be
used by judges, police officers, customs officials, university professors, etc. It is a part of a politician's job description to rely
entirely on their personal judgment, if they deem it necessary, in
those circumstances where emergency action is required. Judges,
police officers, customs officials, university professors may also
sometimes have to take emergency action, which will require the
exercise of personal discretion. But this is not part of their job
description—it is not one of the things that they are paid to do,
and when they do it, they will need to justify their actions retro-
spectively according to the rules. Only politicians can justify their
actions, if strictly necessary, solely by their results. Indeed, politicians may be said to have a special responsibility to ignore the
general rules that hold for everyone else, because politicians are
empowered to judge when the system of rule itself is under threat.
This is part of what Max Weber meant by the idea of political
responsibility, and it is one of the things that he takes to distinguish the vocation of the politician from that of the mere "official".
It is also an aspect of modern political life that many contemporary
political theorists, writing from an essentially liberal and legalistic
perspective, prefer to ignore.

These differences between general guidelines and individual
discretion—and between judges and politicians—lie at the heart
of the arguments that have taken place in Britain about what sort
of anti-terrorist legislation is required in the wake of the attacks
of September 11, and more recently the London bombings of
July 2005. The arguments have continued almost without pause,
and without resolution, since the autumn of 2001, following the
enactment of the Labour government's original emergency legislation that allowed for detention without trial of foreign terrorist

suspects. This legislation was eventually declared unlawful by the House of Lords in 2004, and was replaced by a new set of laws, pushed through parliament early in 2005, which abandoned the option of imprisonment for terrorist suspects who had not been convicted of a criminal offence, and replaced it with a series of "control" orders, up to and including house arrest. The furious debates in both the Lords and the Commons that accompanied the hasty passage of this legislation did not, for the most part, turn on the question of whether control orders were necessary: almost all sides agreed that in some circumstances they were, given the special difficulties of bringing certain kinds of terrorist suspects to trial. The argument was about who should issue these control orders—judges or politicians—and what criteria should be used to decide the level of control needed in any given case. In other words, it was a question of how much individual discretion should be allowed, and whose it should be.

The government, in arguing for the maximum amount of personal discretion on the part of the executive (which in the British case means the Home Secretary) in issuing these orders, placed a great deal of weight on the special responsibility of democratically elected politicians to judge for themselves what constitutes an acceptable level of terrorist threat. It was suggested that politicians have three advantages over judges in making this kind of assessment: first, they have a different appreciation of risk; second, they see the bigger picture when it comes to national security; third, they are less likely to become bogged down in legalistic niceties. Politicians were also said to carry a burden that judges do not share: they will have to take the blame if things go wrong. The result of these claims was a reversal of the more usual line of argument, described by Schauer, which has politicians worrying that judges will not be strict enough in their application of the rules, and will allow their personal discretion to get in the way. Here, the politicians were worried that judges would tend, as a class, to be too strict, and would fail to see that the special circumstances of the terrorist threat demanded discretion in particular cases. And it was the judges, in the House of Lords, who worried that granting such wide discretionary power to individual politicians gave too much credence to the politicians' faith in their own personal judgment.

Inevitably, these disputes turned on a series of stereotypes: stereotypes of judges, stereotypes of politicians, stereotypes of terrorists. Some of these stereotypes were better founded than others. For example, one of the most contested aspects of the legislation concerned the standard of proof that is necessary to justify the issuing of a control order: should the threat posed by individual terrorist suspects be assessed on a balance of probabilities, or merely on the basis of a reasonable suspicion (one that might, by implication, fail to pass the stricter test of being more likely than not to be true)? The government, in arguing for its new special powers, pointed out that it could not afford to abide by the legal standard of a balance of probabilities, because of the catastrophic consequences of failing to act on a reasonable (if more remote) suspicion that turned out to be well founded. This claim relied on a number of generalizations. First, there is the inevitable stereotyping that lies at the heart of any law that works on the basis of mere suspicion—suspects will always tend to be characters of a certain "type" (of race, religion, background, circle of acquaintance, etc.). But the same is true of a law that insists on a more rigorous balance of probabilities: deciding what is more likely than not to occur equally depends on a willingness to generalize on the basis of character types. No assessment of risk can avoid making sweeping assumptions about individual cases. Indeed, all such cases must involve a degree of prejudice, since it is in the nature of risk assessments to seek to prejudge the likelihood of particular outcomes.[3]

However, the government's case involved not merely the stereotyping that is an inevitable accompaniment of risk assessments, but also the stereotyping of certain types of risks themselves. This is much harder to justify. Various speakers on the government's behalf, including the Home Secretary Charles Clarke, made reference during the parliamentary debates on control orders to the case of a potential "shoe bomber" in Gloucester, who had recently been convicted in a court of law. What, they wanted to know, should be done when a suspicion exists about a similar character but the evidence has not been found (unlike in this case, when the incriminating material was discovered in the suspect's home, where it had been hidden for more than two years)? What if, in this case, the suspect had been able to act before his crimes were detected? "The damage that individual would have done," Clarke told the Commons, "is absolutely catastrophic."[4] The implication here is that the risk of allowing a potential shoe bomber to roam free is just too great to be countenanced by any responsible politician, whatever the balance of probabilities. But is it? The Gloucester shoe bomber did not in fact manage to do any damage, despite having the means at his disposal for more than two years. Indeed, notwithstanding their lurid symbolic appeal, recent history suggests that it is extremely difficult for anyone to deploy a shoe bomb to cause catastrophic damage, particularly now that it is so hard to get one onto a plane (and it is especially hard for anyone who arouses the stereotypical suspicions of airport security staff). The government's case for control orders depends on the assumption that the kind of harm threatened by such individuals, however remote, is too great to be assessed on a conventional scale of likely outcomes. It equally seems to rest on the stereotypical assumptions of the Home Secretary about where such threats are likely to lie—we now know it was not shoe bombers in Gloucester but seemingly innocent young men from Leeds with rucksacks who posed the real danger. Two things remain clear following the London bombings. First, politicians exercising their own discretion are just as likely to rely on outmoded stereotypes as any police officer, lawyer or rule-bound bureaucrat. Second, as we saw in Chapter Three, it is far from obvious that the worst a terrorist bomber could do is in fact off the scale of the sort of disasters that governments routinely have to countenance. Even a terrorist bomb on a plane remains relatively, rather than absolutely, catastrophic for anyone other than its immediate victims.

Everything depends on what is meant in such cases by the balance of probabilities. If it means that there must be a better than 50:50 chance of some possible outcome occurring—the strict legal definition—then the standard is indeed too high for certain kinds of risks; it must sometimes make sense to act when the probabilities are lower but the scale of damage that might be caused is sufficient to warrant taking special precautions.[5] But if balancing probabilities simply means that all risks must be weighed on a scale of costs and benefits, and no risk can be assumed to be off the scale, then it is hard to see how a standard of reasonable suspicion can ever stand in contrast to it: any suspicion that

cannot be justified on a scale of costs and benefits is by definition unreasonable. The government feared that the legal profession was bound to remain wedded to the former, stricter definition in control-order cases, because it is the minimal standard of
proof required in all civil legal proceedings (the standard in criminal proceedings—"beyond reasonable doubt"—is even higher).
Lawyers, it was assumed by the politicians, would not know how
to balance probabilities when it comes to dealing with potential
terrorists.

Yet here too the government may have been guilty of unjustified stereotyping. The most cogent statement of the thinking
behind the government's position on the question of standards
of proof—covering both the necessity of stereotyping in all risk
assessments, and the inadequacy of conventional legal definitions
of the balance of probabilities for assessing the risks posed by terrorist suspects—was provided by a judge, in the case of *The Secretary of State for the Home Department vs. Rehman*.[6] This was a case
concerning the right of the Home Secretary to order the deportation of a Muslim cleric suspected of terrorist activities, which
eventually reached the House of Lords. One of the judges who
heard the case there, Lord Hoffman, made two things absolutely
clear in his written judgment. First, in such cases, a degree of
stereotyping is inevitable. As he put it (somewhat legalistically):
"Some things are inherently more likely than others. It would
need more cogent evidence to satisfy one that the creature seen
walking in Regent's Park was more likely than not to have been a
lioness than to be satisfied to the same standard of probability that
it was an Alsatian." Second, in cases involving the assessment of
future terrorist risk, the legal standard of proof is an inadequate
guide:

> In a criminal or civil trial in which the issue is whether a
> given event happened, it is sensible to say that one is sure
> that it did, or that one thinks it more likely than not that it did.
> But the question in the present case is not whether a given
> event happened, but the extent of future risk. This depends
> upon an evaluation of the evidence of the appellant's con-
> duct against a broad range of facts with which they may
> interact. The question of whether the risk to national secu-
> rity is sufficient to justify the appellant's deportation cannot
> be answered by taking each allegation seriatim and deciding

whether it has been established to some standard of proof. It is a question of evaluation and judgment, in which it is necessary to take into account not only the degree of probability of prejudice to national security but also the importance of the security interest at stake and the serious consequences of deportation for the deportee.[7]

Lord Hoffmann is better known as the staunchest judicial critic of the government's original 2001 anti-terror laws, on the grounds that the emergency powers they bestowed on politicians implied a non-commensurable level of threat to national security (that is, a threat to the state's very existence).[8] But on the question of commensurable threats, he is clear that an excessively legalistic interpretation of the balance of probabilities will not suffice.

Given the inadequacy of the traditional guidelines in such cases, the question then becomes whether what are needed are new guidelines, or new powers for politicians to ignore the rules when they deem it necessary. The government has argued that the executive, in the person of the Home Secretary, is best able to see the bigger picture required to make an overall assessment of the threat posed by particular suspects. This assumes that politicians can, when necessary, take account of a wider range of factors, and act more flexibly, than those, like judges, who remain bound to abide by certain inflexible rules. But this, as we have seen, is a fallacy. It does not follow that individuals with wide discretion will automatically have a wider perspective than those who rely on a fixed set of rules. In fact, the reverse may be true, because individuals with wide discretion are less likely to be forced to confront the inadequacy of their own personal stereotypes. Politicians in particular are likely to rely on a set of generalizations that conform to the milieu with which they are most comfortable—the world of security, and secrecy, and power—and thus to ignore the broader ramifications of their actions. Lord Hoffman's judgment in *The Secretary of State for the Home Department vs. Rehman* provides a set of reasonable guidelines to follow when assessing the risk posed by terrorist suspects: these include weighing not only the threat to national security, but also the relative importance of the "security interest at stake", as well as the deleterious consequences for the individual concerned. Politicians, in taking a personal view of the bigger picture, are likely to ignore the second and third of these tests, and narrow their focus to the first.

Eventually, following the debates that preceded the passage of the 2005 legislation, a compromise position was reached which allowed for judicial review of all cases where the Home Secretary decides to impose control orders. This was in order to strike what the Lord Chancellor, Lord Falconer, called "a balance between the need for the Secretary of State to be able to reach judgments on national security issues, and the need to ensure that those decisions are subject to legal scrutiny".[9] But in truth, it is not clear what kind of balance can be struck here, because so much depends on the sequence of decision making in such cases. If the Home Secretary decides first, and then has his decision subject to judicial scrutiny, what is under review is likely to be the scope rather than the content of any decisions taken. As one of Charles Clarke's predecessors as Home Secretary, Kenneth Clarke, put it in the Commons:

> There are many cases in which a judge does not overturn a Secretary of State's decision, even though he personally disagrees with the Secretary of State about its merits and would not have taken it on the evidence before him. The judge lets the decision go ahead if he decides it was within the power of the Secretary of State, that he followed the right process and that he was entitled to do what he did.[10]

Much is currently uncertain in this area, and a lot depends on the precise wording of the act, and on the interpretation of any human-rights legislation that may also be held to apply in control-order cases. But judicial review that is limited to confirming or refusing to confirm the decisions of the Home Secretary once they have been taken, rather than weighing the evidence on which they were made, will do little to counter the bias of the legislation in favour of personal political discretion. If judges are unable to do more than approve control-order decisions, and must stop short of evaluating them, then the best that can be hoped for is that some bad decisions by the politicians might be overturned. What will not happen is that the judgment of the politicians will be subject to wider guidance, allowing for more good decisions to be taken than might otherwise be the case, because the decisions will still belong to the politicians alone.

The government also ran into difficulty on another question of sequence. It repeatedly resisted demands to include a sunset clause in the 2005 legislation, requiring its automatic repeal within a specified period. In the end, a further compromise was agreed under which the Home Secretary made a commitment to introduce new anti-terror legislation within a year, a promise that was described at the time as a "sunset clause by any other name". But in one crucial respect a promise of this kind, however much personal weight is lent it by individual politicians, is not the same as an act that contains a statutory commitment to its own repeal. The difference lies in the possibility that the personal promises of politicians can be rendered obsolete by events. The significance of a sunset clause is that, because it is legally enforceable, it cannot be derailed by an act of terrorism, which might otherwise place politicians under enormous public pressure to consider all previous commitments void. The Labour government has repeatedly stated in parliament that the danger of a sunset clause would be the signal it sent to terrorists that Britain was not serious about its anti-terrorist measures. This need to show seriousness was always liable, in the event of a subsequent terrorist outrage, to trump any promises made in an earlier spirit of compromise. The point of recognizing in a piece of emergency legislation that it is emergency legislation, and must be revoked, is to render it immune from the kind of further emergency that might make it permanent. Here again, the politicians appear to have placed too much faith in the reliability of their own personal judgment, and not enough in the importance of having binding rules. It is true that politicians must retain the ability to act on their own discretion in an emergency. But this ability cannot itself be relied on to establish the limits of the personal discretion of politicians.

Politicians versus the People

At the time of writing, the status of the control-order legislation remains uncertain: the government is set to introduce new anti-terror measures in the wake of the London bombings, while still insisting that the rules governing control orders remain subject to review. The fact that control orders could have done little to prevent the London attack, however, has not altered the government's position that such measures remain essential in the fight against terrorism. The Prime Minister was initially advised of the need for these orders, according to his own version of events, by the security services, whose counsel he has repeatedly said no responsible government can afford to ignore.[11] This claim, though its specific veracity provoked some short-lived political controversy at the time, ultimately laid the basis for what little consensus was achieved in parliament. Even when it was insisted that the evidence provided by the security services in individual cases should be subject to judicial review, no one suggested that judges should advise the government on wider questions of security policy. That had to remain the preserve of the politicians, guided by the experts who serve them.

But where do the public at large, whose protection these new measures are designed to serve, fit in? Should they have any say in the matter? It is all too easy, when elected and non-elected representatives come to debate questions of national security, to assume that the people whom they represent should be discounted in their discussions. When the views of the wider public do feature in these debates, it is invariably in a token capacity—either as the punitive crowd whose patience should not be unduly tried, or as the sensible people "out there", whose unshakeable common sense can be relied on when all else fails.[12] Notwithstanding these stereotypes, no politician truly believes that the public should decide what needs to be done for their own protection—these are never questions that would be put to a referendum, for fear of the populism, ignorance and irredeemable foolishness that are assumed to characterize non-expert opinion on such matters.

Yet there is a case to be made for consulting the public on questions of security risk, trumping the claims of the experts and the politicians to exercise their own personal judgment. The basis of this case is given by James Surowiecki, in his book *The Wisdom of Crowds*.[13] As Surowiecki points out, randomly assembled groups can outperform even the best-qualified individuals in assessing the likelihood of certain kinds of outcomes. Take the trivial instance of trying to guess the number of jellybeans in a jar. If you conduct an experiment with a reasonably large group (say thirty or more) and a reasonably large number of jellybeans (say a few hundred), you will find that the average guess is almost certain to be closer to the truth than your own personal guess.

Moreover, the average guess is likely to be closer to the truth than the guess of the person in the group who is judged in advance the best jellybean guesser (because this is a trivial case, you might be quite prepared to accept that you are not yourself very good at this kind of thing). In fact, there is a reasonable chance that the average guess of the group will be closer to the truth than the best guess of any single individual. In other words, the judgment of the group may be better than the judgment of all the individuals within it, even though the judgment of the group is solely determined by the judgment of its individual members.

This insight can be applied in all sorts of non-trivial ways. For example, professional gamblers who make money out of horse racing do so by having more detailed knowledge and better individual judgment than the average punter. However, no gambler can outperform over time the final market on a horse race (the "starting price"), which is shaped by the collective judgment of everyone who bets on the race, however ignorant, foolish or cavalier. The only way to make money on the horses is to bet early (to "take a price") before the hoi polloi have had their say. This seems paradoxical. After all, when you bet early you are pitting your judgment against that of the bookmaker, who is also likely to be much better informed than the crowd. When you bet late, you are betting against the crowd, to whom the bookmakers have in the end to surrender their judgment. But in the long run, the crowd will win. In ignorance there is indeed a kind of strength.[14] This is an extremely useful insight to have when considering the different ways of making money out of gambling. But perhaps the area in which it is most useful is the one to which Surowiecki (who is mainly interested in the business applications of this principle) devotes least attention: the domain of politics. The wisdom of crowds seems to offer a way out of the impasse that so often bedevils both the theory and the practice of democratic politics. Is it possible that the superiority of crowds to individuals can provide a form of justification for democracy itself?

It might seem strange to think that democracy still stands in need of justification, given its current status as the world's favourite political idea. But in truth, political theorists have always found it hard to explain exactly what it is about democracy that is so compelling.[15] The difficulty can be summarized like this. There are, broadly speaking, two potentially strong defences for democracy, one of which focuses on people's preferences, and the other on their cognitive capacities.[16] The preference-based approach insists that democracy is the best way of finding out what people want. It doesn't matter whether democratic decisions are right or wrong; what matters is that there is no other plausible way to track the desires of the majority. The problem with this approach is that is has become increasingly clear over the last fifty years, since the pioneering work of Kenneth Arrow, that there is no simple way to discern the preferences of the majority. All majoritarian voting procedures turn out to be vulnerable to various inconsistencies and contradictions, whenever there are more than two options to choose from.[17] A cognitive defence of democracy, by contrast, argues that democracies really do provide the likeliest means of making the right political choices, because only democracies allow for the diversity of opinion and freedom of information on which correct decision making depends. John Stuart Mill's *Considerations on Representative Government* is probably the most lucid defence of democracy in these terms. However, the difficulty here is the widely accepted ignorance and fickleness of the masses. Cognitive defences of democracy tend to put the emphasis on elite forms of representation and a "filtering" of public opinion, in order to protect political decision making from the unthinking preferences of the general public; as a result, they often sound distinctly undemocratic. Mill, for instance, favoured a "plural" voting system under which individuals got more votes depending on their intelligence, as judged by their occupation—more for barristers than for tradesmen, more for tradesmen than for foremen, more for foremen than for labourers.[18]

What, though, if the ignorance of the masses turns out not to be a weakness but a strength? This is not an obvious line of defence, but in truth it is relatively easy to find evidence of the perils of "filtering" opinion in order to prioritize elite judgment. Where decision making devolves onto a small group of self-consciously well-informed individuals, it is all too likely that they will lead each other astray if they trust too much in their own judgment and merely reinforce each other's prejudices. Take the most prominent recent example: the Iraq war, and its relation to British public opinion. Tony Blair went to war in the face of widespread (though by

95

no means universal) public scepticism. He justified this course of action on two grounds. First, it was his job to take a lead, even if the public did not like it. The implication here was that the public were against the war because, perfectly understandably, most people prefer not to go to war; but democratic politicians cannot always be guided by popular preferences. The second justification was that Tony Blair, and his security services, knew more about the nature of the threat posed by Saddam than the general public, because they had access to much more information. It now turns out that this information was mostly wrong, or at least wrongly understood by those whose job it was to interpret and judge it. Nevertheless, as Blair has repeatedly argued, no one knew any better at the time. But maybe the public did know better at the time. Perhaps the ignorant masses were actually better equipped to assess the nature of the risk than the experts. It is true that very few people could have said with any degree of certainty that Saddam had no WMD. But then very few people could say with any degree of certainty how many jellybeans there are in the jar.[19] It is also true that different people opposed the war for all sorts of different reasons, many of them pretty unconvincing in their own terms (Saddam's not that bad, we sold him most of his weapons, if Blair's for it I'm against it, George Bush is an idiot, etc.). But it is this very diversity of opinion—and the British newspaper-reading public were probably exposed to more diverse opinions on Iraq than any other—that may explain why the public had a better overall idea of what was going on than those in the closed, secretive, hothouse worlds of Downing Street (and indeed Washington). Although no member of the crowd could claim to be as well informed as the experts, the crowd knew what the specialists did not: Saddam was not an immediate threat.

This does not mean that the crowd is always right. As Surowiecki explains, large groups are only good at making decisions under fairly specific conditions. The members of the group must be willing to think for themselves, they must be more-or-less independent of one another, and the group itself should be reasonably decentralized. There must also be some means of aggregating different opinions into a collective judgment. When people start second-guessing one another, when they follow one another blindly, when they start looking for central direction, the crowd

turns into a herd, and herds are notoriously bad at making decisions. But in the case of the British public's response to the Iraq
war, Surowiecki's conditions seem pretty much to have held.[20]
These conditions are strikingly similar to the ones set out by
Rousseau in *The Social Contract* for determining if a people is capable of self-government. Here is Surowiecki:

> If you ask a large enough group of diverse, independent
> people to make a prediction or estimate a probability, and
> then average those estimates, the errors each of them makes
> in coming up with an answer will cancel themselves out.
> Each person's guess, you might say, has two components:
> information and error. Subtract the error, and you're left with
> the information.[21]

Here is Rousseau:

> There is often a great difference between the will of all [what
> all individuals want] and the general will; the general will
> studies only the common interest while the will of all studies
> private interest, and is indeed no more than the sum of indi-
> vidual desires. But if we take away from these same wills the
> pluses and minuses which cancel each other out, the balance
> which remains is the general will.

> From the deliberations of a people properly informed, and
> provided its members do not have any communication
> among themselves, the great number of small differences
> will always produce a general will, and the decision will
> always be good.[22]

Of course, Surowiecki's terms are much more modest that Rousseau's. There is no talk about a general will or a common good;
rather, it is simply a matter of probabilities, estimates and errors.
Surowiecki accepts that crowds are no better than individuals at
making moral judgments, because moral judgments are nothing
like guessing the number of jellybeans in a jar. Crowds do not
do well when the question is not a straightforwardly cognitive
one. Equally, crowds are not well placed to judge questions that
depend on having detailed knowledge of the particular circumstances of an individual, which by definition can only be known
to those with some first-hand acquaintance. It is for this reason
that crowds would not be well equipped to pass judgment on
individual terrorist suspects—in such cases, a few people might

know a lot but a lot of people would know nothing at all, and rumour and bias would be likely to prevail.

Nevertheless, a large number of the most important questions now facing the world are general problems of cognition—we need to know what we are up against, in order to know how to allocate our resources. Take the question of whether terrorism is more of a threat than global warming. The best way to answer this question would be to know what is likely to happen in the medium term. If there is a good chance that terrorists will get hold of nuclear weapons and then use them, terrorism would seem to constitute the greater threat. But how can we know? One possibility would be to ask the experts and follow their advice. The problem here is that the experts rarely agree, which makes it hard to know which experts to trust. A second alternative would be to see the disagreement of experts as a reason to ask the politicians to exercise their judgment. But a third possibility would be to ask a large group of people that included not just experts and politicians but also members of the public to give it their best guess. This could be done by creating a kind of terrorism futures market, in which a wide range of individuals were invited to estimate the probability of certain eventualities—say, a large-scale nuclear strike over the next decade, or a civil war in Iraq, or even something as specific as the assassination of a particular political leader. In order to guarantee that everyone really gives it their best shot, players could even be encouraged to gamble on the outcome (betting exchanges have tended to outperform both academic experts and polling organizations in predicting the outcome of American presidential elections).[23] This method would have a number of advantages over relying on the usual closed networks of spies, politicians and bureaucrats. It would be open to all, it would be decentralized, it would be leaderless, and it wouldn't have to suck up to anybody. It would pool all available information and intuition, regardless of the source, and turn it into some specific predictions. These predictions might not be right, but they are more likely to be right than the best estimate of any named individual.

There is, though, one obvious disadvantage to this scheme. Most of us would feel pretty appalled at the thought of anyone gambling on real-life death and destruction. When, in 2003, the Defense Advanced Research Projects Agency in the United States tried to set up just such a terrorism futures market (called PAM, or the Policy Analysis Market), the reaction was one of predictable outrage, which killed it stone dead. Two Senators, Ron Wyden and Byron Dorgan, led the assault, calling PAM "harebrained", "offensive", "useless" and "morally wrong".[24] They were, presumably, seeking to articulate the gut instincts of ordinary Americans, for whom the idea that United States foreign policy might be dictated by a group of speculators backing someone to take out the Iraqi Prime Minister would be pretty hard to stomach. It *is* hard to stomach. But the fact remains that such a market can provide information that is simply not available anywhere else. If British policy in Iraq had been guided by the gambling instincts of the British people, who did not think the war was worth the risk, rather than the gambling instincts of George Bush and Tony Blair, who did, then it would have been founded on the sounder intelligence.[25]

Who Knows Best?

The terrorist threat that has come to the fore in the politics of the West since September 11, 2001, has revealed the deep difficulties of knowing whose judgment to trust when assessing certain kinds of risks. It has also revealed the continuing political appeal of emergency powers in dealing with particular types of threat—whether posed by "rogue" individuals or "rogue" states. These powers, precisely because they are so political, can only be exercised by politicians. But the period since September 11 has also revealed the limits of politicians' understanding of their discretionary powers, and the importance of subjecting emergency action to wider tests of impersonal judgment. Politicians, like everyone else, are biased in favour of their own judgment and in favour of the judgment of individuals more generally. This bias leads them to neglect the value of impersonal constraints. In particular, politicians tend to downplay the risk of relying too heavily on their favoured sources of information and advice, and to discount the reliability of rule-based and collective decision making in countering the inevitable distortions that result. Politicians are right when they say that it is their job to make the ultimate decisions on questions of national security, and it would be an abdication of their responsibilities to pass these decisions back either to judges or to the people.

But they are wrong when they insist that their ultimate decisions should be insulated from the influence of judicial or popular opinion. Subjecting personal political judgments to wider impersonal tests need not diminish their decisiveness; it simply makes it more likely that the decision taken will end up being the right one.

The challenge, therefore, is to find ways of combining the need for decisive political action at times of emergency with the kinds of impersonal safeguards that prevent such action from introducing permanent distortions into the idea of national security. There are no easy solutions to this challenge, but there are a number of ways it might be met. One is to ensure that political assessments of risk in individual cases, even if they take priority over purely procedural considerations, are nevertheless subject to some meaningful form of judicial review. Another is to make sure that the advice received by government ministers from their appointed experts is debated as widely as possible by politicians from outside the government: even the most expert advice can be a source of bias if filtered exclusively through the personal judgment of individuals. A third is to make sure that politicians do not ignore the instincts of the public on questions of risk, so long as those instincts have themselves been tested for bias. One way of introducing such tests is through the highly artificial device of a terrorism futures market, although the appeal of markets of this kind is likely to be fairly limited. But there are other tests that already exist, including the test of public opinion. The reliability of public opinion in providing a guide to issues of national security depends on the guarantees that are generated by having a free press, protected from monopoly influence, and offering as wide as possible a range of political views drawn from as diverse as possible a set of information sources. This, in turn, depends on there being an inquisitive public driving the market for news, and willing to read the newspapers it produces. In Britain such a public still exists, though it is not clear for how much longer.[26]

Some of these limitations on executive decision making imply that what we need is more democracy, some that what we need is less. On certain kinds of questions the views of the democratic majority offer a good guide; on others the scrutiny of a non-elected judicial elite provides the best check. It would be absurd to think that the public at large is well equipped to determine which individual terrorist suspects should be subject to control orders, just as it would be absurd to think that judges are in a good position to decide whether or not a state should go to war. But what is clear is that both the challenge of the terrorist threat, and the best ways of meeting it, are not new. What we require are states that allow for decisive political action on the part of their leaders, combined with judicial oversight of particular decisions, robust and diverse legislatures to debate the alternatives (and able, when necessary, to insist on time-limits to emergency legislation), and a well-informed and politically active public to pass its own judgment. We then need the constitutional arrangements in place to ensure that none of these tests of political decision making is allowed excessive influence over the way the government conducts its business. These are the recognizable devices of modern constitutional politics, as it has evolved over the last 300 or more years. Nothing that has happened at the beginning of the twenty-first century has rendered any of them obsolete. Much has happened to make them more important than ever.

WEIMAR IRAQ

Tony Blair has admitted some mistakes in his use of the intelligence that served to justify taking Britain to war in 2003, but he has not been willing to admit that anyone else could have done any better. He has also consistently argued that questions about his personal judgment, and the messy business of who knew what when, can ultimately be discounted in the face of the wider judgment to which the Iraq war will be subjected: the judgment of history. Alongside the rhetoric of good intentions, and the rhetoric of risk, and the rhetoric of decision, Blair has regularly sought to deploy the long gaze of history in order to make sense of some of his difficulties in the present. On one level, this is entirely disingenuous. Blair, like all elected politicians, has tended to invoke the verdict of history at moments of weakness, in order to get him past the judgment that matters most, that of the electorate. But on another level he is, of course, right. History will view the Iraq war in a broader perspective than the personal successes and failures of Tony Blair, or any other individual politician. Yet that has not stopped Blair, in common with other politicians, from trying to predetermine in his own interests the sort of history by which he would wish to be judged.

In June 2004, at one of the low points of his premiership, Blair gave an interview to *The Observer* newspaper, on the occasion of the sixtieth anniversary of the D-Day landings in Normandy. Looking back at the history of the period as a whole, Blair drew comparisons between the opposition he had faced to his own decision to go to war in Iraq and the kind of uncertainty that had preceded Britain's decision to go to war in 1939. "I think it is very interesting," he declared, "when you reread the history of the late Thirties and the Second World War, the degree to which there was a very big disagreement between people as to how to deal with the Nazi threat. Not disagreement that it was a threat, but how to deal with it."[1] This analogy is in many ways typical of the kind of historical arguments that have been employed by British and American political leaders to bolster their case for the Iraq war. Blair prefaced his remarks with a series of routine caveats about how history should not really be used in this way, to justify actions that can only be justified in their own terms. He was insistent that the Iraq war should not be allowed to overshadow the D-Day commemorations, and furthermore he accepted that "it [the history of the period around World War II] should not be used as an argument for or against war in Iraq".[2] Yet these caveats were mere forms of words; in the end, Blair could not resist. Alongside the hypocrisy went some very bad history. Initially, Blair sought to draw the comparison in terms of the "threat" posed by the Hitler and Saddam regimes, but he goes on to collapse this threat into the question of the persecution of the Jews. "You go back in the Thirties to the start of the persecution of the Jewish people ... and you think well these things were there in 1935, 1934 and it was only in 1939 they got round to doing something."[3] The decision to go to war in 1939 was not a decision to "do something" about the Jews, just as the decision to go to war in 2003 was not, when it was made, a decision to do something about the persecution of the Iraqis by Saddam. Because the threat posed by the Saddam regime had to be recast in the language of democratic human rights once the war was over, Blair has to rerun the entire history of World War II in order to conform to this pattern. Which goes to show why these sorts of historical analogies are so hazardous.

What is most characteristic about Blair's use of history, however, is the reference point he chooses. For Blair it goes without saying that if a comparison is to be made, it is with the war against Hitler's Germany. The political advantages of this comparison are obvious, and Blair has not been alone in trying to exploit them. It is not only that the war against Hitler was a just war, and the tyranny of the overthrown regime, once it had been fully exposed, was sufficient to gainsay any objections or misgivings that may have been expressed before its outset. It was also a war that ended with an occupation. This occupation was not easy to begin with, but in the end it produced the desired outcome: the re-establishment of economic security and democratic government. Those who wish to put the problems being encountered in post-war Iraq into perspective have repeatedly cited the difficulties experienced in Germany after 1945 by way of comparison. Following the familiar caveats about the dangers of historical analogy, Condoleezza Rice pointed out during the late summer of 2003, when Iraq was undergoing a period of heightened unrest, that "1945 through 1947 was an especially challenging period [in Germany]. Germany was not immediately stable or prosperous."[4] She went on to remind her audience that the Nazi menace did not simply melt away, and that during the early occupation American forces were under threat from bands of terrorists loyal to the old regime—the so-called "werewolves". Donald Rumsfeld also drew comparisons between Iraqi and German terrorists. Late in 2003, he reminded his audience during an interview on ABC that, notwithstanding the "real differences" between Germany then and Iraq now, "the Nazi faith did linger. And there were people in Germany who kept trying to kill the allies."[5]

In fact, there were very few Germans who tried to kill Allied soldiers after Germany's surrender, and those who did try very rarely succeeded. There were no "werewolves": this band of renegades is simply a myth, extrapolated from the empty threats of the dying regime. But bad history often makes good politics, and Rice and Rumsfeld managed to get their message across: that when it comes to occupation and reconstruction, the early days are not the ones that count. Moreover, this message has not only been for domestic American consumption. In Iraq itself, six months after Saddam fell, the coalition issued a press briefing comparing the state of Iraqi reconstruction with what had been achieved six months after the surrenders of Germany and Japan respectively, highlighting that Iraq was, in those terms, already better off. Given that it was still very early days, this was rather premature, and many things in Iraq got progressively worse over the months that followed (for example, electricity supply was much more limited in the autumn of 2004 than it had been in the autumn of 2003). The terrorism got worse as well, not exponentially, but cumulatively, as the steady drip–drip of car bombings, assassinations and kidnappings continued on through 2004 and into 2005. Iraq was not getting any safer, which is why it became so important to hold safe elections in January 2005. When these elections went off successfully, with a high turnout and relatively little terrorist disruption, the comparison with post-World War II Germany and Japan started to look more plausible. After the inevitable violence and disruption that came with the immediate occupation, the willingness of the allies to hold their political nerve had resulted in some real progress—the first free elections in Iraq for over fifty years. These elections coincided with other changes across the region, including Palestinian elections to find a successor to Yasser Arafat and the stirrings of democratic reform in Lebanon. The "especially challenging" period appeared to be giving way to one of hope.

Of course, not everyone saw it this way. In the immediate aftermath of the Iraqi elections, a *New York Times* report from 1967 was unearthed and widely circulated, describing the results of elections that had just been held in South Vietnam. "United States officials were surprised and heartened today at the size of turnout in South Vietnam's presidential election despite a Vietcong terrorist campaign to disrupt the voting. According to reports from Saigon, 83 per cent of the 5.85 million registered voters cast their ballots yesterday. Many of them risked reprisals threatened by the Vietcong."[6] The game of historical analogy can be played both ways. But for that very reason, one needs to be careful about restricting the range of analogies to the ones that serve the most obvious political purpose. It is unlikely that Iraq will turn out to resemble either the US's greatest foreign policy triumph of the last century, or its greatest foreign policy disaster. The truth is likely to be more complicated. If anything, the place Iraq has come to resemble is post-war Germany, but the war is not World War II; it is World War I.

To compare Iraq with Weimar Germany can appear the most crudely political analogy of all. This is because comparisons with Weimar are invariably extensions of the Hitler analogy by proxy. Weimar has become a kind of shorthand for the sort of democratic chaos that ends in the worst form of dictatorship. But to say that Iraq more closely resembles Germany 1919–23 than it does Germany 1945–49 is to say nothing about Hitler, because Hitler had almost no part to play in the early years of Weimar. Nothing about Hitler's eventual rise to power was inevitable in the initial circumstances of Weimar democracy; it was the result of a series of contingencies that were to play out much later on. What the early years of Weimar do reveal is the inherent difficulty of establishing a stable democracy in unpropitious circumstances, notwithstanding the popular appetite for elections, which is present almost everywhere that genuine democracy has been absent. It is in their origins that Weimar Germany and post-Saddam Iraq can be compared, not their eventual outcomes. This does not mean that the regimes that preceded them must be comparable as well. Saddam's Iraq, as a bestial tyranny, has more in common with Hitler's Nazi state than it does with Wilhelm's imperial autocracy, which though routinely illiberal, and anti-democratic, and militaristic, was not a site of institutionalized torture, mass murder and putative genocide (at least not within Germany; the empire itself was different). But democracies do not stand and fall simply according to the nature of the regimes that precede them. They stand or fall according to how the change to a new political order takes place, and whether it can be sustained.

Like Saddam's regime in Iraq, the Wilhelmine regime fell just a few years after a shocking terrorist incident in which it was not directly involved, but which changed the world in ways that were wholly unpredictable, if not entirely unexpected. The assassination of Franz Ferdinand and his wife in Sarajevo on 28 June 1914 by a small group of would-be suicide bombers—though the bombs missed their target, leaving Gavrilo Princep to shoot the royal couple with a pistol, and the cyanide capsules did not work, allowing the conspirators to be captured and tortured—set in train the series of events which produced World War I, and which culminated in the surrender of the German army to the Allied powers in November 1918 and the simultaneous flight into exile of Wilhelm and his court, leaving political chaos behind. 28 June 1914 was another of the fabled days that changed the world, although, like September 11, the changes that it wrought had to be willed by the political actors who took advantage of the opportunities that it created.

The fall of Wilhelm and the surrender of his army in 1918 did not, by contrast with 1945, also entail the collapse and surrender of the entire German nation. It was the regime that fell apart, and it left in its wake a seething mass of political resentment, social tension, economic uncertainty and widespread deprivation, plus a lot of guns (most of which were held by soldiers returning from the war). It was in these extremely testing circumstances that a proto-government in Berlin sought, with both the support but also the handicap of the involvement of the victorious Allied powers, to build a constitutional democracy. As always in such circumstances, the government had to decide whether to establish a core of social, political and economic stability before calling elections to a constituent assembly, or whether to hope that the fact of elections themselves would help to stabilize the situation. Despite many voices urging delay, it was decided to go ahead with elections, which were successfully conducted and drew wide popular participation, though no consensus for the future direction of the country was clear from the result. Representatives of the many different parties that had contested these elections then gathered in Weimar to draw up a constitution. What eventually emerged was in many ways an impeccably liberal democratic document, though as its critics were quick to point out, it was also a highly aspirational document, and it was not clear how the many liberal, democratic and indeed social aspirations it contained could be reconciled in practice. The Weimar constitution did, however, allow for elections to be held to a new national parliament, following which a democratically constituted coalition government was formed, which began the task of trying to rebuild the German economy. All this took place against a backdrop of routine assassinations, street battles and extensive low-level political violence.

The main problem faced by the government in Berlin, both before and after the drawing up of the constitution, was that it lacked its own loyal military force to uphold its authority. Instead, it had to rely on those forces that were available, which included the freelance *Freikorps*, groups of returning soldiers who were often profoundly alienated by the new regime and shared with the government only a common antipathy towards the communists who were threatening it from the left. Early on, the government also lacked control over various parts of the country, including Bavaria, where a provisional Soviet Republic had been established in the last days of the war (see Chapter Two). In early 1919 Munich had become a kind of no-go zone for the authorities in Berlin, and they feared it might provide the seedbed for wider resistance, as well as fatally hampering any efforts to achieve a lasting constitutional settlement. Without an army of its own, the proto-government was forced to acquiesce in the retaking of Munich by *Freikorps* troops, who were beyond its ultimate control. The result was that Munich was brutally cleansed of resistance to the new regime, but whatever temporary political stability was achieved came at the price of adding to the stock of resentment felt on all sides towards the fledgling German republic.

The parallels between this story and what has taken place in Iraq since April 2003 are striking. So for Munich 1919 read Fallujah 2004? Perhaps not. What most obviously distinguishes events in Munich from what happened in Fallujah is the fact that the Berlin government had to rely on troops whose primary loyalty was to the old, discredited regime. The analogy would hold only if the interim Baghdad government had sought to assert its authority with the aid of roving bands of former Saddam loyalists, allowing them free rein against their erstwhile ideological enemies, the jihadist terrorists. Because the Americans had disbanded and disarmed the forces of the Ba'athist regime, the provisional government in Baghdad had instead to make use of the Americans themselves, plus Kurdish and other sectarian forces, drawn from those parts of the population that had been persecuted under Saddam. The result was a much more thorough cleansing of Fallujah than anything attempted in Bavaria: though many individuals were annihilated, Munich itself was neither destroyed nor depopulated during the counter-revolution of 1919. The other consequence of the reliance of the provisional Iraqi government on American forces to do its dirty work is that the international terrorists and the Ba'athist diehards have become the common enemies of the new regime. In Weimar Germany, reactionary nationalists and revolutionary internationalists spent much of their energies fighting each other. In Iraq, the reactionary nationalists and revolutionary internationalists have come together to fight the forces of occupation.

The fact that Iraq has been occupied by foreign troops following the collapse of the old regime, whereas post-World War I Germany was not, is the clearest point of difference between their respective plights. Occupation was to become a central issue in the politics of Weimar Germany only after 1923, when French and

Belgian troops occupied parts of the Ruhr in an effort to force Germany to honour its reparations obligations. The political and economic catastrophe that ensued—the hyperinflation of late 1923 that wiped out the assets of all German savers and provoked Hitler and his Nazi friends to attempt to seize control of the state from their Bavarian powerbase—did as much as anything to shape the future direction of Weimar democracy. But during 1919–22, the central question of German politics was simply whether the new Weimar regime could establish a coherent identity for itself, which might rescue it from the circumstances of its origin. These circumstances were ones of humiliation and resentment, stemming not from the presence of foreign forces on German soil, but from the financial penalties the victorious powers imposed on Germany at Versailles in lieu of occupation. American and other coalition forces have occupied Iraq in lieu of demanding repayment for the debts incurred by the Saddam regime (in contrast to non-occupying powers, such as France and Saudi Arabia, who have repeatedly sought to get Iraq to honour its financial obligations from the Saddam era). Occupation and reparations are very different sorts of humiliation. But the fact remains that they are both humiliations, and they are also both forms of duress. The question for Weimar Germany was whether democracy could establish itself in the face of such pressures. That remains the question for post-Saddam Iraq.

In the case of Weimar the appearance of humiliation soon came to carry more political weight than the underlying reality of its source. It was not the reparations themselves that threatened the survival of the Weimar Republic (in part because Germany would not pay, in part because Germany could not pay). Rather, what counted was the psychological impact of reparations, which long outlasted any serious attempt on the part of the Allies to uphold the strict terms of the Versailles treaty. During the period when it was supposed to be paying for the war crimes of its predecessor, the Weimar state was also in receipt of significant amounts of financial largesse, in the form of substantial new loans from the United States, which were designed to help regenerate the German economy. The economic ledger of the post-war settlement was by no means entirely negative, but because it was widely assumed that American money was simply being used to equip the German economy so that it could be further squeezed by the other reparations-hungry allies, it often *appeared* to be entirely negative. The American occupation of Iraq has also been accompanied by large amounts of financial largesse. But because the money is being pumped into an occupied state, it is the occupation and not the largesse that remains the salient political fact, as the suspicion persists that the money is simply being redirected by the Americans back to themselves (a feeling not helped by the initial refusal of the occupiers to allow non-American firms to bid for reconstruction contracts). This suspicion is almost certain to endure even as the bare facts of American occupation, including the statistics of American troop numbers in Iraq, start to drop away.

The viability of democracy in Iraq depends on its ability to develop an alternative political narrative to the story of violence, resentment and suspicion that surrounds the circumstances of its birth. The same was true of Weimar Germany. Germany in the early 1920s appeared to have a number of advantages in this endeavour, as Iraq does now. There was widespread popular enthusiasm for real electoral democracy in Germany after the fake democracy of the old Reich (Germany had had a parliament elected by universal male suffrage since 1871, but the parliament elected in this way had been granted no real powers of its own). The fake democracy that had been initiated by Otto von Bismarck in the 1870s and 1880s went along with an attempt to establish a kind of proto-welfare state, and coincided with the rapid industrialization of the German economy and the urbanization of large parts of German society. This resulted, if nothing else, in a population that was increasingly literate, well educated and politically well informed. In the early years of Weimar democracy, a wide range of political parties sprang up to service the divergent interests of this population, as did a huge number of newspapers, catering to every possible political outlook.[7] Some of these parties were ambivalent, at best, about their attachment to the terms of the new constitution. Yet notwithstanding the considerable electoral appeal of extreme parties of both the left and the right, and despite the almost universal condemnation of the terms of defeat imposed on the German state, there was no widespread support in the early 1920s for the most radical alternatives to the status quo (either for Bolshevik revolution or a return to militaristic autocracy). What most people seemed to want was some form of real democracy, and it was a form of real democracy—pluralistic, volatile, potentially divisive but unquestionably dynamic—that they got.

Yet the dynamism of early Weimar democracy was as much a part of the problem as it was a potential solution to the question of how to secure the long-term stability of the regime. A lasting solution could only come through the constitutional workings of the state, and depended on the ability of the state to exercise its power so as to prevent the conflicting interests present within the German population from pulling the state apart. The choice that presented itself to the framers of the Weimar constitution was to seek to create a political system that would reflect the existing political forces at work in post-war Germany, or to seek to create a political system that could deal with them. Perhaps unsurprisingly, given that the constituent assembly was itself elected to provide a reflection of the diverse interests of the German people, the first option came to be preferred. The Weimar constitution devolved most power onto the legislature, which was to be elected according to strict principles of proportional representation, in order to accommodate as many different parties and points of view as possible. The new state therefore lacked a strong central executive, except in times of emergency, when under the provisions of the notorious article 48, the president of the republic, who was otherwise meant to perform a predominantly ceremonial role, was permitted to assume dictatorial powers in order to forestall parliamentary paralysis. The trouble was that when such crises arose, as happened in 1923, and from 1930 onwards, the battle for the constitution, and thus for democracy, was already half lost.

Because Weimar democracy was designed to accommodate rather than to trump the political divisions within Germany, it also served to create a distinctive political class, many of whom came from the opposition movements of the Wilhelm years. These opposition politicians became the new political establishment, and their positions depended on their ability to tap into and reinforce established power bases. What they struggled to do was establish a clear political identity for the new regime, in part because too many of them seemed like hangovers from another political era. Weimar democracy also faced some more practical difficulties in cementing its political identity. There was the problem of the new flag, which had to be different enough from the old flag to mark a clean break but not so different as to alienate those nostalgic for the symbols of past national glory. The result was a messy compromise, which satisfied no one. There was also the real difficulty, given the level of terrorist violence, of finding safe ways for the leaders of the new regime to parade either themselves or the troops on whom their security depended.[8] Yet without the ability to display itself, the Weimar republic could only reinforce its reputation for wishing to conceal some shameful secrets.

A lot of this is already familiar in Iraq, where the new flag has been the source of ongoing hostility, and the political elite have yet to find a way of safely displaying themselves in public. But a lot still remains to be seen, including how the new Iraqi constitution finally comes to distribute power between the legislature and the executive, and between the different factions within the country. Where Iraq is seemingly better placed than Weimar Germany ever was to establish a symbolic break with the past is in the person of Saddam himself, who did not follow Wilhelm into exile, as he might have done. (If he had, it is certain that the Americans would have sought his extradition, as they unsuccessfully sought the extradition of Wilhelm from the Netherlands as part of the negotiations that preceded the Treaty of Versailles; in Saddam's case, however, the Americans are more likely to have got their way.) Once he had been captured, the prospect of trying and executing Saddam offered the regime the chance to re-establish a more plausible link with post-World War II Germany. But the analogy is still a false one: the efficiency and symbolic power of the Nuremberg trials was made possible precisely because they were not conducted by a fledgling German democracy, but by the occupying powers. At the time of writing, the legal proceedings against Saddam—marked by delays, changes of personnel and procedural confusion, and not helped by ongoing political bargaining about which of his crimes should be tried first—seem to symbolize the uncertainty rather than the freshness of the regime's emerging character.

In the end, the problems of Weimar democracy were not just symbolic. The real difficulty lay in establishing a form of constitutional politics that could compete with the politics of resentment that enveloped the republic's founding. The type of politics that the Weimar constitution produced was one founded on compromise, deal making and trade-offs between different interest groups. Tough decisions were too often shirked, and the deals made too often unravelled. For some Germans the new democratic arrangements quickly came to resemble the fake democracy that had gone before—the "smoke-and-mirrors" parliamentarianism of the old Empire, with its horse-trading and its posturing and its empty promises. For others Weimar democracy was seen as a kind of foreign imposition—derisively labelled "Western" liberal democracy—that did not chime with the roots of German self-government, which were taken to lie in the medieval concept of *Genossenschaft* (usually translated as "fellowship", but resonant of an entire, and entirely Germanic, way of life). The democratic manoeuvrings of central government were also perceived by many to be detached from the real business of German politics, which remained local. The new political elite in Berlin seemed removed from people's immediate concerns.

In this respect, the apparent advantages that Germany enjoyed by dint of its industrialization and urbanization in the second half of the nineteenth century turned out to be more of a hindrance than a help for post-war democratic stability. Because Germany was no longer primarily a peasant society, it could not fall back onto a subsistence economy during the desperate, chaotic months following the collapse of the Imperial regime.[9] Urban populations needed some kind of social and economic controls if they were not to starve, and as a result political authority tended to devolve to the local level, and to settle on anyone who was able to provide the most basic social and economic security. The same thing has happened in Iraq, where the population had become largely urbanized by the end of the Saddam years (close to 70% now live in urban areas). The economic ruin that Saddam left behind him meant that an enormous premium has come to be placed on provision of local services—local economic controls, local police forces and militias, local systems of justice, local welfare schemes—and political power has been widely dispersed as a result. Inevitably, these local power blocs represent a serious obstacle to the formation of a national political consensus, because they have hollowed out many of the core functions of the state. In Weimar, when

American money started to come in, a lot of it ended up in the hands of local politicians, who spent it on showy local amenities—swimming pools, cinemas, public buildings. These amenities gave the lie to the idea that all Germany was scratching out a meagre existence under the intolerable strain of the reparations burden. But they did nothing to reconcile people to the claims of central government to be the source of future German prosperity, because local politicians made sure central government received none of the credit.

Still, it was not local politics that brought down the Weimar regime. It was economic and political mismanagement at the national level that destroyed the republic, and not just by German politicians—the terrible difficulties that these politicians faced derived in part from the catastrophic decisions taken by French political leaders during the crisis of 1923–24, and by American political leaders during the crisis that followed the crash of 1929. These crises, both in the political decisions that helped precipitate them and in the political decisions that followed from them, are unlikely to be repeated. It is almost impossible to imagine Iraq being allowed to print money with the reckless abandon of the German government of 1923 (to the point where bank clerks used banknotes as scrap paper for their increasingly astronomical calculations, because they were cheaper than the real thing). It is also almost impossible to imagine that the world in general, and the United States in particular, could repeat the mistakes that led to the global depression of the early 1930s. To compare Iraq to Weimar Germany pre-1923 is not therefore to condemn them to the same fate.

Iraq has the real advantage that the world still possesses the memory of Weimar, which is one of the reasons why politicians, bankers and economists remain so wary of the political risks of runaway inflation and stock market crashes. We currently live in a much less inflationary world than the early 1920s, thanks in large part to the way that information technology has allowed ready access to competing international markets. We also live during a period of relative economic stability compared with the turbulence of the post-World War I years; despite some lurid predictions at the time, September 11 did not have a major negative impact either on the global economy or on American prosperity.[10] Yet it is because the economic backdrop to the attempt to establish democracy in Iraq is relatively benign that the example of Weimar remains a salient one. It will not always be benign—indeed, the deflationary pressures on the world economy may mean that the current extended period of growth will soon be coming to an end, while unforeseen crises like Hurricane Katrina are always lurking around the corner—and the test for any new democratic regime is what happens when the world loses interest, and even the most prosperous nations start to become preoccupied with their own affairs. During the boom years of 1924–29 Weimar democracy stabilized, as did the currency, following the disasters of 1923. The Allied powers, and particularly the United States, worked hard to establish a plausible framework for German economic recovery, seeking to tie in workable (and therefore greatly reduced) reparations obligations to an aid package and strict international financial oversight. But when the American stock market went over a cliff in 1929, and the world economy followed it, Germany was on its own. Left to their own devices, the German people chose to forget the aid and remember only the oversight, which came to appear as a usurpation of national sovereignty and an insult to national pride. This was one of the central, unresolved dilemmas of the Weimar years. In order to help stabilize German democracy, the allies had to take a keen interest in the German economy, and intervene when necessary. The problem was that this intervention helped stoke the resentment that attached to the origins of the new regime, a resentment that bubbled viciously back to the surface once the good times came to an end. Yet without foreign intervention, the good times would never have got going at all. The same dilemma holds in Iraq today.

During the final years of the Weimar republic the Nazi Party was able ruthlessly to exploit the full range of popular resentments against meddling and avaricious outsiders.[11] They did this by feeding on a series of national myths, some of them longstanding but most of a very recent heritage. Above all they harked back to the origins of the republic, and traced its ills to the humiliating circumstances of its birth. They also made full use of the new information technology that was available to them, including radio broadcasts and mass-circulation newspapers. The information technology that is available in Iraq is very different (though it still includes mass-circulation newspapers and radio broadcasts). The world we now live is not only deflationary in economic terms but also, potentially, in mythic terms, in the sense that it may become harder to sustain destructive national myths in the face of the myth-puncturing power of the internet. But it is worth remembering that similar deflationary hopes existed in the early years of Weimar, when the explosion of free speech and new sources of information, after the relative drought of the Wilhelm years, seemed to herald the advent of democratic diversity, and the prospect of a healthy public scepticism. Over time, however, these diverse sources of information tended to amalgamate, both as a result of market pressures, but also in response to the popular success of new kinds of myth-making. The internet, as well as being a deflater of mythic pretensions, is also a formidable source of new myths. For now, market forces in Iraq, being so dependent on American money and influence, are working towards the amalgamation of information resources around the propaganda interests of the new regime. But it is only a matter of time before the competition gets its act together, and someone discovers that there is serious money to be made within Iraq by pandering to the baser political instincts of the wider public. If the baser political instincts of Weimar Germany are anything to go by, it won't only be the stooge American government that comes under attack. It will also be the traitors, turncoats and other "foreigners" who bled the Iraqi people dry when the country was on its knees.

From the perspective of the American occupiers themselves, this is something they still seem ready to take in their stride. They remain optimistic that Iraqi democracy can survive all the insults thrown at it, because they are confident that history is now running its way. For the neoconservative architects of the Iraq war, the biggest single difference between the Weimar period and the early years of the twenty-first century is that then democracy was on the retreat, now it is on the march. But this rather depends on when and where you look. Democracy was also on the march across Europe from 1919 to 1923, when many peoples previously subject to autocratic rule—not just in Germany but in Austria, Poland, Czechoslovakia, Yugoslavia and Finland—became full constitutional democracies. Democracy only started to retreat following the economic crises first of 1923–24 and then of 1929–33. Even so, some of these democracies survived, including Finland and Czechoslovakia, providing a beacon of hope for an increasingly dark continent, until they were finally snuffed out during 1939–40. Sometimes, the march of democracy turns out to be an illusion.

The difference between then and now is that now we know that the abandonment of democracy across Europe during the late 1920s and 1930s was a catastrophe. At the beginning of the twenty-first century we have all the evidence we need about the advantages of democracy over other forms of government—including, above all, its advantages over the other forms of government that were tried in Europe during the inter-war years. But although we know much more about the benefits of democracy, we still don't know that much more about what keeps democracies alive when they start to struggle. We know, for example, that democratic stability is tied to wealth—no democracy has ever fallen in a country with a per capita income of more than $6000 (per capita income in Iraq is currently uncertain, but is estimated to be somewhere between $750 and $2000)—but we don't know how to keep democracies going when the money runs out.[12] We know that democracies, as well as promoting certain social and economic goods like a free press and an independent judiciary, also depend on these things, yet it remains far from clear how they can be rescued if the virtuous cycle of wealth creation and good governance starts to break down. Above all, we still don't know how fledgling democracies in relatively disadvantaged countries can be helped to survive the kind of outside political interference needed to get them off the ground. Neo-imperialism is a part of the problem, not a part of the solution. This gap in our understanding of democracy has been acknowledged by one of the founder members of the "Project for a New American Century", Francis Fukuyama, in his recent book *State Building* (2004). The truth is, Fukuyama says, "we do not know how to transfer institutional capability in a hurry".[13] So the fact remains that we still cannot be sure of what we are doing in our attempts to democratize the world if we lack, as we invariably do, the luxury of time.

We can, though, be reasonably confident of one thing: it is now almost a cliché of contemporary political life that democracies, once established, don't go to war with each other. The attempt to spread democracy to the Middle East is, if nothing else, founded on a belief that this truism can be a guiding principle of international politics, and justifies taking certain risks. But the principle itself only holds for established democracies. It provides no guidance for thinking about the problems that democracies have in establishing themselves, beyond offering good reasons why we should wish them to succeed. The academic version of this truism is called democratic peace theory. It is something of a misnomer. Democracies are good at keeping the peace, but they are bad at making it. The same public pressures that render democratic governments so cautious about confronting each other militarily also tempt them into hasty decisions and quick fixes when dealing with the fallout of the wars they do get drawn into. Democracies are easily distracted, and have a tendency to worry about value for money. Their higher ambitions frequently get lost in the rush to play to the gallery. The massive and enduring commitment of the United States to rebuilding Germany and Japan after World War II is more of the exception than the rule when it comes to democratic peacemaking. Moreover, it was not simply (or even primarily) a peacemaking enterprise: it came in response to the Soviet threat, and the thought that if the West didn't pump money into the economies the war had destroyed, the next war would be lost before it had even begun. Democracies are remarkably good at finding the resources they need when they feel themselves to be under threat. The problems start when the battle has been won, and their electorates begin to want some of their money back.[14]

In this respect, the response of the Western democracies to Germany's fate after World War I is more typical. The noble ambitions of Woodrow Wilson's peace proposals were quickly swamped by the petty politicking that took place at Versailles, where the representatives of the victorious but massively indebted European powers insisted that the real question was who was going to pay. In the years that followed, interest in what was happening in Germany tended to fluctuate according to whether other countries felt threatened by it (as happened during 1923–24) or simply distracted by it (as happened after 1929). Tony Blair is right, of course, when he says that the Western democracies only woke up to the danger of the Nazi regime much too late. But he is wrong when he takes this to be one of the morals of World War II that can be applied to Iraq. Instead, it is the central lesson of the aftermath of World War I.

Whether Iraq proves the exception or the rule in democratic peacemaking only time will tell. There are three kinds of time at work in modern politics: news time, election time and historical time. News time is speeding up, as we learn what is going on in the world faster than ever, and forget it faster than ever, as soon as something new comes on the horizon. Election time is relatively static in stable democracies, but this is not true of democracies that are struggling, which tend to have far too many elections than is good for them. Weimar Germany suffered from too many elections and changes of government, though it was by no means the worst offender among the struggling European democracies of the period (Portugal, for example, got through more than forty governments during its first republic from 1910 to 1926). Even in stable democracies, election time tends to get mixed up with news time, so that electioneering and the results of elections become convenient but entirely artificial staging posts in the never-ending onrush of current affairs. Meanwhile, the speed of historical time can vary considerably, but for the most part it remains pretty slow. It accords with the natural time-spans of human beings: their lives, their careers, their memories.[15] War and the aftermath of war have a tendency to speed historical time up, as does unstable democracy. Too many people died or had their health ruined by the politics of the Weimar years to enable the regime to find its own rhythm. In the end, the steady drip–drip of political violence and assassination took its toll.[16] Still, the fate of Weimar democracy was only settled over a number of years, not just one or two. The fate of Iraq's new democracy will likewise not be played out in news time, or election time. It will be played out in real historical time.

PART TWO

Britain, Europe and the United States

A BEAR ARMED WITH A GUN

Thomas Hobbes, in one of the best-known and most abused phrases in the English language, described the life of man in a state of nature as "solitary, poore, nasty, brutish and short".[1] Less famous, but almost as notorious, is Hobbes's contention that the states that human beings create in order to escape the misery of their natural condition are subject only to the laws that produced that misery in the first place. "The Law of Nations," Hobbes wrote, "and the Law of Nature, is the same thing. And every Soveraign hath the same Right, in procuring the safety of his People, than any particular man can have, in procuring his own safety."[2] This equation of international law with natural law has led many people to suppose that international relations must replicate the terrible conditions of the original state of nature. The adjective "Hobbesian" has become a kind of shorthand for viewing international politics as a scene of conflict and strife, in which something like the law of the jungle prevails. But this view is a mistake, both in Hobbes's terms, and in ours.[3]

It is wrong because states are not like natural human beings. They are, as Hobbes insisted, artificial persons, more like giant automata than people, and with very different qualities. They are stronger, larger and more robust. They are, with good reason, less diffident and less fearful. They are not vulnerable to the same kinds of threat. The problem for natural individuals, Hobbes wrote, is that "the weakest has strength enough to kill the strongest, either by secret machination, or by confederacy with others".[4] This knowledge is enough to make everyone afraid of everyone else. But it is very difficult to slip a knife between the shoulder blades of a state while its back is turned. You can, of course, try to attack individual rulers, those people whom Hobbes called "Soveraign", and no state can guard these with absolute security; but in any state worthy of the name, one sovereign will immediately be replaced by another, allowing the state to live on. This durability makes individual states more certain in their dealings with one another. The social life of states is very different from the natural misery of man as a result.

The life of a state, for example, is not solitary. Indeed, it would be hard to think of a more clubbable bunch than the society of nations, with their endless get-togethers and busman's holidays. States are not poor. Even poor states are not poor, relatively speaking (relative, that is, to the poverty of the poor people who have to live in them). States, both rich and poor, are likely to be heavily indebted, but it is precisely the ability of states to sustain these huge levels of debt that marks them out from natural persons, who are much more easily bankrupted. States can, it is true, be pretty nasty, or at least they can allow unspeakably nasty things to be done on their behalf. It was for Nietzsche one of the few things to be said for the modern state that civilized individuals were prepared to undertake acts of cruelty in its name that they would never dare do for themselves. But states are not, for the most part, nasty to each other, and the life of the state is if anything marked by an excessive gentility, as all parties seek to keep up appearances. Robert Mugabe would not have found himself shaking hands with Jacques Chirac in 2003, nor Colonel Gadaffi in his tent with Tony Blair a year later, if states were as nasty as the individuals they sometimes throw up.

States are not brutish, certainly not on Hobbes's account: it is central to his argument that the law of nations is not the law of the jungle. Because states are not simply men, but machines made in the image of men, states do not share with natural men a tendency to revert to the level of beasts in their dealings with one another. A state is a machine that either works or doesn't, unlike human beings, who can continue to function even when they have lost the ability to make use of their reason. Above all, the life of states is not short. This was the clear message of the highly civilized exchanges that took place between the permanent members of the UN Security Council following Hans Blix's report on the progress of his weapons inspections in Iraq on 14 February 2003. "Old Europe" initiated the conversation, in the person of the then

French foreign minister Dominique de Villepin, who said that he spoke on behalf of "an old country, France, that does not forget ... all it owes to the freedom fighters that came from the United States of America and elsewhere."[5] British Foreign Secretary Jack Straw took up the theme, reminding his audience: "Britain is also a very old country. It was founded in 1066—by the French." Colin Powell had to concede that "America is a relatively new country", before going on to point out that nevertheless "it is the oldest democracy around this table". Here, then, is a world in which being over 200 years old makes you young. But calling these states old barely seems to do them justice. They are practically indestructible, outlasting anything that mere mortal men can do to them. "Vive La France Immortelle!" declared the French press the day after Paris was liberated in 1944. This would be going too far for Hobbes, who insisted that the state was merely "that *Mortall God*, to which we owe under the *Immortal God*, our peace and defence".[6] But whatever else is true about a world in which such newspaper headlines are possible, it is certainly far removed from Hobbes's original state of nature.

The forgetfulness or otherwise of the French about what they owed freedom fighters from the United States and elsewhere provided part of the background to the monumental falling out between France and the United States in the run-up to the Iraq war. It certainly helped to provide the motivation for some of the most pungent neoconservative critiques of European attitudes to the problem of collective security. What became the best-known of these critiques was the one offered by Robert Kagan, who argued in his book *Paradise and Power* (which was an extended version of an article that originally appeared in *Policy Review* in the summer of 2002) that Europeans had forgotten that their ability to champion non-military solutions to the problems of global security depended to a large extent on the willingness of the United States to provide Europe with military protection.[7] Kagan was not the only person making the case that Europe was relying too heavily on American strength, and presuming too much on American goodwill, but what enabled him to stand out from the crowd was a single sentence that appears on the first page of his book. "On major strategic and international questions today," Kagan wrote, "Americans are from Mars and Europeans are from

Venus."[8] This is a one-off remark, and Kagan does not repeat it elsewhere in *Paradise and Power*, though it has since been endlessly repeated by others. What is striking is that he is much more insistent on another distinction he makes on the first page of his book, and which he reiterates throughout what follows. This is the claim that Europeans are Kantians, seeking to inhabit "a self-contained world of laws and rules and transnational negotiation and cooperation". The United States, by contrast, "remains mired in history, exercising power in an anarchic Hobbesian world where international laws and rules are unreliable".[9] He goes on to clarify this distinction by arguing that "one of the things that most clearly divides Europeans and Americans today is a philosophical, even metaphysical disagreement over where exactly mankind stands on a continuum between the laws of the jungle and the laws of reason".[10] But unfortunately this clarifies nothing, because the original distinction makes no sense. Kant is not from Venus and Hobbes is not from Mars. Both were, in their own terms, philosophers of what they each called "Peace". Indeed, to call the Hobbesian world anarchic is to make a mockery of everything Hobbes says. But more than this, the overriding problem with Kagan's account is that the real Hobbesians are the Europeans.

It is the European way, insofar as there is a "European way", to trust that international law can be the basis of agreement if only you recognize the appropriate international actors. It is the European way to prefer to deal with the states you know rather than the unspecified threats about which you can only speculate. It is a right on which Europeans insist to be the best judges of what constitutes a threat to their own security, regardless of what the Americans might tell them. All this makes the Europeans good Hobbesians. In Europe the preference has always been to talk of "failed states", while in the United States the vogue is to describe these same as "rogue states".[11] It is in Hobbes's world, not Kant's, that states simply "fail" or break down, and it is in Hobbes's world that all other judgments about whether states are good or evil are ruled out of court. Kant believed that the test of a state's fitness for peace was whether or not it was what we would call "democratic" (and what Kant himself called "republican"); the question of whether or not it was a state at all, in the sense of having a recognizable government capable of being negotiated with, was at best a secondary consideration.[12] "State building", in the new world order, was initially thought to be a European idea, and one of the reasons Bill Clinton is thought to have flirted with being a "European" president is his willingness to flirt with this idea as well (flirting, it might be said, is also opposed to the martial qualities of true American politics). But "state building" is also *the* Hobbesian idea. It was Hobbes's hope that if you could build enough states, the result would be peace.

It doesn't follow from this, of course, that if the Europeans are Hobbesians, the Americans must be Kantians,[13] though the idea of the "rogue state" is a lot closer to the work of a neo-Kantian political philosopher like John Rawls (with his distinction between "decent" and "non-decent" peoples) than to anything you will find in Hobbes.[14] But it is true that far from being stuck in the past, many American politicians have moved beyond Hobbes, and much of Europe, in one crucial respect. That is, in their preoccupation with the new threat posed by WMD, greatly enhanced by their exposure to one, single, devastating attack, while their back was turned on a sunny September morning. Suddenly, the Hobbesian view that states and states alone have the power and security to operate under conditions of lawfulness is threatened by the knowledge that even the most powerful states are vulnerable to crippling assault from unknown and unpredictable sources. It can now be said that in the international arena "the weakest has strength to kill the strongest", or they would do, if only they could get their hands on the necessary equipment. This, potentially, changes everything. It means that international law can no longer be relied on, and its restraining hand can no longer be expected to control the fearfulness of even those who look from the outside to have least to fear.

The common view that September 11, 2001, marked the return to a Hobbesian world is therefore entirely wrong. If anything, it marked the beginning of a post-Hobbesian age, in which a new kind of insecurity threatens the familiar structures of modern political life. In one sense this insecurity is nothing new, because it carries echoes of the natural uncertainties of individual human beings. But it is new for states, which were meant to be invulnerable to these kinds of paranoiac anxieties. Indeed, it is one of the further ironies of the post-Hobbesian world that there now exists a threat which makes some states feel more vulnerable than their subjects—as evidenced by the endless attempts of democratically elected politicians to assure their publics that they would be as scared as the politicians if they saw what the politicians see across their desks every day. This is something that Hobbes himself could never have foreseen; it is in fact an inversion of the entire Hobbesian order, which supposes that states have less to fear than individuals. And not being designed to deal with this kind of threat, even the most powerful states don't know what to do about it.

It is unsurprising that the result has been confusion and uncertainty from all sides, including from those, like Tony Blair, who have seen it as their job to try to bring the various sides together. In the autumn of 2002, Blair briefly persuaded the Americans to reconfigure their post-Hobbesian concerns into a form that fitted the Hobbesian format of the UN, where it is assumed that states, regardless of their character, can reach agreement on questions of international law. What they discovered is that there is no fit, and the diplomatic manoeuvrings that followed were not good for the United States and they were not good for the UN. The Europeans, whose more traditional view that international law can only work when states take each other seriously, were persuaded to sign a resolution which makes a mockery of that assumption. Resolution 1441 demanded that Saddam Hussein make an "accurate, full, final and complete disclosure" of any chemical, biological or nuclear weapons that Iraq possesses, has possessed in the past, or seeks to possess in the future. Yet Saddam Hussein, all sides agreed, was a tyrant, and tyrannical regimes are no more capable of accurate, full, final and complete disclosure about anything than a dog is of talking French. It is not in their nature. The comparison that was sometimes drawn with South Africa's openness to weapons inspection by the UN in 1993 is therefore entirely misleading. South Africa was in the process of becoming a democracy in 1993, which gave it every incentive to pursue democratic levels of disclosure. Resolution 1441 only made sense if Iraq were in the process of becoming a democracy, though if it were in the process of becoming a democracy, there would be no need for Resolution 1441. The Europeans, by bringing the United States to the UN, found their own concerns reconfigured in post-Hobbesian language. The French would have been truer to their Hobbesian conception of international law if they had refused to sign the first resolution, as well as sparing themselves all the difficulties that followed on their refusal to sign the second. They should have insisted from the outset that the UN only made demands of Iraq that it could meet.

The Iraq war made it clear that there are no clean lines in the new world order, but neoconservatives like Kagan have to insist on them anyway, which helps to explain both the superficial appeal of his book and the horrible mess he makes of his argument as he tries to stretch it out over 100 pages. In order to get the new world order to fit the philosophical disagreement to which he is committed, he is forced into some grotesque contortions. For example, he attributes to the Kantianism of the Europeans the view that the "evil" of Iraq might have been contained in the same way that the "evil" of Germany has been contained within the EU. "Germany was evil once, too. Might not an 'indirect approach' work again, as it did in Europe?"[15] Can there really be anyone in Europe or anywhere else who thinks like this, who thinks that the specific lesson of the defeat of Nazi Germany and the subsequent reconstruction and reunification of the German state is that an "indirect approach" is always best? Kagan attributes to Europeans an inflated sense of the possibilities of moral politics, a sentimental attachment to the view that moral politics means the politics of the EU, and a reluctance to look much beyond their own borders. But if this description is true of some Europeans, it is certainly not true of all. Equally, if you replace "European Union" with "United States" in this litany of wishful thinking, then it is a description that could also apply to many Americans, including the American who occupied the Oval Office between January and September 2001. September 11 changed George Bush, and forced him to look beyond his own borders for perhaps the first time in his life. But if an American politician can be adaptable in this way, why shouldn't a European?

Kagan's answer is to move away from trying to distinguish between Americans and Europeans in terms of intellectual heritage and political temperament. Alongside the Hobbesian/Kantian argument he runs another one, in which the difference between the United States and Europe is described in the more straightforward language of threat. Europeans, he suggests, consistently refused to see Saddam as a threat because they never had the means to do anything about it if he were; Americans, just because they *could* take out Saddam, were able to judge that they *ought*. Kagan offers an analogy:

> A man armed only with a knife may decide that a bear prowling the forest is a tolerable danger, inasmuch as the alternative—hunting the bear with a knife—is actually riskier than lying low and hoping a bear never attacks. The same man armed with a rifle, however, will likely make a different calculation of what constitutes a tolerable risk. Why should he risk being mauled to death if he doesn't have to?[16]

This is hard to square with the view of Europeans as Kantians rather than Hobbesians. But it is also much too simplistic. It would be closer to the truth to say that the Americans seem to have got a glimpse in the woods of a bear armed with a gun. To anyone who hasn't seen a sight like this, it is likely to sound preposterous. But to anyone who thinks they have, the world is going to look a very different place.

Alongside the argument that Europeans are too idealistic, and the argument that they are impotent, Kagan runs a third, which may be closer to the heart of neoconservatism. This is the view that European idealism is at root "self-interested", and that American self-interest is "at times almost indistinguishable from idealism".[17] Kagan wants Europeans to wake up to the fact that their experiments with "postmodern" politics take place in a space that the Americans have bought for them with their willingness to police the world outside. Likewise, he wants the United States to remind the world that the pursuit of American interests can be consistent with the collective interest, something he feels both sides of the transatlantic divide have lost sight of since the end of the Cold War. In a sense, Kagan feels that while the real battles are being fought, the propaganda war is being ignored. Europeans need to be given good reason to recognize what Kagan holds to be self-evident, that "the United States is a liberal, progressive society through and through".[18] But this has proved to be very bad propaganda. If Kagan means "liberal" in its American sense, then it is hard to square with the facts, since liberalism in the United States is on the retreat, and has been for years.[19] If, as seems more likely, he means liberal in something like its European sense, then this can't be true, because a liberal society would by definition have to contain, and find ways of reconciling, progressive and non-progressive elements. This the United States does, but the price of such liberalism is that what look to European eyes like non-progressives must get their turn to operate the levers of American power. Indeed, the problem for many Europeans, given the current electoral hegemony of George Bush's Republican Party, is imagining the circumstances in which the progressives will get another turn.

Can anyone really bridge this gap? Kagan has not been alone in seeing Britain as uniquely well placed to reconcile the diverging perspectives of the United States and Europe, and in placing high hopes in Tony Blair in particular. As well as Britain's advantages of history and geography, Tony Blair has the advantage that he is himself, at least in his own terms, a progressive politician, who nevertheless sees no gain for progressive politics in working against the interests of the United States, whoever happens to be its president. Equally, he sees having to work with the United States as no reason to abandon his progressivism. This line of argument has not gone down well with many in his own party. Yet Blair has the further advantage that his foreign policy agenda has come in part to transcend party politics, precisely because he has been working against the foreign policy instincts of his party for so long. Timothy Garton Ash has suggested that what Britain, and indeed the world, needs is for a pro-American Labour Prime Minister like Blair to be replaced in due course by a pro-European Conservative Prime Minister, also working against the instincts of his party, and for Britain's interests in the wider world.[20] But this is to trust a great deal to the workings of the British party system. One of the most fascinating counterfactual questions of recent British political history is what would have happened if Kenneth Clarke, a genuine pro-European Tory and staunch critic of the Iraq war, rather than Iain Duncan Smith, a Eurosceptic who gave Blair his unstinting support over Iraq, had been elected leader of the Conservative Party on 12 September 2001.[21] There are three broad possibilities. One is that Clarke would have split his party, further diminishing the opposition faced by Blair's government, and probably destroying forever the prospects of the Tories returning to power. The second is that the party would have demanded the repudiation of his "European" attitudes as the price of remaining its leader (as he was forced partially to repudiate them when seeking to become its leader in 2005). The third is that Clarke would have been able to hold his party together while sticking to his principles, in which case his opposition to Blair's Iraq policy would almost certainly have brought down the government, thereby ensuring that the Labour Party never trusted such a staunch pro-American to be its leader again.

It is not at all clear whether the highly personal template of Blair's premiership can be replicated. If the example of Bill Clinton is anything to go by, Blair's triangulation of his party's and the nation's interests is as likely to lead to a reaction, not in favour of a comparable triangulation on the other side, but against such contortions altogether, and in favour of passionate, partisan conviction politics. Blair, like Clinton, may be something of a one-off. But Blair's commanding personal style makes it easy to forget that his perspective is not the same as Britain's perspective, and champions of this style have too often forgotten where Tony Blair ends and the British state begins. In one of the footnotes to his book, Kagan writes: "The case of Bosnia in the early 1990s stands out as an instance where some Europeans, chiefly British Prime Minister Tony Blair, were at times more forceful in advocating military action than first the Bush and then the Clinton administration".[22] Such has been Blair's domination of British politics, and such has been the ubiquity of his presence on the international stage since 2001, that it is hard to recall a time when he was not Prime Minister, as he was not in the early 1990s; he was just another highly promising opposition politician with a glorious if uncertain future ahead of him. Poor John Major, one of the longest-serving premiers of the twentieth century—liberator of Kuwait, breaker of the Tory Party—is no longer even considered deserving of a footnote in the history of the new world order.

Kagan's lack of interest in British electoral politics is understandable. He is keen to emphasize that the divisions he identifies between Europe and the United States are not mere electoral accidents or passing political fashions. The current transatlantic divide, he says, is "not transitory—the product of one American election or one catastrophic event".[23] It is, in other words, not just about George W. Bush and September 11, however much it might sometimes appear otherwise. As a result, Kagan has also been keen to emphasize the continuity of American foreign policy in championing the use of military force against rogue states, long predating September 11, 2001. He points out that Iraq, Iran and North Korea had already been identified as future targets of American foreign policy during the Clinton years, and military programmes to deal with the threat they posed, including a new ballistic missile defence system, were already in train. "Had Al Gore been elected, and had there been no terrorist attacks on September 11, these programs—aimed squarely at Bush's 'axis of evil'—would still be under way."[24] It is in the interests of both sides of the new transatlantic divide to play down the significance of the events of September 11, 2001, because both sides have an incentive to pretend that the US's new anxieties are not merely a passing phase. Yet it is hard to get around the fact that September 11 made the difference. If Al Gore had been elected and the Twin Towers had fallen there is still every chance that American troops would have been sent to deal with Saddam. With George Bush in the White House but no attack on September 11, it is unlikely that an army would have been mobilized. Perhaps because of the hysterical outpourings that followed September 11, in Europe as well as the United States, there is now a tendency to look back with some embarrassment at the certain predictions of the time that this was "The Day That Changed The World". Many of the most lurid of these predictions have not been fulfilled. But at least one thing did change. Europe and the United States would not have split in the way they have if the attack had not happened, nor would they have split if the attack had taken place in Europe. Any attempt to turn this division into a philosophical chasm is therefore certain to be overstated. Early twenty-first-century transatlantic relations do not divide between the Hobbesians and the Kantians but between the Hobbesians and the post-Hobbesians: between those who were and those who weren't spooked by what happened on September 11. As Hobbes knew better than anyone, being spooked is not a good basis on which to try to construct a rational political order. Tony Blair, for all his fine words, has been no more able to do anything about this brute fact of politics than anyone else.

THE GARDEN, THE PARK, THE MEADOW

Imagine that in the near future another terrible famine strikes sub-Saharan Africa, at a time when most Western governments are preoccupied with fighting and funding the never-ending war on terrorism. The ghastly images are duly laid out for public consumption on the nightly news, but the public is jaded by too many images of a suffering world. Then one of the better-funded non-governmental organizations (NGOs) offers individuals the chance to "adopt" particular children or families in the refugee camps, and to keep an eye on their progress through a direct videolink to their mobile phone. Instead of neatly written letters once a month bringing news of clean water and new textbooks, First World benefactors get the chance to monitor, minute by minute, the progress of their beneficiaries: to watch them eat, see them get better, hear them say thank you. The response is overwhelming, and a fully engaged public donates sums that dwarf anything being considered by even the most concerned politicians. Success in this enterprise breeds success, as more money is used to purchase better equipment to offer clearer pictures of the difference that more money can make. The result is that sub-Saharan Africa is better fed, better equipped and better informed than at any time in its history.

But because these parts of the continent would not necessarily be better governed as a result of this experiment—it is not clear that they would be governed at all—some of the equipment, including some medical equipment, falls into the wrong hands. As a result, this newly prosperous region is struck down by a mutated virus that spreads, like HIV, unchecked through swathes of the population. Again, the citizens of the wealthy North are fed direct images of the effect this disease is having on people they have got to know and in many cases to think of as friends, and again their response is swift and overwhelming. Because the disease does not respond immediately to treatment, because it is so obviously contagious, because the doctors needed to treat it are also needed by the donor states, and because the pictures coming back make people feel scared, powerless and betrayed, they turn off their handsets and lobby their governments to quarantine the whole of Africa below the tenth parallel, close all borders, place an embargo on the transport of medical supplies, and to enforce these restrictions with the aid of military force if necessary. This their governments are well equipped to do, having come to specialize above all else in the use of force to restrict freedom of movement and freedom of trade in biological items across the globe. Soon, great chunks of Africa are cut off from the rest of the world, though one or two people continue to receive scrappily written letters detailing the horrors of what is happening inside the diseased zone. The whole continent is written off as a place where good things can happen—a place where, in George W. Bush's memorable phrase, "wings take dream". It is left to rot. Welcome to the world of postmodern politics.

This scenario (or something like it) is laid out by Philip Bobbitt in his book *The Shield of Achilles*, which describes three possible futures for the world we now inhabit, as it makes the transition from a "nation-state" to what Bobbitt calls a "market-state" model of politics and society.[1] The nation state is the model that was generated by, then went on itself to generate, the wars of the late nineteenth and twentieth centuries, including "the Long War" that lasted continuously from August 1914 until it was terminated by the Peace of Paris in 1990: World War I, the Russian Civil War, the Spanish Civil War, World War II, the Korean War and the Vietnam War were merely phases of "a single conflict fought over a single set of constitutional issues", in which only the final outcome of the Cold War was decisive.[2] The nation state had been forged (most notably by Bismarck in Germany) to place the state in the service of the nation, and was at root a welfare state, in the sense that its legitimacy depended on its ability to better the welfare of its citizens. The Long War was fought between the proponents of what were initially three different visions of national welfare—Fascist, Communist and liberal democratic—and then between the champions of the surviving two. When there was only one, it was mistakenly assumed by many that this particular form of the nation state had triumphed, and history was finally at an end.

The irony of this victory, however, was that in achieving it the liberal democratic nation state had started to turn itself into something else. It was now ready to abandon as self-defeating the attempt to provide for the welfare of all its citizens, and instead sought to found its legitimacy on its ability to maximize their opportunities, and to offer them the basic security within which to make those opportunities count. It was becoming, in other words, a "market state", possessed of similar, or even in some cases greater, political and military power than its predecessor, but much more limited in the range of its activities. It was also starting to produce the kinds of leaders who not only recognized but celebrated these limitations. The current special relationship between Britain and the United States becomes on this account something more than an alliance of interests; it is a meeting of minds between types of statesman or stateswoman. Ronald Reagan and Margaret Thatcher were self-consciously the last great leaders in the nation-state tradition, even though it was their regimes that broke the link between the state and welfare. George W. Bush and Tony Blair are among the first market-state political leaders, even though Blair sometimes still talks as though the state can make provision for a more traditional kind of social security through its public services. That is all froth. Deep down they speak the same language, and believe in the same thing: securing through the power of the state the scope for as many individuals as possible (though inevitably not all) to make use of the opportunities the market has to offer. Just as the nation state produced three different versions of itself whose inevitable clashes produced the war that "destroyed every empire that participated in it, every political aristocracy, every general staff, as well as much of the beauty of European and Asian life", so the market state offers us competing visions of its basic character and purpose.[3] Again, there are three, christened by Bobbitt the "mercantile", "managerial" and "market-mitigating" models, or the Tokyo, Berlin and Washington versions, respectively.[4]

Mercantile market politics involves the attempt to retain a kind of alliance between the state and national enterprise within global market conditions; it necessitates large-scale intervention on the side of capital rather than labour, elements of protectionism and the retention of strong cultural identity. This is the Japanese model, and at the moment it doesn't seem to work. Managerial market states look to regional blocs and alliances as the counterweights to national ambition, curtail freedom of movement between these blocs but open it up within them, invest heavily in forms of social insurance to alleviate some of the market pressures on labour, and continue to rely on limited government bail-outs for failing large-scale enterprises. This is the *soziale Marktwirtschaft* that is struggling at present to assert itself in Europe, and is showing minimal signs of progress elsewhere. Finally, market-mitigating states seek to blur the distinction between the welfare of individuals and the welfare of international society, construe opportunities for their citizens in broadly global terms, and seek to make them available as widely as possible within the society of states as a whole; they are suspicious of regulation, intervention and redistribution except in special cases (notably those relating to global security), and rely heavily on deregulated media to protect the public from the worst kinds of exploitation. This is essentially the American wave of the future.

It is in a future world founded on the principles of the Washington model that it is possible to imagine the dereliction of the African continent while the rest of the planet averts its gaze. This is a world in which governments are good at cooperating in matters of security, but when faced with social calamities are in thrall to the vicissitudes of public opinion and to the NGOs and media outlets that service public opinion. It is a prosperous society of states—productive, diverse, but subject to waves of disruption and containing pockets of unobserved and unrelieved grimness (a grimness that will only occasionally reveal itself, as it did when the flood waters rose in New Orleans). Bobbitt labels this possible world the "Meadow", in contrast to the futures we might also enjoy in the "Park", or the "Garden". In the Garden the Tokyo model becomes predominant: political communities turn inwards, and form intricate, discrete and essentially local networks of competition and cooperation; it is a militarily fraught environment, in which each state insists on its own ability to defend itself, and on its right to control its own nuclear arsenal;

but it is a world in which politicians can still seek to cultivate the flower of national identity, and pursue the sublime as well as the merely just or efficient. The Park is the future as seen from Berlin: regular, well fertilized, relatively high maintenance, containing carefully husbanded zones for minority rights and cultures but also a few clear, clean lines of general demarcation; a municipal vision of health and vitality, but in its global application opening the possibility for potentially catastrophic confrontations between lumbering and relatively inefficient trading blocs—Asian, American and European. The life of the Meadow is that of a single political ecosystem under the general supervision of the United States, in which anything is allowed to flourish that can adapt to the fast-moving, evanescent opportunities offered by the global marketplace; a world where the rewards are on offer to anyone who can deal with, indeed relish, impermanence.

Bobbitt himself seems happiest with the thought of life in the Meadow, notwithstanding its horrors, and notwithstanding his own nostalgia for elements of the sublime. But he is convinced that the future belongs to any government that can recognize and transcend the constraints of the form of market state to which it is committed. Each of the three possible futures he sketches out has something to recommend it, though as he describes them not much. In each, the pursuit of a single political vision is limiting and destructive of at least some of the things that make modern life worth living. But the only thing worse than a world in which one of these models becomes predominant is a world in which more than one of them is able to establish itself, and then to square up militarily to its rivals. This would threaten an "epochal" war of the kind that made the twentieth century so terrible for so many of the people who attempted to live through it. Any possible future for the world we now inhabit must contain a fairly limitless supply of local sites of conflict (between North and South Korea, China and Taiwan, China and Tibet, Russia and Ukraine, anywhere in the Middle East, anywhere in the former Yugoslavia), and Bobbitt sketches out a range of these, and a range of possible outcomes (including, in the Meadow, the chilling prospect of a chemical attack on Seoul and the subsequent reunification of Korea under central control from Pyongyang).[5] But these disputes are nothing compared with the possible cataclysm of a war between Washington, Berlin and Tokyo. In a world of states like ours the greatest dangers remain the confrontations between the most powerful states, though these in turn should not blind us to the possibility of allowing small-scale disputes to escalate into the kind of conflicts that overwhelm us. Because this is a world of states, the choice is not between war and peace, but between wars that we have anticipated and can manage, and wars that we haven't and can't.

Bobbitt's book is the best general book on international politics among the swathe to have emerged in the post September 11 era. What makes it stand out is its sense of history, and its insistence that the new world order can only be understood against the backdrop of the long story of the emergence of the modern state, a story that stretches back more than four centuries, rather than little more than four years. *The Shield of Achilles* is really two books rather than one—one a history of the idea of the state, one a speculation about its future. The sheer range of this project, along with its sense of urgency about the risks we currently face, means that Bobbitt ends up both hectoring and unnerving his readers, in the manner of Allan Bloom, Samuel Huntingdon and other purveyors of the slightly unhinged academic diagnostic blockbuster. But he also underpins his account with a sense of the profound historical contingency of early twenty-first-century politics, which includes a recognition that any overarching diagnosis must be less than certain. It is this sense of contingency that is missing from the work of so many other theorists of the new world order, including that of Robert Cooper, a British diplomat who has been a close adviser to Tony Blair during the turbulence of recent years in international politics, and who has helped to provide much of the intellectual ballast for Blairism as a doctrine of international relations. In 2001 Blair appointed Cooper his special envoy to Afghanistan, and he subsequently went on to become the Director-General of the European Union Economic Relations, Common Foreign and Security Policy Council. Cooper's world-view is much easier to summarize than Bobbitt's: indeed, it has occasionally been summarized in a single phrase, "the new liberal imperialism". It is also much simpler. Cooper offers the raw political version of Bobbitt's complex idea of the market state, stripped of all its subtlety and variety.

This is the version that politicians like Tony Blair have been listening to.[6]

Cooper divides the world up into premodern, modern and postmodern states. Premodern states are the ones that attempt, and for the most part fail, to rule those places where modern politics (with its concern for the provision of security and welfare) has broken down or never properly established itself: places like Chechnya and Somalia. Modern states are those that continue to pursue the political ideals of security and welfare in a conventional, nationalistic setting, relying on the well-worn precepts of raison d'état and balance of power to produce the usual sabre-rattling politics; they include India, Pakistan and some of the more successful states of Latin America and the former Soviet Union. Postmodern states have sloughed off these outmoded constitutional precepts and instead gone on to embrace cooperation, mutual interference and a heightened sense of morality in international affairs as their guiding principles; they are exemplified and in many ways defined by the states of the EU. For Cooper, the challenge for the world as it exists now is simply expressed (though harder to put into practice): embrace the postmodern.

Cooper's altogether cruder typology cuts across Bobbitt's in a number of ways, not least in his insistence that the nation state best placed—in every sense except the geographical—to embrace the wave of postmodernity coming out of Europe is Japan. Nevertheless, they have a lot in common. Neither believes that the state is likely to be swept away in the current rip tide of globalization. Indeed, both insist that there is no alternative to the state as the basic unit of political action and political understanding, and that the choice in the conditions of twenty-first century global capitalism is between different forms of the state, not between the state and something else. What they do wish to sweep away are those international institutions founded on a conception of the state which is now outmoded. Neither Cooper nor Bobbitt has a kind word to say about the UN as a promoter of collective security, since both agree that such an enterprise founders on the impossibility of reconciling the idea of international cooperation with the principles of national sovereignty. Would anyone, Bobbitt asks, turn to the UN if international cooperation were a necessity rather than a luxury: if, say, a giant asteroid were heading to Earth? Moreover, a world organized around the UN Charter as its basic constitutional law "would resemble Cold War South Africa ... a small gang of ethnic minorities would own most of the valuable property and keep everyone else confined to 'homelands'."[7] NATO, by contrast, is seen by both as an appropriate vehicle for postmodern political ambitions, because it is no longer limited by the imperative to seek a balance of power (in these arguments NATO intervention in Kosovo in 1999 is held up in contrast to UN intervention in Bosnia in 1992–95). Cooper and Bobbitt also agree that the idea of a European superstate, able to compete with the United States on the international stage, deserves to join the UN on the scrap heap of history. "It is curious," Cooper writes of the architects of European union, "that having created a structure that has transformed the nation-state into something more civilized and better adapted to today's world, there are still enthusiasts who want to destroy it in favour of an idea which is essentially more old-fashioned."[8] Bobbitt more bluntly calls it "rather pathetic that the visionaries in Brussels can imagine nothing more forward-looking than equipping the EU with the trappings of a nation-state".[9]

Where they differ is in their view of the relative strengths of the EU as presently constituted to meet the challenges of the new world order. Cooper is fairly convinced that Europe can and must lead the way; Bobbitt is much more doubtful. But, perhaps surprisingly, both share an ambivalence about the alternative possibility of the United States taking a leading role in the reconstruction of international society. For Cooper, the problem is that the United States is a state that has yet to decide on its identity: it exhibits many of the characteristics of postmodernity in the complexity of its social and economic networks, yet remains wedded to many of the prejudices of modern politics in its dealing with the rest of the world: a lingering unilateralism and a deep suspicion of mutuality. Like Russia (which also exhibits a split personality but faces the added danger of a slide back to premodernity if things go wrong), the United States had too much committed to the Cold War to be able easily to adapt to its outcome—that the defeat of Communism did not fix the world, from the point of view of the United States, but transformed it.

Bobbitt offers a subtler and more convincing explanation for American uncertainties. Uniquely among the world's states, the

United States forged its national identity without having to conjure up the spectre of nationalism. The decisive event was the Civil War, and the key figure Abraham Lincoln, whose presidency left the Union with the trappings of a nation state—onto which in due course a limited kind of welfare state could be grafted—but without the commitment to exclusivity and a closed national consciousness. As a multinational state founded on immigration and cultural experimentation, the United States was in some ways postmodern before the modern age had even reached its apogee. But as the most important player in the crucial battles of the modern world, and the victor in its ultimate war, the United States is now trapped in the past. Its history and constitution leave it well suited to take the lead in making the world safe for opportunity, diversity and conscience (the watchwords of the market state), or they would do if the United States hadn't spent so much of its recent history trying to make the world safe for democracy instead. This is the paradox of the Washington model. If the United States pursues its historic mission to co-opt the rest of the world into its scheme of values, it cannot wholeheartedly embrace the open-endedness of market-state politics. But if it fails to take a lead, then the rest of the world will wonder what they are doing leaving their fate in the hands of those Bobbitt himself calls "the reckless and self-absorbed Americans".[10]

Cooper does not want Europe to go the way of the United States, but he does accept that even Europeans need to accept that in the postmodern world, the challenge is to get used to the idea of "double standards". The postmodern states of Europe and elsewhere still face a threat from the premodern world, which requires them where necessary to adopt aggressive or defensive postures for which they may lack the aptitude or will. This threat—whether in the form of terrorism, instability or simply an affront to conscience—means that states which are increasingly open, trusting and interdependent in their relations with each other may have to be closed, decisive and relatively tough in their dealings with others. The task is to know when to get in and when to get out of the premodern world, from the perspective of a postmodern political environment which no longer maintains any "in" or any "out" in its internal affairs. If this challenge is not met, the threat will expand to include the modern world, whose states will be all too ready to exploit any weakness emanating from the postmodern democracies, and to reacquaint them with the harsh lessons of power politics from an age they thought they had left behind. Postmodern states face a challenge from within, which is to prevent their citizens becoming disconnected from politics altogether. The conditions of postmodernity are designed to focus people's attention on personal rather than public relationships, and the evanescence of market opportunities produces a preoccupation with fleeting over enduring collective experiences (above all, a preoccupation with celebrity). If the state spreads itself too thinly across the disconnected and diffuse networks of personal identity, it will simply dissipate. Something has to hold it all together.

Cooper's difficulty is that he cannot say what that something is, except the will that it should be so. But what he also doesn't say is that this problem is not peculiar to postmodern societies; it is the problem of modernity as well. And unlike the postmodern state, the modern state has an answer to this problem. Its answer is modern politics. The modern state was created precisely in order to be that something which made it possible to live in a world of double standards, a world in which individuals were both separate persons and combined peoples, bearers of private interests and vehicles of collective destiny, citizens and subjects. It is both facile, and wrong, to contrast the simplicity of the modern political world with the complexity of postmodern politics and society. The godless modern world of money and machines has never been uncomplicated; its complexities and inconsistencies have simply been clarified by the order that modern political institutions have been able to bestow on it. In this respect, postmodern politics can sound less like a challenge and more like a straightforward abdication: a concession that in the face of the inevitable double standards of political life we are powerless to do anything but acquiesce.

Indeed, it is not clear that the postmodern state is really a state at all. The state is a quintessentially modern phenomenon, and it cannot be understood without understanding the quintessentially modern forces that went into its creation, including the money and machines that go into fighting modern wars, on a scale that only states can sustain. Bobbitt identifies four forms of the state that preceded the nation state of the late nineteenth and twentieth centuries (the state that could provide the money and machines needed to secure the nation's welfare), beginning with the "princely state" of the Italian Renaissance, as described by Machiavelli. This was superseded by the "kingly state" (whose most notorious champion was Hobbes, but whose greatest practical exponent was Gustavus Adolphus of Sweden), which gave way to the "territorial state" (exemplified in the rule of Frederick the Great), then the "state-nation" (the state of the Bonapartes), which in its turn surrendered to the nation state that Bismarck built (literally so in the case of Louis Napoleon). These transitions were each marked by wars, and by technological and strategic shifts in the ways that wars are fought and won. Each was also ratified by a peace, which temporarily defined a particular constitutional order for the society of states. This is an essentially European story—after the fall of the Italian city states and the demise of the Spanish Empire it is a story of central and northern Europe—and the peace treaties that mark its history tell the tale of its concentrated locale: Augsburg (1555), Westphalia (1648), Utrecht (1713), Vienna (1815), Versailles (1919).

These constitutional shifts brought in their wake spectacular upheavals in politics: the revolutions, liberations and enfranchisements by which European progress is conventionally measured. Yet throughout these transformations the challenge of modern politics remained the one it had been at the outset: how to objectify personal relations in such a way as to sustain the grand collective projects on which individual security was seen to depend. Initially, in the case of the princely state, the individual whose security was at stake was simply the prince himself. Nevertheless, the solution to princely insecurity in a world of mercenaries and newly efficient machines of war was to objectify the prince's identity (hence Machiavelli's insistence that the prince did not have to live by the same moral code as other men, but answered to a set of principles existing beyond the world of personal culpability). So began the gradual shift from individual *status* to the impersonal, administrative *state*.[11]

Once the princely state had objectified the idea of personal service, the task of the kingly state was to reinforce this structure by making the impersonal machine human again. This task took on a new urgency once it was clear that large, well-managed realms (like France) would always defeat small city states (like Florence and Siena). Kings and their dynasties could legitimize the hold of these new, large-scale states over their subjects by giving them a human face (in the language of Hobbes, which came to be the language of the modern world, by "personating" or "re-presenting" them); and where legitimacy is uncertain—as Hobbes knew, and as the famous frontispiece of *Leviathan* illustrates—a human face can be even more terrifying than an inhuman one. But kings and their dynasties were subject to all the weaknesses of the flesh, and the territorial state came into being in order to impose a new and secure identity on monarchical politics, without, it was hoped, destroying it in the process. The challenge of the territorial state was "to make the state, rather than the person of the king, the object of constitutional and strategic concern, without permitting the people to claim the state as their own. 'My land', 'my country', but not 'my nation'."[12]

The territorial state was unable in the end, however, to prevent the emergence of a new form of personal politics, as the newly objectified land offered a vehicle for those politicians who could claim to forge from it an identity for the nation. This was the age of national liberation, and its politics were exemplified, even after his downfall, in the person of Napoleon Bonaparte. Yet from Napoleon's personal style came a reaction, and eventually a re-objectification of the state. Its new object was a nation that did not depend on a leader for its identity, but could be identified with the welfare of its individual citizens, expressed though democratic institutions, but monitored and managed by the giant bureaucratic and military machines of the twentieth century. The history of this form of the state has been punctuated by its own periodic lurches into a grotesque kind of repersonalized (and pseudo-Napoleonic) politics, which even now lingers unhappily on in various parts of the world (North Korea, Cuba, until very recently Serbia). But it is the overarching model, the nation state itself, which both Bobbitt and Cooper believe is now doomed, and has the potential to take us down with it.

The pendulum of modern politics has swung regularly between the personal and the impersonal over the last 500 years, sometimes unevenly but never so erratically as to take the mechanism off its hinges. Now the pendulum is swinging back again. The monolithic structures of national politics are fragmenting under the pressures of opportunistic international capitalism and in conjunction with the increasing personalization of the language of rights. Yet there must be limits to this process if we are to continue talking about a state-based politics at all. If the state is nothing more than the name we give to an indeterminate set of relations between the subjects of rights, then we are no longer living in a world of states, but in a world of governance. Such a world has much to recommend it—or at least it does if it is well organized—but it represents the final uncoupling of the personal and the impersonal whose alliance made possible all that has been good and all that has been bad about modern politics. Governance means rules, laws, codes, audits, accountability, efficiency, regularity, on the one hand, and people, on the other. It is clear how all of the former might benefit the latter. But it is not clear how people are to find the political identity on which states depend in the mishmash of rules and regulations by which they live.

In such a world, politics is unlikely to disappear. But it will be a crude, disjointed and uncomfortable business. Bobbitt gives some indication of what he suspects the new politics will be like: "There will be more public participation in government but it will count for less, and the role of the citizen qua citizen will greatly diminish and the role of the citizen as spectator will increase." Power will be increasingly concentrated, as office-holders accumulate more of it in the fewer places where it is needed. Of the United States system, Bobbitt writes that "it will be important to ensure that the president's ability to govern, in the limited area of responsibility given to market-states, be enhanced."[13] In this role, as in all others, "the market-state merely tries to get the 'best' person for the job", though there are unlikely to be any tests for what is best apart from those supplied by the market (hence Bobbitt suggests that we will soon look back in amazement at our scruples, if we still have any, about the way politics is currently financed in the affluent democracies). Where governments no longer take responsibility, the tests of governance will be straightforward. "The market-state test of the accountability of the NGO is simply this: they are accredited if they can raise enough money to finance successful operations that do not violate international law"—operations like funding telecommunications links between the First and Third Worlds for the relief of famine.[14] This is a world in which everyone, politicians included, is sensitized to personal risk but indifferent to collective fate.

Politics in these circumstances will inevitably become even more personalized than it is at present, as the objects of politics reduce themselves to the subjects of media obsession. Politicians will not abandon the attempt to speak for the state they purport to represent, but it is hard to see how it can be done with much conviction (which will make the appearance of conviction all the more important). The 2002 French presidential election perhaps offered a glimpse of the spectacle to come, not so much in the fleeting success of the Far Right, though perhaps in that as well, but in the crashing of gears as the democratic machine moved at improbable speed from the personal to the impersonal and back again. In the first round the French public had to decide between what were in effect sixteen different personalities offering themselves up for election, and they voted accordingly, choosing to exclude the decent, colourless socialist Lionel Jospin in favour of the flamboyant, preposterous ultra-nationalist Jean-Marie Le Pen; in the second round the vast majority had no choice at all, since Le Pen's rival, Jacques Chirac, was in the enviable position of being able to claim that he represented the last bulwark of respectable politics. So the French electorate had just two weeks to adjust to the sight of a man with a criminal record and a rictus grin, who was first choice of less than one in five of them to be president, commanding their votes as the only possible embodiment of democracy.[15] This may have been the consequence of a poorly designed electoral system, but it was also a caricature of the history of the modern state, and a caricature of the state is potentially all that postmodern politics has to offer.

Both Bobbitt and Cooper accept that the postmodern or market state may not be up to the challenges ahead. Bobbitt is particularly anxious about genetic engineering. He suggests that there may come a point at which science so completely opens up the individualistic basis of market-state politics—by subjecting such things as intelligence, beauty, emotional stability, physical strength, grace, even sociability to the forces of the market—that no state, and especially not one founded on the idea of equality of opportunity, will be able to cope. Cooper is worried about declining birth rates in the West, and more generally that "an excess of transparency and an over-diffusion of power could lead to a state, and to an international order, in which nothing can be done and nobody is accountable because there is no central focus of power or responsibility. We may all drown in complexity."[16] But the implied way out of this—concentrations of power and pockets of opacity in a sea of openness—is simply a restatement of the problem, not a solution, since the problem is how to combine the opposed tendencies of open and closed societies within a unified political system. Cooper says nothing about this, and nothing he does say takes us beyond the concerns of the philosophers of the modern state (Hobbes and Locke, Pufendorf and Spinoza, Kant and Hegel, Madison and Sieyès, Constant, Tocqueville and Mill), who were all engaged in one way or another with precisely this question: how to reconcile the opposed forces of privacy and publicity, of the personal and the impersonal, within a single polity. In this light, it is perhaps more understandable that the architects of European union should seek some reconnection with modern political structures in order to continue this endeavour, even if the way they are going about it at present seems doomed to failure.

Cooper writes about postmodern politics as an opportunity we must seize. Yet postmodern politics is remarkably inert in the face of the challenge of constructing a new kind of state. It sounds more premodern than anything: not so much a world of complexity as a world in which no one has yet worked out a way of facing up to complexity. Certainly, the one active form of politics that Cooper champions has a distinctly premodern ring to it. He wants postmodern states to band together in pursuit of a new kind of imperialism, reconfigured for the moral circumstances of the twenty-first century. Bobbitt is altogether more circumspect. *The Shield of Achilles* is punctuated with poetry illustrating various of its themes (beginning and ending with the verses by Homer and W. H. Auden that give the book its title). The section entitled "The Historic Consequences of the Long War" starts with Philip Larkin's imperial lament, "Homage to a Government", whose last line is a kind of inversion of the much better known coda to "An Arundel Tomb" ("what will survive of us is love"[17]):

> Next year we shall be living in a country
> That brought its soldiers home for lack of money.
> The statues will be standing in the same
> Tree-muffled squares, and look nearly the same.
> Our children will not know it's a different country.
> All we can hope to leave them now is money.[18]

The new world that Larkin was describing is already past. The soldiers will have to go back, have indeed started going back, to places like Sierra Leone, and Afghanistan, and Iraq. Cooper calls this new kind of imperialism variously "defensive", "voluntary" and "cooperative". But it is not clear what these words mean when you put them together. If they mean that states uncertain of their political character should be gently coerced into the club of postmodernity by a series of threats and bribes, as the EU has successfully attempted with some of the states of Eastern Europe, then it is hard to see how this is possible without relying on the basic structures of modern politics. If states are to be offered a set of choices, however loaded, and given the opportunity to take advantage of them, only fairly robust representative institutions will enable their decisions to seem either cooperative or voluntary to the people they represent. Moreover, this form of imperialism looks to be pretty dependent on ideas of territoriality, even though geography is one of the things from which the postmodern state is supposed to emancipate us. It also leaves open the question of what is to be done with states that refuse to cooperate voluntarily (unless the assumption is that, given the right threats and bribes, no state will ever refuse, in which case it is hard to see what is voluntary about it). How would this postmodern imperialism deal with the recalcitrance of a quintessentially modern state like Israel? It is possible to think of both threats and bribes that would bring Israel into line, and on such a scale as to undercut the democratic politics that makes Israel so difficult for the rest of the world to deal with. But threats and bribes on this scale are not going to sit well with the phrase that Cooper takes to summarize the ethos of postmodern international relations: "The world's grown honest."[19]

Cooper suggests that the new imperialism is exemplified by what has been done in Afghanistan since September 11, 2001. But it is far from clear, for now, what kind of state has emerged in Afghanistan since that date. It exhibits signs of all three types of state that Cooper delineates. It is still premodern, to the extent that large parts of the country remain out of control of the central government in Kabul, and that government itself still relies on outside help from American forces to secure what little power it has. It is also quintessentially modern, in that it has conducted successful elections, involving men and women, based on principles of non-discrimination, and securing the victory of a charismatic, national leader who has promised to raise the living standards of his people. But Afghan politics are also postmodern, in that it is not clear what weight any of these promises carry, given Afghanistan's dependence on foreign aid, NGOs and the goodwill of various international financial institutions for any chance of success in rebuilding the country. The new imperialism in Afghanistan seems to call for not just double standards, but triple standards, and perhaps even more than that.

Dealing with the premodern world, Cooper consistently argues, means drawing on the full range of political weapons that we have at our disposal, including those we may wish we had discarded. (Bobbitt, too, makes the point of warning market states not to be queasy about "covert operations", for which he foresees a rapidly increasing need.)[20] It is the ultimate test of political imagination to find a way of reconciling these conflicting impulses. The temptation is to assume that this task can only be performed by emancipating ourselves from the outmoded political imagination of the present, and drawing instead on a different mindset: either the forgotten memories of Europe's imperial past or the intimations of Europe's postmodern future. Yet it is very hard to see how the challenge of postmodern politics can be met without making use of the only political institutions that have yet been devised that are able to reconcile people to a world of double standards. These are, broadly speaking, the pluralistic, democratic and welfarist institutions of the modern state.

Like so many of the writers who have sought to capture the essence of twenty-first-century politics, both Cooper and Bobbitt claim that September 11 did not make the difference; what happened on that day did not shape the world we now inhabit, it merely brought to the surface of international politics features that had previously been concealed. *The Shield of Achilles* was written before the attack on the World Trade Center, but it includes a postscript, entitled "The Indian Summer", in which Bobbitt suggests that those attacks marked the early skirmishes in a new epochal war. In response to the rejoinder that wars can only be fought between states, Bobbitt argues that the multinational, mercenary terror network that Osama bin Laden and others have assembled is a state—"a malignant and mutated form of the market-state".[21] Al Qaeda seeks to possess many of the basic institutions of the state, including a standing army, a treasury, a permanent civil service, even a rudimentary welfare programme for its fighters and their families. All it tries to do without, according to Bobbitt, is "a contiguous territory". It is a "virtual state".[22] The war against this virtual state and others like it will require a big shift in military strategies and priorities, as have all the epochal wars in history. But the market state, as it fights this war, increasingly comes to resemble the virtual state it has made its enemy. The market state, too, is increasingly detached from the narrow hold of territoriality (on Bobbitt's account the state has been steadily detaching itself from the idea of territory since the middle of the eighteenth century). It, too, is a network of intimate but underspecified personal relationships. It, too, is rather shadowy, despite the ubiquity on the nightly news of its grinning figureheads. Market states, like virtual states, are in fact pretty rudimentary political structures, not just in their welfare provisions, but in their inability to establish a plausible objective identity for themselves. Like the postmodern state, the market state more closely resembles the modern state at the beginning than at the end of its history.

The idea of the market state contains both an offer and a threat, as befits the politics on which it would rest. The threat is of a global cataclysm, an epochal war to end all epochal wars. If politicians fail to understand the new world they are dealing with, they will destroy it. Bobbitt doesn't really specify how, but then he doesn't need to. Both he and Cooper pay relatively little attention to China as a possible source of future conflict, not, one feels, because they think the dangers negligible, but because they are so great as to be hardly worth spelling out. Somewhere behind the Washington, Berlin and Tokyo models there lurks a Beijing model of market politics, only nobody is quite sure what it is yet, perhaps not even the Chinese themselves. Politicians who ignore the threats that they are likely to have to deal with, or wish they weren't there, or mistake them for something else, are playing with fire. But that has always been true, just as it has always been true that the best politicians are those who transcend these constraints in the act of recognizing them. No better vehicle for this has yet been devised than the modern state, notwithstanding the number of times that the attempt to transcend it has resulted in disaster. The champions of postmodern politics have yet to suggest the means of doing it any better, though they do open up the prospect of abandoning the attempt altogether.

What is on offer instead is a radical kind of federalism that the idea of the market state places within our grasp. This involves the replacement of sovereign jurisdictions with an "umbrella" form of political rule: a single zone of governance allowing a diverse set of provincial subcultures to coexist under it. This would be the outcome of what Bobbitt calls "a market in sovereignty". Once basic principles of rights and security were established, individuals would be free to seek their own identity within different communities ordering themselves in different ways, and "these may be provinces where feminists or fundamentalist Christians or ethnic Chinese congregate, all within a larger sheltering area of trade and defense".[23]

This is a novel idea, but not an entirely new one. What it most closely resembles is the libertarian vision set out by the late Robert Nozick in his classic text of the 1970s, *Anarchy, State, and Utopia*.[24] Nozick argued that in a world where politics was based on nothing more than a mutual securing of property rights, the possibility would open up for different communities to offer people the full range of political options, subject only to the provision that individuals be free to join and leave these communities voluntarily. There could be Communist communities, and religious communities, and libertine communities, and cooperative communities, and any other kind of community you care to mention, all existing under a single framework of rights-based governance. Nozick called this a utopia of utopias—"an environment in which utopian experiments may be tried out".[25] But it is also utopian in the more straightforward sense that it is a world without politics. The choices that people make and the identities they assume and the relations they establish with one another are entirely divorced from the overarching rules by which they live, which are neutral, indifferent and impersonal. The same is true of what postmodern politics currently has to offer. There is plenty of room for anarchy in such a world, and plenty of room for utopianism, but no real place for the state. For all the hopes and fears that postmodern politics seems to contain, it doesn't contain a coherent vision of the state itself. And without a coherent vision of the state, no form of politics can sustain itself for long.

TWO REVOLUTIONS, ONE REVOLUTIONARY

Evidence of how difficult it may be to sustain any coherent vision of a new world order has been in plentiful supply in recent years, following the American decision to impose its own particular political vision on Iraq. The consequent breakdown in relations between the United States and some of its longstanding allies, above all France, reveals just how easy it still is for states to fall out with one another, notwithstanding the homogenizing forces at work in international affairs. Indeed, the clash between the United States and France was in many ways made worse by all the things that continue to bind them together, including the long history that they share. These deep affinities, and the corresponding tensions, go back to the births of the two republics, when what was essentially a single idea of politics gave rise to two very different visions of how the political world could and should be remade. The story of the origins of the modern state in the events that changed the world on both sides of the Atlantic at the end of the eighteenth century, and above all the story of some of the revolutionary ideas that lay behind them, illuminates various aspects of our current predicament. It shows how a shared understanding of a new political order is always liable to generate its own deep divisions. It also shows how hard it has always been to get the idea of a new political order to stick, in the face of all the mistakes, misunderstandings and misfortunes to which any new conception of politics is prone.

The best illustration of these hazards lies in the respective fates of the two men who did most to make sense of the new world of representative politics at the end of the eighteenth century. Many of the eighteenth-century political theorists with the biggest international reputations came from rather out-of-the-way places, at least in geopolitical terms: Vico from Naples; Hume and Adam Smith from Edinburgh; Rousseau from Geneva; Kant from Königsberg. This is one of the reasons that we like to think of the period as an Age of Enlightened Reason. But because the eighteenth century was also, in the end, the Age of Revolution, its two most important political thinkers do not really belong in this club of international superstars. One, James Madison from Virginia, is more than just a superstar in the United States. He is one of the secular gods of the American republic, as the architect of its constitution, and the author of many of the best-known of the Federalist Papers written in its defence, including Federalist No. 10, which is one of the republic's holy texts. This makes the rest of the world uncomfortable, and Madison's ideas can often seem too American to be true (in contrast to someone like Rousseau, whose ideas can often seem too true to be Swiss). The other, Emmanuel Joseph Sieyès from Provence, is not mistrusted outside of his native France so much as ignored altogether. Even within France he is more of an intellectual curiosity than an object of reverence. The French republic has had too many constitutions, too many false gods and too many false dawns, to go in for the kind of hero-worship of its founding fathers that gives so many Americans such satisfaction. Sieyès contributed to some of the shortest lived of those constitutions, and he was responsible for more than one of the false dawns. Nevertheless, he was a political thinker of genius, to compare with any of the great names of the eighteenth century. And he understood, perhaps as well as anyone, the new world the American and French Revolutions helped to create—a world we still inhabit, however much we may wish to escape it, to this day.

The greatest single obstacle to a wider appreciation of Sieyès's ideas in the English-speaking world has been his name. Not Sieyès, though that is tricky enough (it should be pronounced something like *seeay-ez*, though to English speakers it more often comes out as *c-s*, like the gas), nor Emmanuel Joseph, but Abbé. Where he is known, he is almost always known as the Abbé Sieyès, which he became when he was ordained at the age of 24, in 1772. His formal education had taken place at a seminary in Paris, and then at the Sorbonne, where he read theology. His public life began when, as secretary to the Bishop of Chartres, he was appointed vicar-general of the diocese in 1780, and his involvement in local government started in 1787 when he became a representative of the clergy in the provincial assembly of Orléans. None of this helps his claims to be taken seriously as a theorist of modern politics, and the unsuspecting reader could be forgiven for fearing the worst. But in fact, Sieyès was not a religious man, and his work is free of any kind of theological speculation; it is entirely, almost shockingly, worldly. The Church was a career for him, until 1788, when he discovered his true vocation, which was politics.

The event that made him was the decision of Louis XVI to convene the Estates-General, in a desperate attempt to resolve the financial crisis that was threatening to bankrupt the French state. The Estates-General was a parliament of the three estates of the realm—the nobility, the clergy, and the people—and it was summoned to meet in the spring of 1789. It had not been called since 1614, and no one, including Louis and his advisers, knew what to expect from it this time, though almost everyone had their hopes (Louis hoped for new taxes, the various estates for new rights). Sieyès had no such hopes, because he did not believe the realm should, or could, be divided into three estates, each with separate rights of representation. For Sieyès, only the third estate counted, and the nobility and the clergy had no separate rights from those of the people. By the logic of this argument, there was no such thing as the realm, since the realm was made up of the three estates; instead, there was only something called the "Nation", which was constituted by the 25 or 26 million individuals who inhabited it. During the last six months of 1788, Sieyès wrote three pamphlets in which he pursued this line of thought as far as it would go. The second of them, entitled *What is the Third Estate?*, was published in January 1789, when it caused an immediate sensation. Reading it now, a world away from the events that it describes, it is still easy to see why. It is not a beautiful or polished piece of writing, it is poorly organized and it is probably too long for what it has to say; but it is thrilling in its remorselessness.

Sieyès steadfastly refused to shirk any of the implications of his argument. He begins with three questions, which became the best-known things he ever wrote: "1. What is the Third Estate?— *Everything*. 2. What, until now, has it been in the existing political order?—*Nothing*. 3. What does it want to be?—*Something*."[1] If the answer to the first question was correct, then the answer to the second question was irrelevant, which made the answer to the third question a big mistake. Other champions of the people were hoping that the calling of the Estates-General would be an occasion for the third estate to assert itself against the other two, to make something more of itself. But if the people were *everything*—if the people were the French nation—then it made no sense to demand that they should be better represented within an assembly of the nation. They had to be the whole of that assembly. The obvious rejoinder to this is that one estate cannot be the whole of an assembly made up of three estates. Sieyès's reply could hardly have been clearer: "The Third Estate, it is said, cannot form the Estates-General all by itself. Very well! So much the better! It will form a *National Assembly*."[2] And this, thanks to Sieyès, is what happened.

He made it happen from within the Estates-General, to which the Third Estate of Paris elected him. Once there, he presented on 10 June and 15 June 1789 the two motions that brought about the transformation of the Estates-General into a National Assembly, so initiating the French Revolution. As an elected representative of the people, Sieyès revealed himself to be a successful political opportunist, but he was no orator. He owed his place in the chamber to his three pamphlets, which had made him famous. They do not read like election addresses—they are too intellectually fearless for that—but they do read like the work of someone for whom political thought is a matter of real and almost desperate urgency. In this respect, they are nothing like the Federalist Papers, which had appeared in New York only a year previously. Though these too were motivated by urgent questions, and though they were explicitly written for an election (in order to persuade the people of New York state to ratify the new federal constitution), they are marked by an air of measured calm, which explains much of their enduring appeal. There is no sense of desperation, but a steady confidence that the best arguments will win, from the people with the best arguments. As a revolutionary, Sieyès reads less like Madison, and more like Lenin—not the Lenin of 1917 but the Lenin of 1905, during the first, aborted, Russian Revolution, when he was driven almost to distraction by the unwillingness of his fellow Marxists to seize the moment and make something happen. For most of Lenin's revolutionary colleagues in Russia, the 1905 revolution wasn't quite right for them—it had come too soon, they hadn't had enough time to prepare, the situation on the ground was too confusing, none of the necessary institutions were in place: much better to wait for the right moment. Their tactics, Lenin said, were like the famous advertisement for fly powder: just catch the fly, *then* sprinkle it with the powder, and the fly will die.[3] Sieyès, like Lenin, believed in upending all available stocks of fly powder on the old regime, and seeing who was left standing. "A privileged class," Sieyès wrote, "is like a pestilence upon the nation."[4] In a related image, also somewhat Lenin-like in its apparent ruthlessness, he responded to the anxieties of those who wondered what would happen to the first two estates if the third estate became everything: "It is like asking what place a malignant tumour should have in the body of someone who is ill, as it devours and ruins his health. It simply has to be *neutralised*."[5]

Yet despite all this, and despite the claims of some Marxists that Sieyès provides a naive foreshadowing of their own doctrines (just replace "third estate" with "proletariat" in each of his three celebrated questions), the significance of his writings lies in their conceptual underpinnings, which are nothing like Lenin's. What they are most like, in fact, are the ideas that lie behind the Federalist Papers. Sieyès was not conscious of any intellectual debt he owed to the Americans, in part because he disagreed with them on many of the details of their constitution, but mainly because he claimed that his own ideas long pre-dated the crisis of the French state, or even of the American colonies. He had come to his conclusions about the basic problems of politics in the early 1770s, he said, and he had not shifted. These conclusions revolved around a single word: representation. Sieyès believed that representation was everywhere in the modern world, not just in political life, but in all those social relations that relied on individual human beings acting for each other in various ways: in law, in trade, in manufacturing, in education, in family life, in all "the activities that support society". But this great social network of representation posed a problem for politics. Socially, representation is plural, because different individuals have different representatives for their different activities—different lawyers, tradesmen, suppliers, teachers, parents and so on. But politically, representation is singular, because politics presupposes the single entity of the state. The problem, therefore, was how to find a scheme that could do justice both to the plurality of social representation and the singularity of political representation. It is the basic problem of modern politics: how to keep a diverse society going without the state falling apart.

One answer was to try to make sure that political representation broadly reflected society at large. This was essentially the argument of the American Antifederalists, for whom, as one of their number put it: "The very term, representative, implies that the person or body chosen for this purpose, should resemble those who appoint them—a representation of the people of America, if it be a true one, must be like the people."[6] In particular, political representation should reflect the different orders and classes of people who make up a given society—not, in the United States, nobles and priests, but farmers, manufacturers, artisans, merchants and so on. But there are two difficulties with this argument. First, any political assembly based on the representation of different social groups is liable to be fractious, and the discussions within it uninspiring, as the representatives refer back to the particular interests of their electors. A dynamic politics required what Sieyès called "genuine representatives instead of simple vote-carriers".[7] Second, representation by reflection offered at best only a crude reproduction of certain broad blocks within society; it did not reflect the genuine plurality of individual interests and relationships. Sieyès believed, as much as any of the American founding fathers did, that the only things that counted in politics were individuals and their personal experiences ("Mark well", he once wrote, "the only real happiness is that of individuals").[8] Seeking to represent them as types of individuals was therefore self-defeating: the best you got was a crude caricature of social diversity on the one hand, and politically isolated individuals on the other. The only apparent alternatives, however, were equally unpalatable. To represent France as nothing but 25 or 26 million separate individuals was to invite chaos. Meanwhile, any attempt to represent the people simply as a single, unified whole gave too much power to the people's representatives. Political representation that did not take account of the diversity of social representation was an open invitation to tyranny, as the French experience after 1789 made abundantly clear. Sieyès saw the truth of this argument in principle long before the Jacobins demonstrated it in fact.

The only thing worse than these different kinds of misrepresentation—the misrepresentation of the people's diversity and the misrepresentation of the people's unity—was the crude and hideous combination that existed in France before 1789. The system of estates was a grotesque, medieval parody of social diversity, while the power of the king, as the sole representative of the unified state, went unchecked and unspecified—no one could say where it ended. There were, of course, more subtle combinations than the French one, and the British constitution seemed to many, including many in France, to point the way forward, with its more pragmatic mixture of King, Lords and Commons. But the British example was never going to work for the newly independent Americans, and it didn't work for Sieyès either. If the genius of the British system was that the people had a single representative assembly in the House of Commons, what right had the King and the Lords to interfere in the legislative process? If, on the other hand, the King and Lords also represented the people, on what basis did they make that claim? "Whatever goes into a legislative body is competent to vote on a people's behalf only insofar as it is entrusted with their proxy," Sieyès wrote. "But if there are no free, general elections, where is the proxy?"[9] The people could not be represented in their own, separate chamber and still allow unelected others to speak for them. Yet if no one else would speak for the people, apart from a single chamber of their representatives, who could prevent those representatives from tyrannizing the people in their turn?

Sieyès saw that there was only one way out of this mess of unpalatable choices and unsustainable combinations. The people had to be represented as a single entity, and not divided up into estates or orders or classes; but they had to be represented as a single entity in different ways. The answer to the problem of modern politics lay in the flexibility of the concept of representation, and the most important task of modern political theory was to distinguish the different ways in which the people might be represented. The first, and most important, distinction was between the representation of the people in their capacity as a "constituting power", and in their capacity as a "constituted power".

This meant that the people had to have representatives capable of drawing up a constitution and also to have representatives capable of acting for them within the terms of that constitution; more importantly, it meant that these two sets of representatives could not be the same. The National Assembly of 1789 was to be a representation of the people in their "constituting" capacity: its job was to establish a new constitution for the French state. The authority of this constitution would derive from the fact that it came from the people's representatives, specifically authorized for that purpose. To the objection that the National Assembly of 1789 had not been authorized for that purpose—it was, after all, the old assembly of the Third Estate under a new name—Sieyès replied that somebody had to do it, because France needed a new constitution, and moreover it was not possible to wait for formal authorization, because France lacked a new constitution. This is how it goes with constitution-making: it is unconstitutional. What mattered for Sieyès was that the new constitution should allow for the representation of the people by other bodies than the constituting one. In particular, the people needed separate representation by a legislature and by an executive, and also, potentially, by some kind of constitutional jury to resolve disputes between the two; these would be the "constituted powers". Some of these representatives might be directly elected, some indirectly elected, and others simply appointed. None could claim the sole authority of the people, but all could claim in one way or another to be the people's representatives.

A constitutional gathering acting in the name of the people but not instructed by them; a constitution that produced a separation of powers but presupposed no separation of estates or orders; a mixture of directly elected, indirectly elected, and appointed representatives—this was a case that was being made at roughly the same time on the other side of the Atlantic as well. The circumstances, of course, were very different, but the basic insight was not: political singularity and social diversity could be reconciled if a single people were represented in diverse ways. It meant a clean break with the idea of representation as a reflection of the people at large. It also meant greater freedom for the people's representatives to tell the people what was good for them. For both the Federalists and for Sieyès, the most urgent matter on which the people needed to be guided by their representatives was the question of debt. The popular view of debt, then if not now, was that it was a bad thing, and to be avoided at all costs. The Federalists were worried that representatives acting under instructions from the voters, in a legislature with sole authority to speak for the voters, would try to abolish the debts people already had, and try to prevent them taking on new ones, including a new national debt. For Sieyès, during the winter of 1788–89, the stakes were even higher. He was terrified that the king himself would renege on his debts, and that the people's representatives would not try to stop him. The profligacy of the king and his court had produced the crisis of the state's finances, and it was tempting to think that the king should pay the price for this—with a bankruptcy. Sieyès was adamant that this was a temptation that had to be resisted at all costs. In the first to be written (though the last to be published) and most passionate of his three pamphlets of that winter, he argued that a bankruptcy would ruin not the king, but the French nation, which meant it would be the ruin of the people themselves. The spectacle of a bankrupt king, and the discomfort of those who had grown rich off him, might provide some temporary relief, as Sieyès understood ("The highway robbery perpetrated by speculators on the funds," he reassured his readers, "offends me as much as it offends you").[10] But it would not be the king, nor even the speculators, who really suffered. A bankruptcy would fall most heavily on the king's creditors, including many members of the Third Estate, who might not have to pay new taxes, but would also be receiving no more income from their government bonds. The destruction of the king's credit would not go unnoticed by his foreign enemies either. England, Sieyès predicted, would certainly attack a bankrupt France, knowing that she had no credit in the money markets, and no ready sources of income to pay for her defence. What choice would the people have then, except to agree new taxes in order to provide the nation with the means to fight? A king with no credit will always require more money, but a king with no credit need have no compunction about how he gets it. A royal bankruptcy, Sieyès declared, would be "the ruin of all hope". But it would not be the ruin of the regime. Instead, "its hand would be free to use the great mechanisms of fear and money, and again it would be able to spread them around with profusion."[11]

So, the people had no choice but to service the king's debts. Yet this was an abhorrent idea, because it meant that the people would pay the price for the king's irresponsibility. The only solution was for the people not merely to service the debt, but to bite the bullet and adopt it as their own, and this is what Sieyès advocated. The Third Estate, he argued, acting for the entire Estates-General, should "adopt the debt in the name of the nation". If the debt belonged to the people themselves, then the state's finances might finally acquire some stability. But the people themselves could not take the decision to adopt the debt. It had to be done on their behalf, by their representatives. If such a decision were left directly up to the people, or to representatives awaiting their instructions, then it would be shirked, because the prospect of more debt, and someone else's debt to boot, would frighten them off. Only if the nation had an assembly capable of taking these kinds of decisions for it would the difficult decisions be made. Yet the assembly that institutes a national debt cannot also be the one that decides how the money is raised or how it is spent—that would take the people back to where they were under the king, responsible once again for what are essentially someone else's spending habits. Different representatives, answerable to the people in different ways, have to decide on questions of taxation and expenditure, and on much else besides, including the root cause of most taxation and most expenditure, which is war.

It is an immensely powerful argument but it is not a simple one, and it can look somewhat paradoxical. It appears to rest on a series of double standards. The people need to be united in order to save the state for themselves, but they cannot act for themselves in order to save the state. The people must be represented as though they possessed a single identity, but maintaining that identity requires that they should not be represented in only one way. This line of thought contains echoes of the ideas of earlier political theorists, including Hobbes, Locke, Montesquieu and Rousseau, but is not quite like any of them. Sieyès's genius through 1788 and early 1789 was to take this complicated, multifaceted argument and make it straightforward, obvious, unarguable. It is an achievement to compare with that of the authors of the Federalist Papers, who were attempting much the same thing. It was only after his triumph of June 1789 that the complications returned, as Sieyès struggled to turn the people's constituting power into the correct arrangement of constituted powers for the new state. In this struggle his divergence from the American constitutional model became clear. He was adamantly opposed to an executive power of veto, which he thought would make a mockery of the distinction between executive and legislature. He believed in a separation of powers, not a balance of powers, which he called "a vicious idea".[12] Moreover, the powers that Sieyès was willing to grant the executive were far less extensive than the powers of the American presidency. The Great Elector, as Sieyès called his head of state, was primarily a symbol of the unity of the nation; he would have the real and not simply symbolic power to appoint ministers, but certainly no power to make appointments to a supreme constitutional court. In the United States, the president decides on war but it is up to Congress to make the formal announcement; Sieyès believed that the legislature should make the decision, and the executive simply the declaration. Sieyès was opposed to a Bill of Rights, believing that the people needed no separate rights when they had a constitution; this was a battle the American Federalists fought and lost. Above all, Sieyès did not believe in the idea of federalism itself. France had to be, in the famous phrase, "*une et indivisible*", which was consistent with the people being represented in different ways, but not in different places. Though the Federalists successfully asserted the rights of central government, the question of the rights of the people's representatives in the various states remained unresolved, including the great unspoken question of their right to secede from the union, which was to haunt the republic years later. Sieyès insisted that the constitution of the new French state had to include a re-division of the country into a series of 83 departments that cut across the traditional boundaries of local government, and undermined them. Local assemblies, and larger provincial assemblies, existed in order to move men, money and votes upwards to the centre, and to organize the administration of national laws that came back down. They were to be, Sieyès wrote later, "more than confederated states; they are true, integral and essential parts of one and the same whole. This observation is important so that one never compares us with the United States of America."[13]

Yet the most important difference between Sieyès and the Federalists is not one of substance, but one of timing. The formulation by Madison, Hamilton and Jay of an intellectual defence of the new American system of representative government came at the end of the revolutionary process, and in the aftermath of the drawing up of a new constitution. Sieyès set out the core of his ideas at the very beginning of his revolution, before there was a constitution or even a constitutional assembly to defend. It is one of the tragedies of the French Revolution that the best ideas—the most far-sighted as well as the most flexible—came first, while it is one of the saving graces of the American revolution that the best ideas came last. Having got their constitution up and running, the three authors of the Federalist Papers were able to reap the benefits: John Jay went on to be the first Chief Justice of the United States Supreme Court; Alexander Hamilton became Secretary of the Treasury; and James Madison became the fourth president of the United States. Sieyès spent the years between 1789 and 1799 trying desperately to find a constitution that worked, and trying to find the politicians who could make it work. He was still trying in the summer of 1799, when he was elected to the Executive Directory in Paris and given one last chance to reform the constitution in order to save the nation, which was by then under severe threat both from within and without. He decided that the existing regime in Paris had to be overturned, in order to see off the threat of a resurgent Jacobinism and to provide him with the political security to proceed with his reforms. He organized a coup, but realized he needed a general to guarantee its success. By chance, Napoleon Bonaparte had returned to France from Egypt in October 1799, and Sieyès decided, after some hesitation, that he had found his man. On 10 November power was transferred from the legislature into the hands of a provisional Consulate, consisting of only three members, including both Sieyès and Bonaparte (the third was a lawyer named Ducos). A new constitution did emerge before the end of the year, but by then Bonaparte had asserted himself, and it was his constitution, formally enshrining the power of the new Consulate, with Bonaparte himself at its head. Sieyès had lost. He retired from public life, saddled with the unenviable reputation of the man who had started the French Revolution, and the man who had ended it.

The decade Sieyès spent trying to find a constitution that could do justice to his core ideas, and that could also accommodate the vicissitudes of French politics during the most turbulent period in its history, earned him another reputation, as a kind of bespoke constitution-maker for all seasons, determined to be adaptable, indeed so adaptable as to be almost deranged. He was mercilessly mocked on this score by the scourge of the revolution, Edmund Burke, who wrote in 1796:

> Abbé Sieyès has whole nests of pigeon-holes full of constitutions ready made, ticketed, sorted, and numbered; suited to every season and every fancy; some with the top of the pattern at the bottom, and some with the bottom at the top; some plain, some flowered; some distinguished for their simplicity, others for their complexity; some of blood colour; some of *boue de Paris*; some with directories, others without direction; some with councils of elders, and councils of youngsters; some without any council at all. Some where the electors choose the representatives; others where the representatives choose the electors. Some in long coats, some in short cloaks; some with pantaloons, some without breeches. Some with five-shilling qualifications; some totally unqualified. So that no constitution-fancier may go unsuited from his shop, provided he loves a pattern of pillage, oppression, arbitrary imprisonment, confiscation, exile, revolutionary judgment, and legalized premeditated murder, in any shapes into which they can be put.[14]

Sieyès was no revolutionary terrorist, but it is easy enough to see his various constitutional experiments as opening the door to those who were. It is also easy to parody him as a kind of super-rational fantasist, playing with his abstract schemes of government while the real and bloody business of politics went on unchecked and unnoticed. This is in obvious contrast to the American Founders, whose reputation has long been as supreme pragmatists, sensitive to political reality, cautious, modest, but ruthless in their determination to make their preferred scheme stick. The American constitution has lasted for more than 200 years, while none of Sieyès's got off the ground at all, so who is to argue? And yet, if we look at the history of the last 200 plus years, Sieyès was right about more things than Madison was. For example, he realized early on that no system of government that sought to preserve both social diversity and political unity could survive without political parties to animate it. "The existence of two parties," he wrote, "is inseparable from any kind of representative system."[15] Madison accepted there would be parties, but wished to limit their effects, as dangerous to representative government. Yet Madison's version of representative government could not have survived without political parties, which have seen it through its various crises. The most serious of these, including both the Civil War and the Great Depression, helped to transform Madison's original constitutional settlement into something more like a national representative system as envisaged by Sieyès: bureaucratically centralized, dominated by party, and funded by a large national debt (in this respect, Hamilton was closer to Sieyès than Madison was). But the office of president, as it has developed through these crises, has come to exercise powers that go well beyond those Sieyès would have approved, interfering in all aspects of government, making wars, opposing laws, drafting budgets, curtailing rights, and all the while choosing the judges who can decide whether or not this is constitutional. The ability of the legislature to act as a national forum for the nation's combined interest has been usurped by the executive, in ways that Sieyès's constitutional schemes sought to forestall. Meanwhile, the consequent pressure on the executive to respond directly to the twists and turns of public opinion has grown, in ways that Sieyès could have predicted.

Sieyès did not advocate a presidential system. Indeed, he believed for a while that the best figurehead for the new French state would be a king. Unfortunately, the only king available at the time was Louis XVI, and Sieyès had to make the best of it. This accommodation with the monarchy earned Sieyès a further reputation as someone less than fully committed to the principles of the republic. But in an exchange of letters with the most fashionable political theorist of the day, Thomas Paine, he defended himself against the charge that in the great struggle between Republicanism and Monarchy, he was on the wrong side. The exchange took place in the summer of 1791, following Louis's secret flight to Varennes and subsequent arrest, which had left his supporters among the revolutionary leaders looking rather exposed. Sieyès had already been subject to a fierce attack in the Parisian Jacobin club, first from Robespierre, and then from Danton, and he took the opportunity of Paine's letter to defend himself. Paine had written in response to Sieyès's declared preference for a monarchical form of government, reminding him that "it is against the whole hell of Monarchy that I have declared war" (Paine's rather grandiloquent list of reasons for this included "my predilection for humanity, my anxiety for the dignity and honour of the human species, my disgust at seeing men directed by infants and governed by brutes, and the horror inspired by all the evils which Monarchy has scattered over the Earth").[16] To "the misery of Monarchy" Paine directly opposed "the Republican System", which he defined "simply as a Government by Representation".[17] For Sieyès this was a horrible confusion of terms. The representative system could not be identified with a particular form of government, but only with the idea of constitutional government itself—it was the case, he maintained, "that every social constitution of which representation is not the essence, is a false constitution".[18] The argument between Republicans and what Sieyès called "Monarchicans" (to distinguish them from dyed-in-the-wool Monarchists) was not about the principle of representation, but about its form, and in particular the form it should assume in the executive branch of government. Sieyès supported monarchy because he believed it was useful to have "an individual of superior rank, in whom is represented the stable unity of the government", able to appoint ministers and to monitor their independence.[19] By contrast, his Republican opponents (and here he had in mind Robespierre and Danton as much as Paine) wanted an executive council at the head of the state, directly answerable to the people or to the single chamber of a popular legislature. Sieyès believed that this would result in a concentration of what he called "irresponsible power", and he was of course correct. But his tone was conciliatory, which is understandable given the circumstances. The opponents of monarchy, he suggested, should really be labelled *"Poliarchists"*, because they championed a many-headed executive whereas he supported an executive that culminated in a single point—"the *triangle* of Monarchy", as he put it, as opposed to "the republican *platform*". In other words, he was happy to suggest that this was a fairly technical difference of opinion, concealing broader points of agreement ("They are for the public interest," he wrote somewhat nervously, "and certainly we are so too").[20] "Poliarchist" is an ironic title nonetheless— the many-headed executive of the Poliacrats resulted in a single-headed constitution, so collapsing "that division of powers, which is the true bulwark of public liberty"; as a result, the many heads of the new executive did not remain in place for long, and some were soon rolling around in baskets on the Place de la Révolution.[21]

Sieyès's preference for monarchy over Jacobin republicanism was motivated more by a suspicion of what he called "crude democracy" than any attachment to the person of the king. When it became clear just how inadequate Louis was to fulfil the role of Great Elector in the new constitutional scheme, Sieyès readily abandoned him, and as a member of the National Assembly he voted for the king's execution in 1793 (which meant that, as a regicide, he had to go into exile in Brussels following the restoration of the Bourbons in 1815). In fact, he never really settled how the position of Great Elector at the summit of the executive should be occupied, or by whom. He was certainly unlucky in the cast of characters the revolution offered up to him, from the tyrant he was stuck with at the beginning to the tyrant he wound up with at the end. The Americans, by contrast, were remarkably fortunate in whom they had available. If ever a new nation was blessed with an individual of superior rank, in whom could be represented the stable unity of the government, it was the United States, in the person of George Washington. The three presidents who followed him—Adams, Jefferson, Madison—were all lucky men (of the founders, only Hamilton's luck really ran out, when he was fatally wounded in a duel with Vice President Aaron Burr in 1804); equally, the United States was very lucky to have them. Timing, luck, circumstance were all against Sieyès's schemes for France, and instead France got the Terror, and then the chaos that followed the Terror, and then the arbitrarily imposed order that followed the chaos. France also got, as a result of these experiences, a different conception of representative politics from the one Sieyès had championed. As Michael Sonenscher has argued, the French experience of politics in the late eighteenth century produced an alternative version of liberal politics for the nine-teenth century.[22] This version of liberalism is usually associated with Benjamin Constant (like Rousseau, a peripatetic Swiss émi-gré who eventually found his voice in France), and particularly his celebrated speech of 1819 to the Parisian Royal Academy, com-paring the liberty of the ancients with the liberty of the moderns. Constant argued, along with Sieyès, that modern politics is impos-sible without representation, because modern citizens do not have the time or the inclination to take many political decisions for themselves, and are better off leaving those decisions to others whom they appoint. Indeed, the most famous line from the speech was a direct quotation from Sieyès: "Rich men hire stewards."[23] But Constant had a more straightforward conception of what was involved in popular representation than Sieyès. He believed that the people's representatives would always seek too much power if the people were not vigilant, and that the great danger of mod-ern politics was that the comforts of modern living would lead individual citizens to neglect politics altogether, leaving them vul-nerable to exploitation by their politicians. Rich men who don't keep an eye on their stewards can suddenly find themselves poor. As a result, Constant advocated a system of direct elections where possible, and more popular participation in politics between elec-tions, through the exercise of what he called "public opinion"—in newspapers, debating societies, political clubs and so on. He wor-ried that a more indirect and complex system of representation of the kind advocated by Sieyès was likely to lead to apathy rather than engagement. Modern citizens, Constant recognized, partic-ularly modern French citizens who had experienced the political traumas of 1789–1815, needed no excuse to turn their backs on politics. But the experiences of 1789–1815 should also serve to remind them what their political representatives were capable of doing while their backs were turned.

Unlike both Sieyès and Madison, who believed in their different ways that the people's representatives could keep an eye on each other, Constant believed that it was up to the people to keep an eye on their representatives. Constant's version of liberalism rested on the idea of a watchful scrutiny of all political representatives, whereas Sieyès founded his political system on the idea of variety in all forms of political representation. Yet, just as Sieyès's commitment to variety did not prevent him from being deceived when it came to dealing with Napoleon Bonaparte, so Constant was also deceived by Napoleon, notwithstanding his commitment to vigilance. Having been a persistent critic of Napoleonic rule, Constant allowed himself to be persuaded in 1815, during Napoleon's One Hundred Days, to draw up a new "liberal" constitution for the old Emperor. This constitution entrusted Napoleon with executive power precisely because he "transcended" the system of popular representation, and would therefore be able to preserve the people from the excesses of their representatives. The basic problem with this arrangement is that it implied that the people were better off entrusting power to someone they hadn't chosen for themselves, which went against the presumption in favour of popular election. The other problem was that it meant trusting Napoleon. Sieyès at least had the excuse in 1799 that Bonaparte was a relatively unknown quantity. In 1815 Constant should have known better.

Yet despite the humiliations that this period of French history heaped on their respective claims to understand how politics works, the argument between Sieyès and Constant—between variety and vigilance as the possible linchpins of a genuinely liberal democratic political order—still makes sense today. Both schemes of politics have their perils. Constant was right to suspect that excessive complexity and multiplicity in representative arrangements can turn people off politics altogether, if they cannot find a clear, direct line of accountability to their political masters. On the other hand, it is also true that too much emphasis on vigilance can lead to suspicion, and suspicion can lead to mistrust.[24] The challenge of modern politics is to find a form of representative government that is not so complex that it makes a mockery of the idea of popular representation, but not so simple that it sets the people against their politicians. Both Sieyès and Constant understood this dilemma, even if they did not ultimately resolve it. It remains the central dilemma for all constitution-makers and state builders to this day. It is one that the current architects of European constitutional order are still struggling to resolve, and show little signs of even having understood. Their strategy of trying to sell an extremely complicated and cumbersome constitution (in its way, a much more obfuscatory document than anything proposed by Sieyès) through the excessively crude device of the plebiscitary referendum has clearly failed. But for now they have nothing to put in its place, certainly nothing that can compare with the clarity and political insight of the solutions put forward by Constant and Sieyès.[25]

Meanwhile, across Europe and beyond, well-established states are finding that their citizens are starting to lose interest in representative politics. Turnout is on the decline almost everywhere, and many people are starting to wonder what their elected representatives are for. For Sieyès, the guiding principle behind any satisfactory representative system was the idea of the nation. The French people had a clear political identity because they constituted a nation, just as the French nation had a stable political character only when it was constituted by its people. It is not clear that this is true any more. The idea of the nation state is under threat, from broader political and social interests. The question no one has yet resolved is whether it is possible to transcend national politics while still retaining the coherence of a popularly constituted representative system. Contemporary democratic theory has for the most part studiously avoided this question, preferring to concentrate on academic schemes of deliberative democracy and international justice. But this is the question that matters. If politics is to move beyond the nation state, we are at the beginning and not the end of the political revolution that will bring this about.

Political thought does not currently lack revolutionary thinkers who, having tired of the sterility of so much academic political theory, are on the lookout for radical alternatives to the status quo, ranging from global parliaments to new versions of the politics of the streets. There is also no shortage of world-weary voices ready to point out that these schemes are invariably founded on nothing more than the advanced stages of wishful thinking. But what we do currently lack are political thinkers, and indeed politicians, willing to argue for radical alternatives to the status quo in terms that can make sense of, rather than merely repudiating, the complexity of our current political arrangements. The danger of revolutionary political thought is that it can end up wishing the past away. The danger of conservative political thought is that it can end up mistaking the past for the future. The hardest thing of all is to find a way of harnessing the possibilities contained in the present. This can only be done by remaining sensitive to the simultaneous pull of simplicity and complexity in political affairs, and recognizing the risks of trying to combine them. It also needs a certain amount of luck. A well-known recent book on Europe by an American—Larry Siedentop's *Democracy in Europe*—whose title aped that of a better-known, earlier book on the United States by a European—Alexis de Tocqueville's *Democracy in America*—posed the question, "Where are our Madisons?"[26] But it is not just another Madison we need. It is another Sieyès.

CHAPTER TEN

EPILOGUE: VIRTUAL POLITICS

The aide said that guys like me were "in what we call the reality-based community", which he defined as people who "believe that solutions emerge from your judicious study of discernible reality". I nodded and murmured something about enlightenment principles and empiricism. He cut me off. "That's not the way the world really works anymore", he continued. "We're an empire now, and when we act, we create our own reality. And while you're studying that reality—judiciously, as you will—we'll act again, creating other new realities, which you can study too, and that's how things will sort out. We're history's actors ... and you, all of you, will be left to just study what we do."

Ron Suskind, *New York Times Magazine*, October 2004

There often seems to be something unreal about contemporary politics. Certainly, politics seems unreal to many of the people who have lost interest in it. The complaint of those who increasingly choose not to vote, to participate, to follow, to take any interest at all in the doings of their elected representatives, is that politics means nothing to them. It is a game, played by initiates for their own delight, cheered on by their hangers-on in the media, who understand the rules but can no longer explain them to their diminishing, distracted, fragmented audiences. Of course, the politicians and their hangers-on in the media are aware of this, and are constantly looking for new ways to make the game accessible to outsiders. They talk up what they do whenever they can, emphasizing the real difference that politics can make to the lives of even the most distracted individuals. But this constant insistence on the significance of politics in the face of widespread popular indifference often serves to make things worse. Listening to politicians boast of their own indispensability before a sceptical public simply reinforces the impression that politics is a self-important, self-referential, self-indulgent activity. Politics is all of these things, and has always been so. But it is the impression that counts, and for now the pervasive impression is that the politicians are puffing themselves up, for no one's benefit but their own.

This impression has been reinforced over the past few years by the war on terror. On the one hand, the attacks on September 11 provided politicians with a perfect illustration of how much politics still matters, and how foolish it would be for the electorates of the West to assume that nothing was at stake in the choices that they make. On the other hand, voters in many Western states have become suspicious of all claims that politicians make about the significance of what they do. The war on terror is so obvious a means by which to enhance both the power and prestige of national politicians that it is easy to assume that this must be its primary purpose. As a result, it is also easy to assume that the ongoing threat of terrorism has been inflated by the politicians, or even invented by them altogether, in order to keep politics and political power centre stage in the life of the nation.[1] On this view, the very thing that is supposed to have reconnected national politics with a sense of reality is itself essentially unreal.

This view has much more pull in some places than in others. For large swathes of European public opinion the war on terror is assumed to be a political contrivance, but this assumption is not widely shared in the United States, where the war on terror seems much more real. The obvious explanation for the difference is that Europe was not attacked on September 11, whereas the United States was. The emotional impact of the attacks was sufficient to persuade many Americans that they faced a real enemy, against whom they had no choice but to fight. That emotional impact was felt elsewhere, but it did not last more than a few weeks. Because it did not last, other terrorist attacks outside the United States have not had the same effect on public opinion as the original attacks of September 11. For example, the Madrid train bombings of March 2004 did not significantly alter the scepticism of many Europeans concerning both the war on terror and

the politicians who were leading it. There were two main reasons for this. First, the bombings were seen by many as a consequence of Spain's involvement in the US's wars, and therefore
in part the fault of the politicians who had chosen to embrace
these conflicts. Second, the Spanish government was widely perceived to have sought to cover-up Al Qaeda's involvement in the
attacks, which occurred three days before a national election, by
blaming them on Basque separatists. Together, these factors combined to reinforce, rather than to counter, the sense that the war
on terror was a politicians' war, and that it was the politicians
who should pay the price (as José Maria Aznar's government
did).

The bomb attacks that struck London on 7 July 2005 were different from those in Madrid, but not that different. They took
place shortly after, rather than immediately before, a general election, so that the question of the government's survival was never
remotely at stake. Moreover, the Labour government had learned
the lessons of Madrid—as it had learned the lessons of September 11—and conducted itself in the immediate aftermath of the
bombings with calm, openness and dignity (though the same cannot be said of the London Metropolitan Police). At no point in
the days and weeks that followed did Tony Blair or his ministers
appear to have their eye on any party-political advantage that
might be derived from the attacks (a stance which worked to the
advantage of their party very well). But equally Blair could not risk
deploying the rhetoric of war in order to bolster party-political or
wider national unity. The reasons for this were fairly clear. First,
he was determined to challenge any link that might exist in the
public mind between the carnage in London and the carnage that
was taking place almost daily on the streets of Iraq—the London
bombings were emphatically not to be seen as a consequence of
the war in Iraq, even as they were understood to be a continuation of the wider struggle against terrorism that had prompted
it. Because of Iraq, the language of a war on terror has come to
cut both ways for Blair, as it did not for George Bush in the days
and weeks following September 11. Second, the discovery that the
London bombers were home-grown—regular, workaday citizens
who had passed almost unnoticed under the blanket surveillance
of the British security services—meant that any characterization

of the attacks as part of a wider war raised the possibility that such a war might become a civil one. Bush had had a foreign enemy to attack, and did so with gusto. Aznar also confronted a foreign enemy but chose, catastrophically, to target a domestic one. In July 2005, Blair found himself in the unenviable position of having to pass off a domestic threat as essentially foreign in nature. It is small wonder that his martial rhetoric was a little subdued.

There is also a question of scale. The London bombings killed 56 people (including the 4 suicide bombers), the Madrid bombings 190, compared with the 2749 now believed to have died in the attack on the World Trade Centre (the earliest estimates for the September 11 attacks, which stood for a number of weeks, put the death toll at around 7000). The London and Madrid attacks, terrible as they were, were both less terrible and less surprising than the attacks on New York and Washington. Nor did they produce any images that could compare with the mesmerizing pictures of the two planes crashing into the Twin Towers; indeed, it is hard to imagine any images that could compete with those generated on September 11 for sheer aesthetic and emotional power. Yet even in a world that is now much more used to acts of terrorist violence on a grand scale, it is still possible to imagine some future atrocity, costing many thousands of lives, that would rally the peoples of Europe behind their politicians—as Americans rallied behind theirs—and dispel any sense that the war on terror is simply a facade for something else. In these circumstances, the politicians would no longer need to insist on the significance of the struggles in which they were engaged. Terrorism—terrorism of the right kind, the most shocking kind—retains the unique capacity to make those struggles real.

The possibility that some event may occur that will either galvanize an electorate, as American voters were galvanized after September 11, 2001, or antagonize them, as Spanish voters were antagonized in March 2004, or simply unsettle them, as happened in London in July 2005, explains much of the uncertainty that hangs over the politics of the West. We are, all of us, waiting for something to happen. National politicians know that their fate depends to a large extent on events they can readily imagine but cannot reliably anticipate, and whose impact on their own futures is largely beyond their control. Many politicians are also, unsurprisingly, torn in how they think about these events. They know that a sceptical public is likely to remain sceptical in the absence of some catastrophic confirmation of the politicians' worst fears. But they also know that no sane politician could wish for catastrophic confirmation of the dangers they have been warning against. The kind of shock to the system that national politicians need to remind people that politics still matters is also the kind of shock that no politician can really want, and all of them must fear, knowing that it is impossible be sure how the voters will apportion the blame. So we keep waiting—waiting for Osama—and as we wait we cast around absurdly for other events, other catastrophes, to supply the kind of meaning we are looking for.

"Could the tsunami disaster be a turning point for the world?" asked the front page of *The Independent* newspaper on 4 January 2005. The answer, of course, is no, because such disasters, though they can engage the emotions of onlookers powerfully, only engage them briefly, before the onlookers return to their more everyday concerns. The tsunami calamity was routinely described in the days after it happened as the worst natural disaster in history, when it was simply the worst disaster to occur within the operative memory of an information-crazed age. Saturation coverage of the event, and of the substantial but still relatively trivial amounts of aid it conjured up, gave a fleeting impression of a more cooperative and charitable world. But there was no enduring political content to this vision, which has since faded away. Still, the tsunami disaster was not without political consequences, both for the national governments of the countries affected,[2] and also for the politicians who sought to capture and channel the glancing interest of the wider world. The common run of political affairs is always vulnerable to acts of God, and such events have the capacity to raise politicians up and to cast them down, seemingly at random. Politicians also retain their own capacity to exploit unforeseen challenges and disasters, and to use them to champion the causes on which they had already set their hearts. There is nothing new in politics being subject to the vicissitudes of fate, and in politicians being tested by their ability to cope with what is thrown at them. Why should the war on terror be any different?

In many respects, grand acts of terrorism are no different from any other twists and turns of political fortune. The victims who died on September 11, 2001, were hideously unlucky, but George Bush was lucky to be in office on that day, and like many politicians before him, he rode his luck, turning it to his electoral advantage. He also tried to make his own luck in Iraq, with much more limited success. Politicians are always liable to be made or broken by events beyond their control. But what is new about the world at the beginning of the twenty-first century is that these events are no longer anticipated as intrusions into the familiar, ongoing narrative of political life, where politicians, parties and governments contend for power on the basis of their private desires and public ideologies. The anticipation of these events has now become a kind of public ideology in its own right. Waiting for Osama currently provides a large part of the narrative of politics itself.

What does this new ideology consist in? It has three central components. First, it rests on the assumption that global terrorism has no ideology of its own beyond the perpetration of acts of violence in and for themselves. Terrorism is understood as a nihilist phenomenon, and the terrorists themselves, from the perspective of a political universe in which morality still holds sway, as "evil". Because terrorism is simply destructive, it cannot be negotiated or engaged with. It stands outside the conventional structures of credible politics, which is why terrorist acts remain intrusions into political life, rather than a part of it. Second, the threat of this form of terrorism is understood to be pervasive, and the possibility of intrusion to be a permanent one. It could come at any time, in almost any place, for reasons wholly unrelated to the political positions adopted by national governments: on this account, everyone in the West should see themselves as equally vulnerable, regardless of any concessions or evasions that might be suggested by particular political leaders. France is no safer than Britain or Spain, just as neither Britain nor Spain turned out to be any safer than the United States. There is therefore nothing to lose by confronting the threat head-on, with force. Third, lurking somewhere in the background of this sense of pervasive threat is a glimpse of a world without threat, in which the terrorists have been vanquished, and freedom reigns. The war on terror is understood by those who prosecute it as a war without any conventional limit or time-frame, but nevertheless as a war that can ultimately be won.[3]

This is the ideology that is shared by George Bush and Tony Blair. Still, for all the clarity of vision that is claimed on its behalf, it remains an elusive doctrine. It is hard to know what it really means. For example, it rests on the assumption that acts of terrorist violence are inevitable, yet it insists that individual politicians must behave as though each particular act of violence is avoidable. Politicians like Blair are required to behave as though such an attack is simply a matter of time, while also conducting a policy that is designed to protect the public at large from all possible attacks of this kind. Once an attack comes, the argument does not change, but is merely reinforced: what happened in London in July 2005 was taken to confirm both the unavoidability of terrorist violence and the imperative to avoid the possibility of all such violence in the future. In the tortured words of Sir John Stevens, then Chief of the London Metropolitan Police, speaking a year before the July bombings: "We do know that we have actually stopped terrorist attacks happening in London but, as the Prime Minister and Home Secretary have said, there is an inevitability that some sort of attack will get through, but my job is to make sure that does not happen."[4] Meanwhile, the distant glimpse that is simultaneously offered of a world without terrorist threat, with its promise of a final escape from political violence, ignores the potential for violence that lurks in all forms of politics, and all forms of policing, however successful. In politics, as all responsible politicians understand, there can be no final escape from the possibility of violence. This is a war that can never be won. So the war on terror treats as inevitable the violence that it is designed to avoid, and it treats as ultimately avoidable the violence that politicians know to be inevitable. It is not surprising, therefore, that a lingering air of unreality clings to it, and to contemporary politics as a whole.

Yet the very elusiveness of this ideology is part of its appeal, for the politicians who choose to promote it. It is simultaneously a highly flexible, and a more-or-less impermeable doctrine. This combination has proved an extremely successful vote-winning strategy. The all-or-nothing view of the war on terror, which sees the terrorist threat either everywhere or nowhere, is a very difficult one to counter. Certainly, it proved very hard for John Kerry to counter during the American presidential campaign of 2004, because it is not, in the words of one commentator, a "fact-dependent" picture of the world.[5] The fact that global terrorism is not as pervasive as it is often presented—there were no WMD in Iraq; the Saddam regime was neither a sponsor nor an ally of Islamic jihadism; international terrorism is not a well-organized global network of terror cells, but an ill-defined collection of groups with often disparate goals—did not prevent Bush from gaining re-election, because Bush was campaigning on the basis that the war on terror only makes sense if everything hangs together; and conversely, that if things do not hang together, then the war cannot be fought at all. The choice Bush presented to the American people was either to continue the struggle regardless of the facts, or to give up on it altogether. It was a false choice in its own terms, but it generated a real political one, between Bush and his opponent. Bush was able to present his false choice with more conviction than Kerry was able to present the alternative, which was to offer a real choice between the many different ways of confronting the terrorist threat, some more reasonable, reliable, sustainable than others. By a narrow margin, the American public found Bush's false choice to be more real than Kerry's real one.

Bush was aided in his campaign by having a clear, resonant, sanctified language in which to express his convictions. "We are in a conflict between good and evil, and America will call evil by its name," he told the graduating class at West Point. But it is a sign of the flexibility of this ideology that it equally well serves the purposes of Tony Blair's New Labour Party, and can be couched in an alternative language of secular, pragmatic progressivism. Addressing the Labour Party conference in September 2004, for the last time before the general election, Blair sought to connect the war on terror with the traditional centre-left cause of social progress. In his speech, Blair sketched two competing views of international terrorism. "One view is that there are isolated individuals, extremists, engaged in essentially isolated acts of terrorism … If you believe this, we carry on the same path as before 11 September. We try not to provoke them and hope in time they will wither." On the other view, "you believe September 11 changed the world; that Bali, Beslan, Madrid and scores of other atrocities that never make the news are part of the same threat and the only path to take is to confront this terrorism, remove it root and branch." Blair then invited his audience to choose.[6]

There are two things to say about this choice. First, it was and remains a nonsensical one, even after London has been added to that list. It does not follow from the fact that you believe that separate acts of terrorism can be isolated, that you must also believe either that they are the work of "isolated individuals", or that the only thing to do is to avoid provoking the terrorists. You might equally believe that, having isolated the causes of terrorism in different parts of the world (and the causes of terrorism in Leeds and London are not simply the same as the causes of terrorism in Baghdad and Kabul), the only thing to do is to confront them, with as much force as possible. But second, Blair has consistently understood this choice as essential to the future of progressive politics as an electoral force. Indeed, he believes that it is this choice that will determine whether his own preferred brand of politics can survive at the polls. Yet because the choice is a false one, it is a bizarre inversion of progressivism that he has to offer the British electorate. It rests on the presupposition that all future progress may be threatened by any given act of terrorism, because all acts of terrorism must be related. Blair's view of what he calls "the reality of the future" is that it is a place where everything is connected in a great chain of being, where it is not possible to sever the links between separate political challenges in order to identify what can be changed, and what cannot. In the United States, this world-turned-upside-down version of progressive politics, in which conservative certainties are simply annexed from the past so that they can be played out at whim across the vast, uncharted terrain of the future, isn't called progressivism, or even neoprogressivism. It's called neoconservatism.

What Blair has been consistently unable to offer, any more than George Bush, are good reasons why this view of the future should be true. Blair cannot simply let it rest, as his American counterpart has been willing to, on a question of faith. Instead, he has been forced to fall back on the claim that September 11 changed the balance of risk for all politicians, including progressive ones. Yet September 11, 2001, did not change the balance of risk in the way that Blair implies, and nor did July 7, 2005. If it is the case that terrorism is an all-or-nothing struggle between order and chaos, then no single event, however dramatic, can have made the difference. But if what he means is that September 11 gave huge impetus to worldwide terrorism, and inspired terrorists across the globe to raise the stakes, and seek to link their disparate activities in a common cause, then it is hard to understand why the enemies of terrorism should acquiesce in their collective struggle. Better surely to attempt to disaggregate global terrorism, and to sever the links, than to build them up at every opportunity. It is true that Iraq has become an excellent place for any terrorist with global ambitions to further the common cause of chaos. But the people who made it such a good location for global terrorism can hardly use the fact of global terrorism to justify what they are doing there.

If Saddam had had WMD, and if the war had successfully disarmed him of those weapons, Blair's progressivism might make some sense. He could then argue that Saddam's regime presented a particular problem, which had to be resolved in its own terms, unpleasant as the resolution might be. But in the absence of those weapons, Iraq can only be justified as part of a struggle in which nothing makes sense in its own terms, and everything is of a piece with everything else. "The irony for me", Blair declared in the autumn of 2004, "is that I, as a progressive politician, know that despite the opposition of so much of progressive politics to what I've done, the only lasting way to defeat this terrorism is through progressive politics." And how did he, as a progressive politician, choose to characterize this endeavour? As "the oldest struggle humankind knows, between liberty or oppression, tolerance or hate; between government by terror or by the rule of law."[7] These are not the antitheses of a genuine progressivism; they are the antitheses of neoconservatism, which is, as the name suggests, simply another form of conservatism. The twist is that whereas traditional conservatives assume nothing can be made better without making something else worse, neoconservatives assume that, so long as an action is undertaken in the cause of freedom, nothing can be made worse without making something else better. This, essentially, is the neoconservative defence of the occupation of Iraq. At the time of writing, it is hard to see it as anything more than mere superstition. The genuine antitheses of progressivism are between truth and superstition, knowledge and ignorance, common sense and ancestor-worship. But truth, knowledge and common sense—the vestiges of enlightenment principles and empiricism—are not what motivates the war on terror.

In a domestic context, Blair's inverted progressivism offers another twist on conservative assumptions, this time concerning fear. Blair and his ministers have repeatedly argued that, since September 11, it has become necessary to allay the public's fears, as a precondition for making progress on wider questions of social justice. One of the chief architects of this strategy, as well as its most enthusiastic exponent, was Blair's Home Secretary from 2001 to 2004, David Blunkett. In the autumn of 2004, Blunkett was driven from office by a scandal about a lover, a nanny and a visa application; a scandal which, in the way of such things, now seems somewhat unreal. (Blunkett subsequently returned to government, Tony Blair having decided that the result of the 2005 election served to wipe the slate clean. In his new role, Blunkett continued to play the part he had carved out for himself in his previous one—after the London bombings he left flowers of condolence at the scene of one of the attacks with the handwritten message: "In sorrow that I was not able to do more to save you.") Before his initial departure, Blunkett did his best to set out the case for a progressive form of politics founded on an engagement with fear. His defence of the British government's programme of anti-terror measures, which included the indefinite detention of foreign suspects without trial, and the proposed introduction of compulsory identity cards, was as follows.

> People do not open their hearts and minds, and hear messages, particularly progressive messages, if, underpinning that, subliminally, is a fear of what's happening around them, and if they're more insecure when they go out, and they walk on the street. If they fear, because of September 11, and its aftermath, what is happening in terms of the new forms of threat, then we have to provide that stability and security, if they're going to be able to hear the messages about reducing

the fear of difference, about being able to create a civilized
and caring and compassionate society.[8]

In other words, you have to tackle fear head-on if you ever want
to move beyond it. In narrow party-political terms, this strategy
made a good deal of sense, and it helped Blair's government out-
flank the conservative opposition on questions of national security. It also conformed with the central political lesson of George
Bush's presidential campaign of 2004: terrorism will serve the
interests of the politician who can make it an all-or-nothing issue.
But outside the close confines of electoral power politics, the case
for progressive politics founded on the conquest of fear is an
empty one. Progress cannot be predicated on the absence of fear,
because fear is endemic in any system of politics. You cannot bully
people into leaving their fears behind.

The war on terror has not, and will not, succeed in conquering
people's fears. But it has succeeded in giving them something else
to be afraid of: fear itself, which has been demonized, and pushed
to the margins of democratic life.[9] This demonizing of fear means
that terrorism can no longer be compared with any of the other
threats we might face, because terrorism represents nothing less
than the threat of a fearful existence per se. Terrorism threatens
us with terror, whereas global warming merely threatens us with
disaster. Yet the idea that a terrorist attack—any terrorist attack—
is something to be feared above all else is unsustainable in the
long run, whatever short-term electoral gains may be reaped from
promoting it. During any lengthy hiatus between terrorist attacks,
it will become increasingly hard to remember what it is we have
to be afraid of. On the other hand, whenever an attack comes, then
we will discover, as Londoners discovered in July 2005, that we
have no choice but to confront our fears, and deal with them; life
will carry on, and politics with it. The individual politicians who
are currently conducting the war against terror must know this,
though they also know that if they get the blame for the attack
in question, politics will carry on without them. In this sense,
the politicians have more to fear from acts of terrorism than the
public they are trying to protect, which is why the threat has to
be overplayed.

Yet the same politicians who exaggerate the threat that individual acts of terrorism pose to the political life of the established

democracies are also forced to downplay the threat they pose to the political life of the states they wish to democratize. Britain and the United States, robust and enduring democracies, must be protected from each and every terrorist attack that threatens them. Meanwhile in Iraq, no single terrorist attack, however terrible, can be allowed to derail the democratic process. The aftermath of the Iraq war offers a kind of mirror image of the democratic life of the nations that brought it about. The democracies of the West are to be protected against terrorism at all costs; yet no amount of terrorist activity in a country like Iraq can be set against the value of democracy there. In the run-up to the Iraqi elections of 2005, George Bush and Tony Blair insisted that each and every terrorist atrocity was to be discounted against the worth of what they were trying to achieve by introducing democracy to Iraq, however token and fragile that electoral process might seem. So, depending on where you look, democracy can be both infinitely vulnerable and more-or-less invulnerable to the threat of terrorist attack.

Here, finally, the charge of hypocrisy seems impossible for politicians like Bush and Blair to avoid. The all-or-nothing approach to terrorism means that in some parts of the world the threat to democracy of individual acts of violence is held to be everything, and in others it is nothing. The truth lies somewhere in between. Democracies like Britain and the United States are well able to withstand acts of terrorist violence, and the threat of terrorism to the life of these nations should not be overplayed.[10] At the same time, the prospects for democracy in Iraq have been gravely damaged by the scale of the terrorist assault unleashed there since the American occupation. But the occupiers do not accept this. The war on terror requires that after each act of terrorist violence in Iraq, the struggle simply begins again, because anything else would be handing a victory to the terrorists. The deaths of the many thousands of real victims of this terrorism cannot be weighed against the prospects of a peaceful, democratic future for Iraq, however remote. At the same time, in the West, where real victims of terrorism since September 11 remain notably thin on the ground, nothing can be weighed against the prospect of adding to this slender toll. In the war on terror, real deaths count for less than unreal ones.

Hypocrisy is nothing new in politics. Politicians, including all democratic politicians, have always valued the lives of their own citizens over those of foreigners. No politician, particularly no democratic politicians, can afford to worry more about the past than the future. It is part of the brutal reality of politics that deaths, once they occur, simply become part of the political fabric, to be spun as the politicians chose; it is the deaths that are to come that matter, because it is in the future prospect of death that uncertainty lies. It is for this reason that national politicians will go to almost any lengths to secure the lives of their own citizens. Equally, it is why, in the cause of that security, they will be cavalier with the lives of almost anyone else.

This sort of brutal, pragmatic political reasoning—the nasty side of modern politics—is often associated with the thought of Thomas Hobbes. The world we now inhabit, dominated by a few, immensely powerful, intensely paranoiac states, and one state above all others, is routinely described as Hobbesian. It is true that Hobbes's political thought was founded on fear, and that he reduced all fear down to the anticipated fear of death. But ours is not a Hobbesian world, because Hobbes was not a hypocrite. His conception of politics was realistic, but it was also genuinely progressive, because he understood that political progress depended on not being hypocritical about fear. Hobbes believed that a state founded on a recognition of the centrality of fear to all human struggles could rescue individuals from the fearful lives they endured in the state of nature, where they were prey not only to an endless suspicion of each other, but also to peddlers of vain and false philosophies, scaring them with empty tales of ghosts and fairies and demons, "as men fright Birds from the Corn with an empty doublet, a hat, and a crooked stick".[11] The state existed to free us from these needless anxieties, and to provide us with something of which it made sense to be afraid. Political fear, for Hobbes, was reasonable fear, and the more reasonable it was, the less there was to fear in it. In the end, Hobbes believed that fear might wither away, if only we would stop trying to resist it, and sought to make sense of it instead. It was the state—the only institution that could make sense of fear, if it chose—that would guide us towards the goal of all politics, which Hobbes called "peace". In this sense Hobbes's political philosophy is more utopian than is usually supposed, though how utopian it appears depends on how distant the ultimate prospect of peace has become. The fact that it looks almost entirely utopian viewed from the perspective of Blair, and Bush, and the world that they represent, shows how far we have come from Hobbes's vision of the state, and how far we have to go to get back to it.

NOTES

CHAPTER ONE
Introduction: September 11 and the New World Order

1. Hugo Young, "The free world must decide how its values are protected", *The Guardian*, 13 September 2001 (www.guardian.co.uk).

2. Matthew Parris, "The bigger they come, the harder they fall", *The Times*, 15 September 2001 (www.timesonline.co.uk).

3. Tony Blair, "The opportunity society", Speech to Labour Party Conference, 28 September 2004 (www.labour.org.uk).

4. Dick Cheney, Speech to Republican Party Convention, 1 September 2004 (www.gopconvention.com).

5. The same applies to critics of the restrictions on civil liberties introduced in the aftermath of the terrorist attacks. One of the staunchest of these in Britain has been the journalist Simon Jenkins, who wrote of a debate in the House of Commons in December 2004 on the introduction of identity cards: "One MP after another stood up to parrot that '9/11 changes everything'. Like Reds under the bed, this slogan has become the catch-all for any restriction on civil freedom." (Simon Jenkins, "I never thought I'd say this, but thank you to the Lords, the Libs and the law", *The Times*, 22 December 2004 (www.timesonline.co.uk).)

6. See John Kampfner, *Blair's Wars* (London: Free Press, 2003), especially pp. 140–41 and 263–64, where he quotes an unnamed British official: "Bush listens politely, agrees that the points being made are good. He says things like: 'I'll do what I can.' As soon as Tony is in the air on the way back home Bush forgets the conversation and we know he has forgotten. There have been several moments when Tony felt Bush had got it. Tony would say things like: 'We really are on the same page. Bush has finally clicked.' Then a few hours later soberness would set in and he would realise he hadn't."

7. Tony Blair, "Doctrine of the international community", in *Neo-Conservatism*, ed. Irwin Stelzer (London: Atlantic Books, 2004), p. 107.

8. Ibid.

9. Tony Blair, "The threat of global terrorism", Speech in Sedgefield, County Durham, 5 March 2004 (www.scottishlabour.org.uk).

10. See Peter Stothard, *30 Days: A Month at the Heart of Blair's War* (London: HarperCollins, 2003), especially pp. 106–07.

11. Michael Ignatieff, *The Warrior's Honor: Ethnic War and the Modern Conscience* (New York: Henry Holt, 1997), pp. 18–19.

12. This was a repeated remark in Cheney's stump speech during the campaign (see, for example, "Vice President's remarks in Los Lunas, New Mexico", 31 October 2004 (www.whitehouse.gov)), following a quote attributed to John Kerry in a *New York Times Magazine* interview published on 10 October 2004 ("We have got to get back to the place we were, where terrorists are not the focus of our lives, they're a nuisance").

13. David Hare captures the full flavour of this cynicism in his play about the build-up to the Iraq war, *Stuff Happens*: "**Cheney**: OK, I admit it, if we want him, Blair's good at the high moral tone. If you want to go into battle with a preacher sitting on top of a tank, that's fine by me. But bear in mind, preacher's one more to carry. Needs rations, needs a latrine, like everyone else." (David Hare, *Stuff Happens* (London: Faber and Faber, 2004), p. 104.)

14. Ulrich Beck, *World Risk Society* (Cambridge: Polity, 1999), p. 137.

15. The journalist Simon Hoggart, commenting on Blair's performance in the House of Commons on 23 February 2005—Blair had said on that occasion: "If there were to be a serious terrorist act in this country, and afterwards it was thought that we hadn't taken the measures necessary, believe me, no one, no one, would be talking about civil liberties"—captured the essence of this appeal. "Suppose hundreds of people died in a mass bombing, and the government knew the identity of the suicide bomber whose limbs were being carried away in the same body bags as his victims—and had been unable to do enough to stop him? And suppose this happened just before an election? There are horrors of which those of us who are not elected never have to face." (Simon Hoggart, "Howard's fury at lack of time for desperate choice", *The Guardian*, 24 February 2005 (www.guardian.co.uk).)

16. Blair, "Doctrine of the international community", p. 109.

17. Tony Blair, Speech to the United States Congress, 18 July 2003 (www.number-10.gov.uk).

18. See, for example, Dennis Thompson, *Restoring Responsibility: Ethics in Government, Business and Healthcare* (Cambridge University Press, 2004), especially "Introduction: the need for institutional responsibility".

19. See, for example, *The Norwegian Study of Power and Democracy* (www.sv.uio.no/mutr/english/index.html). A summary of some of the findings of this study is given in "Wealth and decay", Stein Ringen, *Times Literary Supplement*, 13 February 2004 (www.the-tls.co.uk).

20. *European Constitution*, Article 1–3: "The Union's Objectives" (www.europa.eu.int/constitution).

21. If this does happen, it will not happen in the short term. "*Perhaps* over decades such functional arrangements, if made subject and properly answerable to national parliaments, can develop along institutional evolutionary lines into organs of representative federal government." (John Gillingham, *European Integration 1950–2003: Superstate or New Market Economy* (Cambridge University Press, 2003), p. 484.)

22. For example, see Jeremy Rifkin, *Why Europe's Vision of the Future Is Quietly Eclipsing the American Dream* (Cambridge: Polity, 2004) and Mark Leonard, *Why Europe Will Run the 21st Century* (London: Fourth Estate, 2004).

For a more balanced view, see Timothy Garton Ash, *Free World: Why the Crisis of the West Reveals the Opportunity of Our Time* (London: Allen Lane, 2004).

23. A good example of this was provided by the acrimonious exchanges in the *London Review of Books* between European and American intellectuals in the weeks immediately following September 11, 2001. A fairly narrow constituency of highbrow readers was deeply and profoundly divided in their emotional response, on the basis primarily of national identity (see *London Review of Books*, Volume 23, Numbers 19–23, especially contributions by Mary Beard and Marjorie Perloff).

24. Francis Fukuyama, *State Building: Governance and World Order in the Twenty-First Century* (London: Profile Books, 2004), p. 159.

25. A similar case for politicians and the publics they represent to get used to having it both ways has been provided by Anne-Marie Slaughter. She writes: "National governments and national government officials must remain the primary focus of political loyalty and the primary actors on the global stage. If, however, they are to be actors in national and global policymaking simultaneously, officials would have to be able to think at once in terms of the national and the global interest and to sort out the relative priorities of the two on a case-by-case basis... In short, to avoid global government, national government officials will have to learn to think globally. Following the old Roman god of gates and doors, or beginnings and endings, they must become Janus-faced, with one face pointing forward and the other backwards. In this case, however, one face must look inward and the other outward, translating quickly and smoothly from the domestic to the international sphere." (Anne-Marie Slaughter, *A New World Order* (Princeton University Press, 2004), pp. 234–35.)

26. The shining exception to this is Philip Bobbitt, *The Shield of Achilles: War, Peace and the Course of History* (London: Allen Lane, 2002) (see Chapter Seven).

27. Constant's most resonant account of the temptations and perils of seeking to escape the public domain and indulge in the delights of mere privacy is provided in his novella *Adolphe* (1816) (see Benjamin Constant, *Adolphe*, ed. Leonard Tancock (London: Penguin, 1964)).

28. Benjamin Constant, *Political Writings*, ed. Biancamaria Fontana (Cambridge University Press, 1988), pp. 327–28.

29. For the definitive neo-Kantian statement of this position, see John Rawls, *The Law of Peoples* (Cambridge, MA: Harvard University Press, 1999), p. 36: "I follow Kant's lead in *Perpetual Peace* in thinking that a world government—by which I mean a unified political regime with the legal powers normally exercised by central government—would either be a global despotism or else would rule over a fragile empire torn by frequent civil strife as various regions and peoples tried to gain their political freedom and autonomy."

30. For instance, Isaiah Berlin identified Constant as unequivocally on one side in the great political divide between the advocates of "negative" and "positive" liberty (see Berlin, *Four Essays on Liberty* (Oxford University Press, 1969)).

CHAPTER TWO
Tony Blair and the Politics of Good Intentions

1. "Rumsfeld's hostage", *The Guardian*, 1 April 2003 (www.guardian.co.uk).

2. *Hansard's Parliamentary Debates* (CXCIII, June–July 1868), col. 525.

3. Ibid, col. 522.

4. Ibid.

5. Ibid, col. 525–26.

6. See, for example, Tony Blair, Speech to the United States Congress, 18 July 2003 (www.number-10.gov.uk).

7. In the most recent English translation, the title is given as "The profession and vocation of politics", to capture the double sense of the term *Beruf* (see Max Weber, *Political Writings*, ed. Peter Lassman and Richard Speirs (Cambridge University Press, 1994), p. 309).

8. See Richard Grunberger, *Red Rising in Bavaria* (London: Barker, 1973).

9. See M. J. Bonn, *Wandering Scholar* (London: Cohen and Bent, 1949), p. 213.

10. Weber, *Political Writings*, p. 362.

11. Ibid.

12. Ibid.

13. Ibid, p. 355.

14. Ibid, p. 356.

15. Ibid.

16. See Marianne Weber, *Max Weber: A Biography*, ed. Harry Zohn (New York: Wiley, 1975).

17. Bonn, *Wandering Scholar*, p. 207.

18. Michael Walzer, "Political action: the problem of dirty hands", *Philosophy and Public Affairs* (2:2, 1973), p. 177.

19. Ibid.

20. Ibid.

21. See H. C. G. Matthew, *Gladstone 1809–98* (Oxford University Press, 1997). Matthew summarizes Gladstone's own account in his diaries of these episodes as "a strange mixture of detail, thoroughness, generality and principle, carried through with cool efficiency, passion, self-confidence and religious repentance" (p. 92). Gladstone described his dealings with prostitutes as "the chief burden of my soul" (ibid).

22. Weber, *Political Writings*, p. 342.

23. Blair acknowledged at the time that these encounters were part of a political strategy, rather than just a horrible mistake, though he did seem taken aback by some of the hostility he had to endure as a result (see Stothard, *30 Days*, p. 5). The phrase "masochism strategy" came into everyday journalistic parlance during the early days of the 2005 general election campaign, when journalists were encouraged by Downing Street insiders to describe Blair's television encounters with studio audiences in these

terms—the idea being to assemble groups of disgruntled voters in order to allow Blair to treat them with a kind of long-suffering, earnest, sympathetic loftiness. This was meant to show Blair at his best. The difference between Blair and Gladstone is well captured by the thought that it would be hard to imagine the latter deploying his masochistic impulses as a vote-winning strategy, never mind briefing the press about it.

24. Weber, *Political Writings*, p. 357.

25. W. E. Gladstone, *Midlothian Speeches*, ed. M. R. D. Foot (Leicester University Press, 1971), p. 129.

26. Ibid.

27. On Lincoln's Weberian qualities, see James E. Underwood, "Lincoln: a Weberian politician meets the constitution", *Presidential Studies Quarterly* (34:2, 2004), pp. 341–65.

28. Abraham Lincoln, *Speeches and Letters 1832–65*, ed. Paul Argyle (London: John Dent, 1957), p. 269.

29. Ibid, p. 180.

30. *Hansard (House of Commons Debates)*, Volume 330, col. 335 (www.publications.parliament.uk).

31. Weber, *Political Writings*, p. 358.

32. See Noam Chomsky, *The New Military Humanism: Lessons From Kosovo* (London: Pluto Press, 1999).

33. "Interview with Ian McCartney", *New Statesman* (12:563, 1999), pp. 18–19.

34. Siôn Simon, "The Dome may be a failure, but it's a heroic failure", *The Daily Telegraph*, 13 November 2000 (www.telegraph.co.uk).

35. See Blair, "The opportunity society".

36. For a less political, but equally damning, assessment, see *UK National Audit Office Report: The Millennium Dome* (HC 936, 1999/00) and *National Audit Office Report: Winding-up the New Millennium Experience Company Ltd.* (HC 749, 2001/02).

37. Matthew Parris, "Are we witnessing the madness of Tony Blair", *The Times*, 29 March 2003 (www.timesonline.co.uk).

38. Weber, *Political Writings*, p. 367.

39. On Blair's relationship with Brown, see Andrew Rawnsley, *Servants of the People: The Inside Story of New Labour* (London: Hamish Hamilton, 2000), especially pp. 151–56; also Robert Peston, *Brown's Britain* (London: Short Books, 2005).

CHAPTER THREE
Taking a Chance on War: The Worst-Case Scenarios

1. Blair, "The threat of global terrorism".

2. Martin Rees, *Our Final Century: Will the Human Race Survive the Twenty-First Century?* (London: Heinemann, 2003). See also Richard Posner, *Catastrophe: Risk and Response* (Oxford University Press, 2004).

3. Blair, "The threat of global terrorism".

4. Ibid.

5. See, for example, *Protecting Public Health and the Environment: Implementing the Precautionary Principle*, ed. Carolyn Raffensperger and Joel Tickner (Washington, DC: Island Press, 1999).

6. Cass Sunstein, *The Laws of Fear: Beyond the Precautionary Principle* (Cambridge University Press, 2005).

7. Blair, "The threat of global terrorism".

8. Ibid.

9. Ibid.

10. "What amazes me is how many people are happy for Saddam to stay. They ask why we don't get rid of Mugabe, why not the Burmese lot. Yes, let's get rid of them all. I don't because I can't, but when you can, you should." (Stothard, *30 Days*, p. 42).

11. The warning was revealed in the House of Commons Intelligence and Security Committee Report, *Iraqi Weapons of Mass Destruction—Intelligence and Assessment* (September 2003), p. 34 (www.cabinetoffice.gov.uk).

12. *Financial Times*, 16 March 2004 (www.ft.com).

13. Lord Hutton, *Report of the Inquiry into the Circumstances Surrounding the Death of Dr David Kelly C.M.G.* (London: The Stationery Office, 2004), p. 654.

14. Ibid, p. 589.

15. *Hansard (House of Commons Debates)*, Volume 401, col. 760.

16. Ibid, Volume 423, col. 1431.

17. Ibid, Volume 423, col. 1432.

CHAPTER FOUR
Taking a Chance on War: Suez and Iraq

1. See Bob Woodward, *Plan of Attack* (London: Simon & Schuster, 2004), pp. 117–18.

2. Tony Blair, "My pledge to the refugees", BBC News online, 14 May 1999 (www.bbc.co.uk/news). The background to this very personal pledge is described in Kampfner, *Blair's Wars*, pp. 54–55.

3. Blair's support for the London Olympic bid was seen at the time as a big gamble, but again it seems likely that Blair only threw his full personal weight behind the bid once he had been persuaded that London stood an excellent chance of winning. This coincided with the appointment of Sebastian Coe as team leader of the London bid, and the knowledge that Coe could rely on the support of former IOC president Juan Antonio Samaranch if Madrid's bid failed. Blair's risk temperament suggests that the frantic last-minute lobbying he undertook before the IOC vote in Singapore was less a cause of London's ability to triumph than an effect of it.

4. The event is described in D. R. Thorpe, *Eden: The Life and Times of Anthony Eden, First Earl of Avon 1897–1977* (London: Chatto & Windus, 2003), p. 523. (Thorpe records that he was a 13-year-old eyewitness to the event.)

5. Hugh Thomas, *The Suez Affair* (London: Weidenfeld & Nicholson, 1967), p. 163.

6. See ibid, p. 126.

7. Ibid, p. 214.

8. These were: *Iraq's Weapons of Mass Destruction: The Assessment of the British Government* (London: The Stationery Office, September 2002); and the so-called "dodgy dossier", *Iraq—Its Infrastructure of Deception, Concealment and Intimidation* (London: The Stationery Office, February 2003). This second dossier was discovered by Dr Glen Rangwala of Cambridge University to have been extensively plagiarized from an article in the *Middle Eastern Review of International Affairs* by Ibrahim Al-Marashi, entitled "Iraq's Security and Intelligence Network: A Guide and Analysis", first published in September 2002.

9. Dwight D. Eisenhower, *The White House Years. Waging Peace 1956–61* (London: Heinemann, 1965), p. 52.

10. See Leon D. Epstein, *British Politics in the Suez Crisis* (London: Pall Mall Press, 1964).

11. See Peston, *Brown's Britain*, pp. 324–54.

12. In a *Political Studies Association* poll of the best Prime Ministers of the last 100 years taken among academics and published in December 2004, Eden came 20th out of 20 (and was some way behind the 19th placed candidate, Alec Douglas-Home). Blair was ranked 6th. Clement Atlee came top.

CHAPTER FIVE
Who Knows Best?

1. Frederick Schauer, *Profiles, Probabilities and Stereotypes* (Cambridge, MA: The Belknap Press, 2004).

2. Ibid, pp. 259–60.

3. The desire to stamp out prejudice in making these kinds of risk assessments lay behind the conclusion of the 1996 Gore Commission on Airport Security and Racial Profiling, which argued that such assessments should avoid "stereotypes and generalizations" as far as possible. This conclusion is absurd, because risk assessments are impossible without the deployment of some stereotypes and generalizations. (See Schauer, *Profiles, Probabilities and Stereotypes*, pp. 182–83.)

4. *Hansard (House of Commons Debates)*, March 2005, col. 1858.

5. This is distinct from the precautionary principle described in Chapter Three, which states that it always makes sense to take precautions when the risks are unknown. In fact, the reverse it true: it only makes sense to take precautions when you have a reasonably clear idea of the level of risk you are facing.

6. *Judgments—Secretary of State for the Home Department vs. Rehman (AP)*, 11 October 2001, Sections 55–56 (www.parliament.the-stationery-office.co.uk).

7. Ibid. Charles Clarke made the same case in the Commons, though he put it in slightly different terms: "Making control orders requires not only

an examination of factual matters, but an analysis of the overall security situation and assessments of the risks posed by particular individual." (See *Hansard (House of Commons Debates)*, March 2005, col. 1575.)

8. I discuss this wider question of whether terrorism can threaten the state's very existence in Chapter Ten.

9. *Hansard (House of Lords Debates)*, March 2005, col. 859.

10. *Hansard (House of Commons Debates)*, March 2005, col. 1583.

11. "Let us get back to the central question at the heart of this legislation. The reason we are introducing it has nothing to do with people making protests, it is because the police and the security services are advising us that they need these control orders." Tony Blair, House of Commons, 9 March 2005 (*Hansard (House of Commons Debates)*, March 2005, col. 1509).

12. For example: "I intervene early today on the basis that I am not a lawyer and will not make legal points, but I am someone who is in touch with people out there, who feel very threatened and nervous that the dilution of the Government's original policy will be such that they will not have protection." Baroness Wall, House of Lords, 10 March 2005 (*Hansard (House of Lords Debates)*, March 2005, col. 866).

13. James Surowiecki, *The Wisdom of Crowds: Why the Many are Smarter than the Few, and How Collective Wisdom Shapes Business, Economies, Societies and Nations* (New York: Little Brown, 2004).

14. It could be argued that horse racing is a case where everyone is a kind of expert, and that professional gamblers are simply acknowledging that specialist knowledge is not hard to come by (anyone can study the form). But the fact is that not everyone who bets on horses does study the form—some bet on superstition, names, colours, favourite jockeys, mood, impulse, etc.— yet even a crowd containing many individuals of this type will outperform the experts. The reason ignorance can contribute to knowledge in this case is that a crowd that includes everyone, including the ignorant, is highly unlikely to exclude any sources of real information and insight, whereas a group preselected for expertise may be blind to some important details.

15. For a recent account of the durability of this puzzle, see John Dunn, *Setting the People Free: The Story of Democracy* (London: Atlantic Books, 2005).

16. See Ian Shapiro, *The State of Democratic Theory* (Princeton University Press, 2003). Shapiro suggests the possibility a third kind of strong defence, based on the idea that institutionalized competition for power is capable of generating genuinely democratic outcomes. However, this essentially Schumpeterian argument (see Joseph A. Schumpeter, *Capitalism, Socialism and Democracy* (New York: Harper, 1942)) is usually taken as a weaker justification than either the preference-based or cognitive defence (see, for example, Adam Przeworski, "Minimalist conception of democracy: a defense" in *Democracy's Value*, ed. Ian Shapiro and Casiano Hacker-Cordon (Cambridge University Press, 1999)).

17. How debilitating these contradictions are for democratic politics in practice has nevertheless remained a subject of some controversy. For the view that the difficulties with democracy identified by Arrow have been

overstated, see Gerry Mackie, *Democracy Defended* (Cambridge University Press, 2003).

18. John Stuart Mill, *Utilitarianism, On Liberty, Considerations on Representative Government*, ed. J. M. Dent, p. 309 (London: Orion, 1993).

19. Of course, if someone happened to know that the jar containing the jellybeans was distorted in some way, offering a false picture, that person would be better placed to judge the true picture than the crowd. It could be argued that this was the situation with regard to intelligence about Iraq— a number of experts knew that the picture being offered to the general public was distorted, and these were the experts who knew best. However, because the evidence of these distortions only came out after the war, it remains true that the public were better equipped than the balance of expert opinion (which did not acknowledge these distortions but either conspired to produce them, or failed to notice them, depending on how you read the motives of those involved) to judge the nature of the risk, because the public contained many individuals who assumed that the picture being presented was biased in some way. In other words, it was the ignorance of the public that made public opinion better equipped to identify distortion than the expertise of the insiders, which created that distortion in the first place.

20. This is one reason why it could be argued that the British public were better placed to judge this question than the public of other, more sceptical, European nations. It is precisely because the British public were more divided on this question, and political and media coverage reflected these divisions, that there was less risk of the aggregate of public opinion representing a collective prejudgment, as in the case of Germany or France.

21. Surowiecki, *The Wisdom of Crowds*, p. 10.

22. Jean-Jacques Rousseau, *The Social Contract*, ed. Maurice Cranston (London: Penguin, 1969).

23. One notable exception to this was on the night of the 2004 American presidential election, when internet reports of John Kerry's lead in various exit polls led to a sharp contracting in his odds on becoming president (at one point, shortly before the first official results came in, Kerry was trading at 1/3 and Bush at 9/4). This skewering of the odds was the result of an internet cascade of information that distorted the range of opinion that is usually necessary to make an accurate book on a particular event. Anyone who trusted in the long-term betting forecasts of the result (which consistently predicted a Bush win) over the short-term distortions of election night was able to make a lot of money.

24. For a detailed account of the fate of this project, see Surowiecki, *The Wisdom of Crowds*, pp. 77–83.

25. In a YouGov poll (www.yougov.com) conducted between 10 and 12 January 2003, two months before the war, respondents were asked "Have George Bush and Tony Blair convinced you that Saddam Hussein is sufficiently dangerous to justify military action against him?" 34% said yes, 58% said no. Although polling figures for British attitudes to the war varied considerably at different times (and in response to whether the possibility of military action with UN sanction were included as an option), these figures

are fairly typical of the long-term trends. When, in another YouGov poll conducted on the eve of war in March 2003, respondents were asked "Taking everything into account, would you support or oppose Britain going to war against Iraq now?", 36% said support, 57% said oppose.

26. For the view that this is in large part the fault of the newspapers themselves, see John Lloyd, *What the Media are Doing to our Politics* (London: Constable & Robinson, 2004).

CHAPTER SIX
Weimar Iraq

1. Tristram Hunt, "D-Day's outcome was the beginning of a new Europe", *The Observer*, 6 June 2004 (www.guardian.co.uk).

2. Ibid.

3. Ibid.

4. Speech to "104th National Convention of the Veterans of Foreign Wars" in San Antonio, TX, 25 August 2003 (www.whitehouse.gov).

5. www.defense.gov.transcripts.

6. The report went on: "A successful election has long been seen as the keystone in President Johnson's policy of encouraging the growth of constitutional processes in South Vietnam. The election was the culmination of a constitutional development that began in January, 1966, to which President Johnson gave his personal commitment when he met Premier Ky and General Thieu, the chief of state, in Honolulu in February. The purpose of the voting was to give legitimacy to the Saigon Government, which has been founded only on coups and power plays since November, 1963, when President Ngo Dinh Deim was overthrown by a military junta." ("United States encouraged by Vietnam vote", *New York Times*, 9 April 1967.)

7. Many of these newspapers, as in Iraq, were scrappy, homemade productions, reflecting both the diversity of political opinion and the lack of material resources available to conduct popular politics on a wider scale.

8. "The Republic eschewed military parades, partly because of socialist anti-militarism, but also because the loyalties of the new Reichswehr were too tenuous to march its units safely though the streets." Michael Burleigh, *The Third Reich: A New History*, p. 45 (London: Macmillan, 2000).

9. In Russia, by contrast, which was still a largely peasant society, the economic crisis that followed the collapse of the Tsarist regime in 1917 did return much of the country to a subsistence economy. This meant that it was easier than in Germany for central government to reassert its authority, once there was a central government in place with the will to do so.

10. For example, the current American budget deficit, although relatively high by recent historical standards, is tiny compared with the massive debts run up by the major combatants (apart from the United States) during World War I.

11. The Nazis won only twelve seats in the May 1928 national elections, the last ones held before the crash of 1929. The number of seats they won in

the elections that followed were: 107 (September 1930), 230 (July 1932), 196 (November 1932), 288 (March 1933).

12. See Adam Przeworski, "Institutions matter?", *Government and Opposition* (39, 2004), pp. 527–40.

13. Fukuyama, *State Building*, p. 141.

14. See James MacDonald, *A Free Nation Deep in Debt: The Financial Roots of Democracy* (New York: Farrar, Straus & Giroux, 2003).

15. Perhaps the single most significant event in the recent politics of the Middle East came from a natural human lifespan, not an artificial electoral one: the death of Yasser Arafat.

16. The figures for the numbers of political murders in Weimar Germany remain uncertain, but appear to have run into the hundreds per year during the most violent periods. One estimate for the years 1919–22 puts the number killed at 356. Another estimate is that 300 were killed in the year up to March 1931, and another that 155 died as a result of political violence during 1932 in Prussia alone (see Richard J. Evans, *The Coming of the Third Reich* (London: Allen Lane, 2003), pp. 269–70). The numbers who suffered serious injury as a result of the incessant street violence of these years ran into the thousands.

CHAPTER SEVEN
A Bear Armed with a Gun

1. Thomas Hobbes, *Leviathan*, ed. Richard Tuck (Cambridge University Press, 1996), p. 89.

2. Ibid, p. 244.

3. For a full account of the ways in which Hobbes's thought has been simplified and misconstrued in contemporary international relations theory, see Noel Malcolm, "Hobbes's theory of international relations" in his *Aspects of Hobbes* (Oxford University Press, 2002).

4. Hobbes, *Leviathan*, p. 87.

5. Dominique de Villepin's Statement to the UN Security Council, 14 February 2003 (www.globalpolicy.org).

6. Hobbes, *Leviathan*, p. 120.

7. Robert Kagan, "Power and weakness", *Policy Review* (113, 2002); Robert Kagan, *Paradise and Power: America and Europe in the New World Order* (London: Atlantic Books, 2003).

8. Kagan, *Paradise and Power*, p. 3.

9. Ibid.

10. Ibid, p. 91.

11. "As a French official once told me, 'The problem is "failed states", not "rogue states" '." Ibid, p. 30.

12. See "Perpetual Peace" in Immanuel Kant, *Political Writings*, ed. H. Reiss (Cambridge University Press, 1991), especially pp. 99–102 ("The First Definitive Article of Perpetual Peace: The Civil Constitution of Every State shall be Republican").

13. For example, it is hard to reconcile present American foreign policy with the following: "The concept of international right becomes meaningless if interpreted as a right to go to war. For this would make it a right to determine what is lawful not by means of universally valid laws, but by means of one sided-maxims backed up by physical force. It could be taken to mean that it is perfectly just for men who adopt this attitude to destroy one another, and thus to find perpetual peace in the vast grave where all the horrors of violence and those responsible for them are buried." Kant, *Political Writings*, p. 105.

14. See Rawls, *The Law of Peoples*.

15. Kagan, *Paradise and Power*, p. 60.

16. Ibid, p. 31.

17. Ibid, p. 78.

18. Ibid, p. 41.

19. See John Micklethwait and Adrian Wooldridge, *The Right Nation: Why America is Different* (London: Allen Lane, 2004).

20. Garton Ash, *Free World*, p. xxx.

21. In the final round of voting among members of the Conservative Party, Duncan Smith defeated Clarke by 60–40% (the declaration of this result had to be delayed until 13 September, because, unsurprisingly, on 12 September 2001 no one was paying any attention). However, in the vote earlier that summer among Conservative MPs to select the two candidates for the run-off, Clarke came first with 59 votes, and Duncan Smith only defeated the third placed candidate, Michael Portillo, by a single vote (54 to 53). If the run-off had been between Clarke and Portillo, it is quite possible, though by no means certain, that Clarke would have won.

22. Kagan, *Paradise and Power*, p. 7, note 2.

23. Ibid, pp. 3–4.

24. Ibid, p. 92.

CHAPTER EIGHT
The Garden, the Park, the Meadow

1. Bobbitt, *The Shield of Achilles*.

2. Ibid, p. 24.

3. Ibid, p. 63.

4. Bobbitt's alternative title for the "market-mitigating" model is the "entrepreneurial" model.

5. See Bobbitt, *The Shield of Achilles*, pp. 732–33.

6. Robert Cooper, *The Breaking of Nations: Order and Chaos in the Twenty-First Century* (London: Atlantic Books, 2002). Cooper's thesis has been published in a number of versions over the past few years. But part of it began life as "a short note for the Prime Minister to read at Christmas" (see p. vi).

7. Bobbitt, *The Shield of Achilles*, p. 475.

8. Cooper, *The Breaking of Nations*, p. 37.

9. Bobbitt, *The Shield of Achilles*, p. 234.

10. Ibid, p. 744.

11. The best account of the intellectual history behind this change is given in Quentin Skinner, "From the state of princes to the person of the state", in his *Visions of Politics*, Volume II (Cambridge University Press, 2002).

12. Bobbitt, *The Shield of Achilles*, p. 139.

13. Ibid, pp. 238–39.

14. Ibid, p. 339.

15. In the first round of the election, Chirac polled 19.88% of the popular vote; Le Pen came second with 16.86%; Jospin third with 16.16%. In the second round run-off against Le Pen, Chirac was elected with 82.21% to his rival's 17.79%.

16. Cooper, *The Breaking of Nations*, pp. 79–80.

17. Philip Larkin, *Collected Poems* (London: Faber & Faber, 2003), p. 117.

18. Quoted in Bobbitt, *The Shield of Achilles*, p. 212.

19. Cooper, *The Breaking of Nations*, p. 32.

20. See Bobbitt, *The Shield of Achilles*, pp. 321–24.

21. Ibid, pp. 820–21.

22. Ibid.

23. Ibid, pp. 801–02.

24. Robert Nozick, *Anarchy, State, and Utopia* (Oxford: Blackwell, 1974).

25. Ibid, p. 312.

CHAPTER NINE
Two Revolutions, One Revolutionary

1. Emmanuel Joseph Sieyès, *Political Writings*, ed. Michael Sonnenscher (Cambridge, MA: Hackett, 2003), p. 94.

2. Ibid, pp. 147–48.

3. See V. I. Lenin, "Two tactics of social-democracy in the democratic revolution", in *Selected Writings*, Volume I (London: Lawrence and Wishart, 1947).

4. Sieyès, *Political Writings*, p. 157.

5. Ibid, p. 162.

6. *The Federalist with Letters of "Brutus"*, ed. Terence Ball (Cambridge University Press, 2003), p. 456.

7. Sieyès, *Political Writings*, p. 12.

8. Quoted in Murray Forsyth, *Reason and Revolution: The Political Thought of the Abbé Sieyes* (Leicester University Press, 1987).

9. Sieyès, *Political Writings*, p. 131.

10. Ibid, p. 63.

11. Ibid, p. 27.

12. Ibid, p. 50.

13. Quoted in Forsyth, *Reason and Revolution*, p. 155.

14. Quoted in ibid, p. 167.

15. Quoted in Sieyès, *Political Writings*, p. xxxiii.

16. Ibid, p. 166.

17. Ibid, p. 165.

18. Ibid, p. 168.

19. Ibid, p. 169.

20. Ibid, p. 172

21. Ibid, p. 171.

22. See Michael Sonnenscher's introduction to Sieyès, *Political Writings*, pp. lx–lxiii.

23. See Constant, *Political Writings*, pp. 325–26.

24. In this respect, France has followed Constant more than it has followed Sieyès. The constitutions of the various French republics have inclined towards relatively straightforward and direct forms of popular representation (either parliamentary or presidential), accompanied by repeated injunctions to the people to get involved in politics. The French people, meanwhile, have tended to organize themselves into a variety of entrenched interest groups in order to keep their politicians in check. This corporatist style of politics reinstates the idea that society consists of a number of different orders (farmers, workers, students, etc.) without returning to the view that representative politics should "reflect" the full range of these orders. Instead, a system of direct popular representation is forced to seek a series of accommodations with society at large. It is one of the apparent paradoxes of Constant's liberalism, by contrast with that of Sieyès, that the more straightforward the representation of the people, the less straightforward the politics that can result.

25. The obvious alternative to the referendum is the one suggested by eighteenth-century historical precedent: to hold elections to representative assemblies, whose job is then to decide whether or not to ratify the constitution. There are two problems with this idea for the architects of European integration, however. First, it is too American (this was the way the American constitution was ratified during 1787–88). Second, it is too democratic, not in any classical sense, but in the distinctively modern sense that it places too much power in the hands of the people's representatives to make up their own minds. Plebiscitary politics may be unpredictable, but they are at least open to fairly straightforward manipulation (that, indeed, is part of their point). Popularly elected representative assemblies, given the power to debate important questions on their own terms, need much more careful handling. The Federalist Papers alone are testament to that.

26. See Larry Siedentop, *Democracy in Europe* (London: Allen Lane, 2000), Chapter 2.

CHAPTER TEN
Epilogue: Virtual Politics

1. This was the thesis of one of the most influential television programmes to be broadcast in Britain since September 11, 2001, Adam Curtis's "The Power of Nightmares" (BBC series, 2004).

2. For example, the Thai Prime Minister Thaksin Shinawatra was able to turn popular approval of his handling of the disaster into an overwhelming victory in the general election held two months later.

3. "As Reagan had dared to go beyond staunch anticommunism and imagine a world after communism's collapse, so Bush looked beyond the present chaotic state of the world of terror to a blessed land of freedom. ('In this election, my opponent has spent a lot of time talking about a day that is gone. I'm talking about the day that is coming.')." Mark Danner, "How Bush really won", *New York Review of Books*, 13 January 2005.

4. Mayor of London press conference, 16 March 2004 (www.bbc.co.uk/news).

5. See Danner, "How Bush really won".

6. Blair, "The opportunity society".

7. Ibid.

8. Interview on BBC Today Programme, 13 November 2004.

9. See Corey Robin, *Fear: The History of a Political Idea* (Oxford University Press, 2004).

10. "This is a nation which has been tested in adversity, which has survived physical destruction and catastrophic loss of life. I do not underestimate the ability of fanatical groups of terrorists to kill and destroy, but they do not threaten the life of the nation. Whether we would survive Hitler hung in the balance, but there is no doubt that we shall survive Al Qaeda. The Spanish people have not said that what happened in Madrid, hideous crime as it was, threatened the life of their nation. Their legendary pride would not allow it. Terrorist violence, serious as it is, does not threaten our institutions of government or our existence as a civil community ... For these reasons I think that the Special Immigration Appeals Commission made an error of law and that the appeal ought to be allowed. Others of your Lordships who are also in favour of allowing the appeal would do so, not because there is no emergency threatening the life of the nation, but on the ground that a power of detention confined to foreigners is irrational and discriminatory. I would prefer not to express a view on this point. I said that the power of detention is at present confined to foreigners and I would not like to give the impression that all that was necessary was to extend the power to United Kingdom citizens as well. In my opinion, such a power in any form is not compatible with our constitution. The real threat to the life of the nation, in the sense of a people living in accordance with its traditional laws and political values, comes not from terrorism but from laws such as these. That is the true measure of what terrorism may achieve. It is for Parliament to decide whether to give the terrorists such a victory." Lord Hoffman, House

of Lords Judgment on anti-terror legislation permitting foreign suspects to be detained without trial, 16 December 2004 (Judgments—A (FC) and Others (FC) (Appelants) v. The Secretary of State for the Home Department (Respondent) (www.publications.parliament.uk)).

11. Hobbes, *Leviathan*, p. 465.

INDEX

nuclear war, nuclear weapons, 7, 56, 59, 61–62, 75, 98, 128, 138
Nuremberg trials, 113

Paine, Thomas, 168–69
Pakistan, 62, 141
Parris, Matthew, 1, 3, 50
Policy Analysis Market (PAM), 99
political time, 120
Portillo, Michael, 202n.21
Portugal, 120
"postmodern politics", 19, 21–22, 25, 27, 130, 136, 142–44, 148–49, 151, 153–54
Powell, Colin, 125
Powell, Jonathan, 63–64
precautionary principle, 56–60, 62, 64–66, 196–97
Project for the New American Century, 20
public opinion, 13, 72, 95, 100, 138, 168, 171, 176, 199n.19, 199n.20
Putin, Vladimir, 39

Rangwala, Glen, 197n.8
Rawls, John, 127, 193n.29
Reagan, Ronald, 137, 205n.3
Rees, Martin, 55
referendums, 17, 77–78, 93, 173, 204n.25
representation, 23, 49, 95, 112, 157, 159–62, 169–72, 204n.24
Republican Party, 3, 131, 191n.4
Rice, Condoleezza, 67, 105
risk, x–xi, 9–13, 23, 31, 33, 51, 53, 55–66, 68–74, 76–79, 81, 86–90, 93, 96, 99–103, 119, 130, 140, 148, 174, 177, 184, 192n.14, 195n.2, 196n.3, 197n.3, 197n.5, 197–98n.7, 199n.19, 199n.20
Robespierre, Maximilien, 169
Rousseau, Jean-Jacques, 97, 156, 164, 171
Rumsfeld, Donald, 105, 194n.1

Russia, 39, 75, 136, 139, 142, 159, 200n.9
Russian Revolution, 158

Saudi Arabia, 110
Schauer, Frederick, 82, 84, 86
Second World War, *see* World War II
Security Council (UN), 50, 75, 124, 201n.5
September 11, 2001, ix, 1–13, 19, 27–28, 41, 60, 85, 99, 107, 115, 127, 129, 133–34, 140, 151, 176–78, 180, 183–85, 187, 193n.23, 205n.1
"September dossier", 64–65, 75, 197n.8
Serbia, 50, 146
Shinawatra, Thaksin, 205n.2
Short, Clare, 72
Siedentop, Larry, 174
Sierra Leone, 150
Sieyès, Emmanuel, 23, 26, 149, 156–74, 204n.24
Simon, Siôn, 47–49
Skinner, Quentin, 203n.11
Slaughter, Anne-Marie, 193n.25
Smith, Adam, 156
Somalia, 141
South Africa, 128, 142
South Korea, 139
state building, 20, 118, 127
stereotypes, 82, 87–90, 93
Stevens, Sir John, 181
Stothard, Peter, 62
Straw, Jack, 63, 125
Sunstein, Cass, 58
Surowiecki, James, 93–97
Switzerland, 34, 36–37

terrorism, 2, 7, 9–12, 16, 27, 41, 55–62, 65, 69, 75, 81, 83–90, 92–93, 97–101, 105–07, 109, 113, 133, 135, 143, 167, 176–87, 191n.5, 191n.9, 192n.12, 192n.15, 205–06n.10
Thatcher, Margaret, 48, 137

Thomas, Hugh, 74
Tocqueville, Alexis de, 149, 174

United Nations (UN), 2, 7, 33, 50,
    57, 68, 74–75, 124, 128–29,
    141–42, 199–200n.25,
    201n.5
United States, ix, xi, 1–9, 13–14,
    18–20, 27, 40, 72, 74, 82–83,
    98–99, 106, 110, 115–16, 119,
    125–33, 137, 139, 142–43,
    147, 155–56, 160, 165–66,
    170, 174–77, 180, 183, 187,
    192n.17, 194n.6, 200n.6,
    200n.10
utopia, 21, 153–54, 188–89,
    203n.24

Versailles, Treaty of, 34, 110, 113,
    119, 145
Vico, Giambattista, 156
Vietnam, Vietnam war, 106, 136,
    200n.6
Villepin, Dominique de, 125

Walzer, Michael, 39
war on terror, 4, 12, 16, 56, 81,
    135, 176–78, 181–82,
    185–87
weapons of mass destruction
    (WMD), 2, 9, 33, 52–57,
    61–66, 75, 96, 127, 182, 184,
    196–97
Weber, Max, ix, 23, 34–45, 47–51,
    85, 194n.7, 194n.16
Weimar Republic, 34, 36, 41,
    106–17, 120
Wilhelm II, Kaiser, 107, 112–13,
    117
Wilson, Woodrow, 119
World War I, 106–07, 109, 115,
    119–20, 136, 200n.10
World War II, 20, 104, 106, 113,
    119, 136
worst-case scenarios, 55–62
Wyden, Ron, 99

Young, Hugo, 1